T0314189

# SOFT CORRUPTION

## Rivergate Regionals

Rivergate Regionals is a collection of books published by Rutgers University Press focusing on New Jersey and the surrounding area. Since its founding in 1936, Rutgers University Press has been devoted to serving the people of New Jersey and this collection solidifies that tradition. The books in the Rivergate Regionals Collection explore history, politics, nature and the environment, recreation, sports, health and medicine, and the arts. By incorporating the collection within the larger Rutgers University Press editorial program, the Rivergate Regionals Collection enhances our commitment to publishing the best books about our great state and the surrounding region.

# SOFT CORRUPTION

How Unethical Conduct
Undermines Good Government
and What to Do About It

WILLIAM E. SCHLUTER

**R**

RUTGERS UNIVERSITY PRESS

New Brunswick, Camden, and Newark, New Jersey, and London

Library of Congress Cataloging-in-Publication Data
Names: Schluter, William E., 1927– author.
Title: Soft corruption : how ethical misconduct undermines good government and what to do about it / William E. Schluter.
Description: New Jersey : Rutgers University Press, 2017. | Series: Rivergate regionals | Includes bibliographical references and index.
Identifiers: LCCN 2016024606 | ISBN 9780813586175 (hardcover : alk. paper) | ISBN 9780813586182 (e-book (epub)) | ISBN 9780813586199 (e-book (web pdf))
Subjects: LCSH: Political corruption—New Jersey. | Misconduct in office—New Jersey. | Campaign funds—New Jersey. | Conflict of interests—New Jersey. | Patronage, Political—New Jersey. | Political culture—New Jersey. | New Jersy—Politics and government.
Classification: LCC JK3545 .S45 2017 | DDC 320.9749—dc23
LC record available at https://lccn.loc.gov/2016024606

A British Cataloging-in-Publication record for this book is available from the British Library.

∞ The paper used in this publication meets the requirements of the American National Standard for Information Sciences—Permanence of Paper for Printed Library Materials, ANSI Z39.48 1992.

www.rutgersuniversitypress.org

Manufactured in the United States of America

I dedicate this book and all that it stands for to Samuel A. Alito Sr. In the minds of most Americans, the name Sam Alito connects with the associate justice of the United States Supreme Court. But the Sam Alito I am honoring was his father, who served for many years in charge of New Jersey's nonpartisan Office of Legislative Services and whose influence over the legislature from the 1960s until he retired in 1984 was pervasive and profound.

During this time and under his guidance, New Jersey earned the reputation as having one of the most effective and best-run legislatures in the country. In his position, Sam Alito and his staff researched and drafted all legislation for both the state senate and the general assembly. His abilities and expertise on New Jersey government matters made him an indispensable authority on the Trenton scene.

Sam Alito was more than just a straight arrow and solid researcher. He was a mentor, a total professional who would go the extra mile for any legislator who sought his help. He served as secretary on two of the legislative commissions on which I was appointed: Election Law Revision and County and Municipal Government. The Election Law Revision Commission, guided by its members and Mr. Alito, produced a landmark report in 1975 exposing the way that candidates and political parties were financed in New Jersey as well as how the electoral process was not always managed fairly.

This report and the work of the Commission inspired me to take up the banner of reform, which has been the backbone of my political career ever since. Sam Alito was a major influence, instilling in me the importance of justice, fairness, and integrity in the role of government service.

# CONTENTS

# PREFACE

Twenty years in the New Jersey legislature, and many more years of activity in local, county, and state politics, gave me a thorough understanding of how government in New Jersey works. And the picture has not been pretty.

This is not to say that all officials are miscreants and that all government activity is shady. Indeed, many go into public office for the right reasons: to serve fellow citizens faithfully, honestly, and efficiently; to try to make life better for everyone; and to carry out the American dream of government of the people, by the people, and for the people. Through the efforts of these well-intentioned officials, government has been able to implement policies to protect precious natural resources, help small businesses to create jobs, support home ownership, expand higher education opportunities, promote public health and safety, and advance other programs for the public good.

But there are lawmakers and public servants who are not so inspired, who spoil it for the rest by gaming the system to reap personal benefits and power. These are the public officials who engage in unethical conduct, activities that break no laws but fail to meet acceptable standards of morality. This is *soft corruption.*

The history of government is filled with accounts of the corrupting influence of political power. In the words of James Madison, "The essence of government is power, and power, lodged as it must be in human hands, will ever be liable to abuse." Events in New Jersey have shown that not all government and political leaders are motivated by altruism and integrity. Rather, many succumb to accommodation, expediency, and then, subterfuge.

The various stories and episodes in this book have been taken from the public record going back fifty years. The ones that draw on my own experiences are limited to those that have special significance in explaining a certain event or activity, and will be so noted.

My commitment to government reform evolved over the years. It started in 1965 when I was picked as the Republican sacrificial lamb to run for state senate against a popular Democratic incumbent whose party dominated the district. I ran a bare-bones campaign, sharply criticizing my opponent who, as a lawyer/legislator, engaged in conflicts of interest (legal at the time) by representing private clients before state agencies. Although I was defeated by more than 22,000 votes, I did earn the endorsement of the *Times of Trenton* for my efforts at reform.

Later as a legislator, I was appointed to the Election Law Revision Commission, where my eyes were opened to two stark realities: the campaign contribution is a major force in determining government decisions, and the process of selecting candidates to make these decisions is too often manipulated in secret by backroom power brokers. These conclusions were borne out by the words of John Gardner, founder of Common Cause, who said in 1975: "The two chief obstacles to responsive government are money and secrecy: the scandalous capacity of money to buy political outcomes, and the bad habit of doing the public's business behind closed doors."

Despite recommendations made by the Election Law Revision Commission in its 1975 report, and by numerous good government groups over the years, almost no serious measures for reform have been adopted into law. Yes, there have been some minor changes, nibbling around the edges but leaving plenty of loopholes. The New Jersey legislature seems intent on maintaining the status quo so that the system will continue to produce for the benefit of those who manage it.

It was not long before I became seriously committed to all aspects of reform, focusing my attention on the many failings and shortcomings in government. The more blatant issues that cry out for reform as described in detail in this book include: senatorial courtesy, dual office-holding, influence peddling by lobbyists, patronage abuses, partisan redistricting, wheeling of campaign funds, and, above all, concentration of power by those who control political money. Taking a pro-reform position on these issues did not endear me to many of the leaders of my party or of the legislature. Although I was able to pass a significant campaign finance disclosure bill in my early years in office, other efforts at reform were not as successful. In fact, many of these efforts were not only rejected, but led to reprisals.

My career in the senate was done in by Republican members of the 2001 Apportionment Commission who, as reported in the press, were complicit in permitting my hometown to be switched from a safe Republican district to a heavily Democratic one that included the city of

Trenton. Unwilling to withdraw completely from the political scene, I entered the race for governor in 2001 as an independent. This move gave me a platform to continue the campaign for reform—but I received only 1 percent of the popular vote.

Later, my service as chair of the Citizens Clean Election Commission and as a member of the State Ethics Commission continued to whet my appetite in the fight against unethical conduct. But even with all the bad government behavior taking place in New Jersey there was no public clamor for reform. The people seemed to consider ethical failings by public officials "business as usual," and were convinced there was no prospect for change.

Something has to be done. I decided to continue my efforts to expose soft corruption by writing this book. My hope is that these stories will help raise the level of public outrage to the point where we see a genuine citizens' uprising that forces change.

Given the present depth of public lethargy, this will be a difficult task. But our American values demand that we reverse the defects associated with soft corruption before they create further dysfunction and disarray in what should be a representative democracy.

# ACKNOWLEDGMENTS

I wish to acknowledge the help of numerous friends, family members, associates, and professionals who gave of their time and talents in the production of this book. The finished product would never have emerged in its present form without their assistance.

Although it is difficult—and perhaps unwise—to give greater credit to some contributors over others, I will single out one individual whose support and guidance have been absolutely essential: Richard L. McCormick, president emeritus of Rutgers University. Dick McCormick became interested in the book's mission early when he learned that the subject matter was about New Jersey's addiction to government corruption. This topic is a familiar one for McCormick, whose specialization in scholarly research and writing has been political corruption in this country as well as national reform initiatives. Dick McCormick spent countless hours reviewing and critiquing the manuscript drafts of this book. His wisdom and suggestions on this entire issue area have been invaluable, and I am eternally grateful to him.

Other individuals who have served as readers, consultants, and advisors include: George Amick, Jeff Brindle, Joe Donohue, Matt Friedman, Susan Henkel, Fred Herrmann, Judy Jengo, Kyle Keiderling, Peter Mazzei, Leslie Pell, Mary Pinney, Ingrid Reed, Bill Schluter Jr., Nan Thurston, and Andrew Tirpok.

Special recognition should go to Ross Holley, whose research and computer skills added much to the quality of the material in the book and to efficiencies in authoring it.

Of course the patience and understanding of my wife, Nancy Schluter, was crucial in providing the supportive environment so necessary for me to keep a clear focus and to persevere through the many frustrations that an author experiences.

The professional editing supplied in the early stages by Matt Reilly, Polly Kummel, and Diana Groden is respectfully acknowledged. Since January 2015 I have benefited from the editing services of Michael Meagher, whose knowledge of New Jersey government and editorial craftsmanship have strengthened the tenor and quality of the writing in this book.

Finally, my literary agent, Marie Galastro, has been an effective ally in guiding me through the maze of manuscript publication.

# SOFT CORRUPTION

# 1 ▸ SOFT CORRUPTION— THE PROBLEM

$\bigwedge$ WEALTHY SCULPTOR with family problems makes generous campaign contributions in the hope of influencing legislators to enact
a law that will help him stop his daughter from receiving a share of the
family inheritance. He nearly succeeds. A state legislator dips into his publicly funded office budget to pay the assistant editor of his district's largest
newspaper $2,000 for unspecified general services. The speaker of the state
assembly invites lobbyists to contribute $1,500 to her reelection campaign
in exchange for the opportunity to talk with her about "your concerns
and those of your clients." Employing an unwritten but tradition-honored
practice, a senator single-handedly blocks the governor's highly qualified
nominee for commissioner of education from even coming up for a confirmation vote. A longtime legislator, defeated on Election Day, is handed a
position at the state's parole board, at more than double his legislative salary. He leaves the job a year later, as soon as the resulting 78 percent bump
to his state pension takes effect. His response to critics: "If anybody don't
like it, that's too bad. Let them go spend thirty-three years in office."

Welcome to New Jersey, home of sandy beaches, bucolic small towns, entertainment legends, high-technology industries . . . and an unfortunate history of government corruption.

Most people associate government corruption with the spectacle of an elected official paraded before news cameras and reporters after being arrested or indicted in connection with crimes committed in public office. We shake our heads, utter a disparaging comment, and then just change the channel or turn the page, resigned to the notion that this is the way things are. A politician breaking the law has become so commonplace that it's hardly news. Who cares? It happens all the time.

And certainly it happens far too often. Every November, we go to the polls and choose the people who will represent us in government. Later, we watch as they place their left hand on a Bible, raise their right hand, and swear to faithfully uphold the laws of the state. Then time passes, and some of those same hands wind up handcuffed together under a trench coat as the offender is led off to a jail cell.

In recent decades, New Jersey has earned a reputation for criminal corruption at all levels of government—the result of numerous cases that have been exposed and prosecuted.[1] But the political culture associated with such malfeasance also breeds another level of wrongdoing that should offend us all as members of a participatory democracy. It occurs when the people who hold public office figure out how to game the system in ways that enrich them and their cronies *without* breaking any laws. This is soft corruption: unethical transgressions carried out in the quest for political power or personal benefit, achieving results that work against the public interest; and it's all legal. Most writers about corruption generally define it as political behavior that violates the norms of public office for private, selfish reasons.[2] That definition is fine, except that such behavior can be perfectly legal.

Soft corruption is much more pervasive in public office than most people realize. Consider just a handful of examples, which will be covered in greater detail later in this book:

- In 1989, four legislators who would soon occupy their party's top-ranking seats in the assembly invited twenty high-powered lobbyists to a meeting, ostensibly to solicit their ideas regarding the upcoming election campaign. The real purpose: to shake them down for major campaign contributions from their clients. Those who failed to comply could lose any chance of having legislation favorable to their clients see the light of day.

- In 2011, the capable, respected executive director of the state commission charged with investigating violations of the conflict-of-interest law was pressured to resign, so that the governor's office could replace her with someone of its own choosing.

- County clerks are responsible for deciding "by lot" which party's candidates will be listed on the preferred first line of the general election ballot. By remarkable luck—or something more—the Republican county clerk in Hunterdon selected the GOP for Column A every year from 1999 to 2009. In heavily Democratic Essex County, the Democratic clerk drew his party for the first column thirteen times in a fourteen-year stretch—a streak broken only in the year that the county party was feuding with the Democratic governor.

- In 2002, the prominent head of a Newark congregation was appointed as state commerce secretary while retaining his pastorate. It was an unusual arrangement that would soon become untenable. At the same time that the church's community development program, which he controlled, was actively seeking funding from nearby Jersey City for a housing development with the pastor directly lobbying council members, Jersey City was applying for grants from a state authority chaired by the very same man. Jersey City received funding from the state, and the project proposed by the pastor's church got its approval and financing from Jersey City.

- In the city of Elizabeth, the school board acts as a political machine. Its nine members have accounted for the appointment of twenty relatives to jobs on the district payroll, and the board has leaned on teachers to purchase tickets to political fund-raisers—soliciting right on school property.

- When the police director of New Brunswick retired in 2010, he received more than $375,000 in unused vacation and sick time, along with a $115,000 annual pension from the police and firemen's pension fund. Six months later, he took advantage of a provision of the fund and applied to be rehired. He soon was earning an annual salary of $120,000—while still collecting his $115,000 yearly pension for the exact same position.[3]

Soft corruption is found in the exploitation of such political and governmental activities as campaign finance, lobbying, patronage, and the electoral process, as well as potential conflicts of interest where a public official acts on government matters that provide personal rewards. Engaging in these processes is not, per se, engaging in soft corruption. They are necessary functions of government that can be performed honestly, fairly, and with integrity. Money has to be raised for political campaigns and can be done honorably; lobbying to represent and express the concerns of interest groups is a normal and desirable phenomenon in our system of self-government; patronage can involve filling government jobs with individuals who are fully qualified; the electoral process can be used to select competent candidates for public office in an open, fair, and transparent manner; and a lawmaker can decline to participate when confronted with a matter that may affect his or her private interest.

It is only when individuals manipulate government functions for reasons of greed, personal advancement, or political advantage that soft corruption occurs. When legislative leaders seek large campaign contributions from special interests that have a stake in pending legislative proposals with an unspoken quid pro quo, that's soft corruption. When lobbyists conduct fund-raising events for legislative candidates, that's soft corruption, too. Such practices, all of which pass legal muster, are unethical and work against the public interest. And no one should dismiss them by saying, "That's politics."

These examples of soft corruption are part of a political culture in which certain people behave as if the system exists to facilitate their personal gain, not to do the greatest good for the community. Soft corruption leads to the dysfunction we see today at the national and state levels of government, contributing to the public's lack of confidence in how we the people are represented. Lawmakers who are part of this culture subvert the quality of public policy, thus adversely affecting traditional government responsibilities such as education, health care, transportation, and social services every time they make a decision for reasons other than an honest assessment of the public policy at stake.

A good explanation of the difference between soft and criminal corruption comes from George Washington Plunkitt, a leader of the Tammany Hall political machine of New York City more than one hundred years ago. Plunkitt made a distinction between "dishonest graft" and "honest graft." The former is bribery, extortion, or other criminal acts used by a government official to gain an advantage or benefit. The latter occurs when the official uses inside information or the power of office to gain a personal benefit. To Plunkitt's way of thinking, only a fool would engage in dishonest graft when there is plenty of honest graft—soft corruption—to go around.[4] More recently, former New Jersey governor Brendan Byrne captured the distinction this way: "If somebody wants a permit from a local government, and he goes to the mayor and gives him $10,000 cash in an envelope, he's guilty of a crime. If he . . . handles it right and . . . makes a campaign contribution to the mayor's campaign, which is perfectly legal, it gets him exactly the same result."[5]

The struggle against both forms of corruption has been a theme running through many periods of American history. One such period was in the late nineteenth century, when the railroads, utilities, and other corporate giants were able to tell many state legislatures how to vote on such matters as taxes, business charters, and the selection of U.S. senators (who were chosen by the legislatures back then). These commercial enterprises understood the power of states over corporations' economic well-being and used their money to buy the support of state legislators and political bosses. Such blatant abuses were challenged by President Theodore Roosevelt's trust-busting reforms—aided by the muckraking journalism of Lincoln Steffens, Ida Tarbell, and others—and to the Progressive movement at the beginning of the twentieth century. A leader of the Progressives, Robert M. La Follette of Wisconsin, realized that government corruption was facilitated by the ability of moneyed interests to put their people into elective office. At the time, candidates for government office were chosen by the bosses and then stood for election. La Follette championed the direct primary to "emancipate the legislature from all subserviency to the corporations," reasoning that this reform would fumigate special interests from the internal workings of the political parties. Through La Follette's efforts, Wisconsin approved the direct primary in 1904,[6] and by 1915 all but three states had adopted this reform.[7]

More recently, in the aftermath of the Watergate scandal, public pressure, good-government groups like Common Cause (founded in 1970), and aggressive reporters who exposed unsavory practices prompted state and federal lawmakers to pass reforms designed to bring a higher level of ethics and integrity to government.[8] Added stimulus came from advances in electronic data processing, which provided greater transparency in government and made concealing unethical deeds more difficult. Until that point, New Jersey law contained virtually no restrictions on campaign financing or on lobbying. Public officials did not have to make financial disclosures that would reveal conflicts between their public duties and their private business interests. And manipulating the primary ballot structure in the selection of candidates for office was standard operating procedure among political pros. After Watergate, New Jersey enacted laws regulating campaign financing and lobbying, and the conduct of public officials became subject to conflict-of-interest regulations. By the early 2000s, the state had guaranteed open public records and meetings and had partially curtailed "pay-to-play" practices that granted access only to those who contributed to political campaign coffers.

But ever-resourceful politicians and public officials have been able to carve out exceptions and loopholes in these reforms. Moreover, New Jersey has done little to ban dual office-holding, correct patronage excesses, and tackle the reasons for the lack of competition among those seeking elective office.

The most significant temptation to engage in soft corruption has been the increasing amount of money now on the political scene. The need to amass enormous campaign war chests places inordinate emphasis on fund-raising and, through it, creates opportunities for major donors to influence policy outcomes and obtain government benefits.

The most dramatic event associated with raising enormous amounts of campaign money was the U.S. Supreme Court's ruling in *Citizens United* on January 21, 2010. This decision removes any restrictions on political spending by corporations and unions, so long as the expenditures are made independently. In other words, corporations and unions are now treated the same as individuals and can give unlimited sums on behalf of or in opposition to an identified candidate or issue, providing these expenditures are not coordinated with a specific campaign. State and federal laws still impose restrictions on *direct* contributions to candidates and parties, such as limiting the amount, disclosing the donor, prohibiting corporate and union giving, and regulating pay to play.

Since *Citizens United*, special interests have poured vast amounts of money into election campaigns, primarily for federal office but increasingly on the state and local level as well. Clearly, results in these elections will mean that the political agendas of the winners will comport more with the interests of the corporate, union, and fat-cat donors than with the interests of Jane Q. Public. To the extent that *Citizens United* distorts our principles of representative democracy, this decision is an enabler of soft corruption.

Meanwhile, the volume of direct campaign contributions has also escalated. And these, when made in the context of the unspoken quid pro quo, are the more sinister examples of soft corruption. Laws requiring disclosure of the identities of the donors and recipients of campaign contributions have made it easy to see correlations between the interests providing the money and specific government actions. Examples of donors and the rewards they receive include law firms appointed as counsel to government bodies with high-value retainers, businesses that receive narrowly targeted tax breaks through legislation, labor unions that obtain sweetheart contracts, and developers who receive unwarranted permit approvals. Such arrangements lead cynics to say that the offer of a campaign contribution is a legal bribe, and the solicitation of a contribution is legal extortion. Pretty harsh words, but they all add up to soft corruption.

Countless thousands of public officials—unquestionably a substantial majority—are honorable and do not participate in soft corruption. Likewise, many direct campaign contributions are given to support a candidate or political party whose public policy objectives already match those of the donor and are not meant to influence a specific government outcome. The distinction must be made. Not all contributions are suspect. But contributions that do not pass the smell test—that lead to direct benefits to the donors through government actions that otherwise would not have been taken—are soft corruption at its worst.

In this book, I examine soft corruption in five areas of political and governmental activity: campaign financing, lobbying, conflicts of interest, patronage, and the electoral process. In order to get the sense of how soft corruption creeps into the functions of all levels of government in New Jersey, it is absolutely necessary to understand thoroughly how government operates in the state. Accordingly, I take great pains in the following chapters to explain the procedures and practices of political government activity in sufficient—and sometimes simplistic—detail for the reader to understand how the culture of ethical transgressions permeates the state, and why this problem has become so intractable.

1. Without question, *campaign financing* is the most dominant and all-encompassing of the five forms of soft corruption. It includes the process by which money is raised from donors and the ways in which that money is spent. It pertains to the funding of a particular campaign but also the formation of a political action committee, the spending by a political party, the transfer of dollars from one war chest to another, the funds spent to influence voters to vote yes or no on a public question, and much more. The other four areas of soft corruption all have a component of political money, thereby connecting them directly and indirectly to the campaign contribution.

2. *Lobbying* is advocacy to influence government decisions. Over the years, lobbying has become institutionalized, and today its practitioners are paid handsomely to achieve results for their clients.

   Virtually all states regulate lobbyists by requiring them to register, identify their clients, and disclose how they spend their money. In many states, the law limits campaign contributions made by lobbyists. These regulations add to the transparency of the system and help to prevent outright buying of government decisions, but they do little to diminish the power of lobbyists over public officials. This power comes in two forms: the campaign money they raise and deliver to lawmakers whose support they are soliciting, and the electoral assistance from the lobbyist's clients such as labor unions, business associations, developers, gun owners, farmers, and others. When lawmakers do the bidding of lobbyists against the best interests of their constituents and the general public, they are engaging in soft corruption.

   As with campaign financing, not all lobbying is soft corruption. Active lobbying is undertaken in the public interest to protect the environment, enhance consumer protection, and advance good government. In fact, not all lobbying paid for by commercial interests solely benefits those interests. There can also be good outcomes from these lobbying efforts, such as the 2012 bond act for higher education capital construction, supported by New Jersey's business and commerce associations.

3. *Conflict of interest* occurs when a public official is faced with taking action on a government matter that affects, or could affect, the personal and business interests of the official, members of the official's family, or business associates. As a result, most states now have laws requiring elected and appointed officials to disclose their personal finances and have promulgated codes of ethics to prohibit specific practices that constitute conflicts of interest. Full and total disclosure is key to ending corruption in government. In the words of former U.S. Supreme Court Justice Louis Brandeis: "Sunlight is said to be the best of disinfectants." Alert reporters who reveal information on personal financial disclosure forms and campaign contribution records often help to expose ethics violations.

One important aspect in preventing and addressing conflicts of interest is the enforcement process. Too often members of ethics enforcement commissions are political appointees who are not enthusiastic advocates for strict enforcement. As a result, those agencies gloss over situations rife with conflict of interest and allow them to continue.

4. *Patronage* in its broader sense is more than government jobs. It also covers the perks, benefits, and favors doled out by government, including purchasing goods, hiring personnel, funding programs, granting pension benefits, and such lesser practices as the use of government cars. Patronage becomes soft corruption when officials award government jobs without competition to unqualified people or dispense benefits as political payoffs.

5. *The electoral process* is critically important in determining the quality and effectiveness of who governs. Obviously, campaign money is a major factor in deciding which side wins an election. But campaign money might be crucial in only a small percentage of New Jersey's legislative districts. In the vast majority of elections there is little competition, because one party is dominant in so many districts. Races for seats in the New Jersey statehouse see little competition because of the strong political party influence over the redistricting process, which allows those who control the process to tilt the distribution of partisan voters to the advantage of their party.

Primary elections are crucial starting points for candidates to advance to elective office. But when strong party bosses control the selection of candidates, real competition is snuffed out. Many candidates who emerge from this process as elected officials owe their loyalty to the political machine and have little interest in taking independent or controversial stances that might be of greater benefit to their constituents. Manipulation of the candidate selection process by party insiders is a blatant example of soft corruption.

Among the many consequences of soft corruption, three are particularly troubling for states like New Jersey: higher-cost government, bad governmental decisions, and an apathetic public.

## SOFT CORRUPTION MEANS
## HIGHER-COST GOVERNMENT

Soft corruption practices in campaign finance, lobbying, conflict of interest, patronage, and electoral manipulation are interrelated; the political pros mix and match strategies in each of these areas to maximize their power and achieve their governmental objectives. And all of these practices contribute to higher-cost government.

Those who do business with government factor campaign contributions and lobbying expenses into the cost of services and products they provide and for which government pays. Despite enactment of pay-to-play measures that attempt to negate the quid pro quo connection between government contract awards and campaign contributions, resourceful vendors circumvent these laws. They donate directly to candidates and to PACs, which are exempt from pay-to-play regulation. And pay-to-play laws do not apply to contracting by most county and local government agencies.

Genuine competition in awarding vendor and professional service contracts does not always exist when lawmakers who have related business holdings and connections intercede in influencing awards to favor themselves, associates, or relatives. This often means that government pays more for something of inferior value.

Consider also the abuse of patronage in the appointment of unqualified people to public jobs and sweetheart deals that result in lucrative retirement payouts of unused sick and vacation compensation. There are cases of pension padding where some government workers are paid a generous pension for past services while they are reemployed by government in positions with high salaries. This practice increases the burden of raising revenue for pensions without producing added value to taxpayers. Double-dipping undermines the basic principle of pensions, which is to provide income for services rendered in public jobs for those who have retired—and stay retired.

A recent example of a political maneuver, costly to the public, was seen in the effort of Governor Chris Christie to rack up an overwhelming majority in his 2013 reelection. U.S. Senator Frank Lautenberg had died in office that June, and the most logical timing for the special election to fill his seat was Election Day in November. Instead, by gubernatorial decree, Christie advanced the date of the special U.S. Senate election in the fall of 2013 by three weeks ahead of the regular election date, when he would be on the ballot. This meant that the large number of voters who would be drawn to the polls to vote for the very popular Democrat, Cory Booker, for U.S. Senate would not be voting at the same time for governor. This stratagem helped Christie achieve an astounding 22 percent majority win over his Democratic opponent. But the separate election cost the state an extra $12 million, and in the words of *Star-Ledger* columnist Tom Moran, "this was a forced donation to the Christie campaign by the taxpayers of New Jersey."[9]

In these and other ways, soft corruption drives the cost of government higher than it should be, and the result is that the public pays more in taxes, or essential services do not receive as much funding as they should—or both.

## SOFT CORRUPTION LEADS TO BAD GOVERNMENT DECISIONS

The second area where soft corruption shortchanges citizens is in the quality of governance delivered by public officials. And indeed, the quality of governance is not abstract. When political power brokers influence public policy in their quest for campaign money, the true interests of the public are of secondary importance. And if raw patronage is allowed to dictate who is named to important government positions, talent and ability are no longer the determining factors in making these appointments. The same applies to the selection of candidates for elective office by political bosses under conditions that are often secret and closed.

Instead of attracting the best and brightest into government service, New Jersey has a propensity for rewarding those whose primary attribute is political loyalty. Competition has always been considered a touchstone of American success, but healthy competition among talented aspirants is largely absent when it comes to advancing in government office.

Representative government is one of the core principles on which this nation was founded. In seeking a government that makes good legislative and administrative decisions, citizens look for quality in their representatives—leaders with integrity, courage, and good judgment who will thoughtfully use their knowledge and experience in government to vote in the best interests of the people they serve. Citizens expect lawmakers to have a reasonable measure of independence to do what is right and not kowtow to special interests or party bosses.

In New Jersey, it is easy to question whether the people receive this high-quality representation from their elected officials, many of whom occupy safe seats and depend upon campaign dollars, political power brokers, and the demands of the patronage system to continue to hold their office and enjoy its perks. The failure of the principle of representativeness in New Jersey government is even more pronounced when one considers the many cases where unelected political powers—party bosses like George Norcross, "Big Steve" Adubato, and others who will be discussed later in this book—have a direct influence over government policy and decisions. How can public officials buffeted by such pressures truly represent their constituents?

It is useful to consider an example of a bad government decision: the pension bond proposal advanced by the administration of Governor Christie Whitman in 1997 (see chapter 3), which history has shown to have been fiscally unsound. Soft corruption entered into this major policy initiative when three recalcitrant senators were pressured on the floor of the senate to vote for the proposal, despite their very strong reservations. They finally relented and voted to approve the measure. They subsequently received substantial campaign contributions from the senate campaign fund—only to lose the ensuing election. But all was not in vain, as they were awarded lucrative patronage appointments following their electoral losses.

## SOFT CORRUPTION CONTRIBUTES TO PUBLIC APATHY

Instead of being outraged at a government where lawmakers regularly engage in soft corruption, New Jersey citizens have become immune to the litany of ethical transgressions that occur in their state. There seems to be an attitude of "what's the use?" and "it's just politics as usual." Too many New Jerseyans are turned off by their government.

In a 2009 opinion survey conducted by the Monmouth University Polling Institute, only 29 percent of the surveyed voters judged New Jersey's government to be good or excellent, and 61 percent believed that their state legislators look out for their own financial interests rather than for the public good.[10] Is it any wonder that this sentiment prevails when lawmakers make no effort to challenge and reform soft corruption? The few attempts at reform are undercut by clever loopholes devised by compliant legislators to circumvent the purpose of these attempts.

Can we blame the public for its despair and cynicism when the state senate, after voting unanimously to pass a reasonable measure controlling gun ownership by people with possible mental illness, faced a veto by the governor—and then failed to override the veto when eleven Republican senators defect and vote against the override?[11]

Under these conditions, alienation from government has set in with John Q. and Jane Public. The resultant apathy has produced lower voter turnout and general uninterest in government. In the 2015 general election, less than 22 percent of registered New Jersey voters showed up at the polls, a record for the lowest participation rate in the history of the state.[12] This leads to the question: How can we expect government to be responsive to the people it is supposed to serve if they have given up on it?

The five areas of soft corruption have overlapping and intertwining features. Figure 1.1 illustrates the interdependence of these five areas and the centrality of campaign financing. Lobbyists raise campaign funds and take part in elections, patronage provides a source of tribute from job holders as well as a cadre of election workers, and conflicts of interest exist when patronage results in a public official holding more than

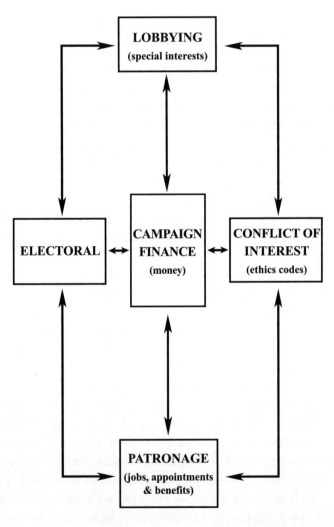

FIGURE 1.1. Interrelating Areas of Soft Corruption

one government job or when contributions are received from special interest donors.

Soft corruption is a national problem, and I will cite some examples from other states, but the focus of this book is on the problem in my native New Jersey. Each of these five soft corruption issue areas will be treated in separate chapters that follow (campaign finance will require two chapters: numbers 2 and 3). After this examination of these problems and their consequences, chapter 8 offers a comprehensive agenda for reform, with recommendations related to each area of soft corruption. In the pursuit of such answers, states must be careful to avoid populist reforms that seem appealing but in reality create new problems; I conclude with a warning against such "faux reforms" and instead recommend a novel approach to enabling citizen-led solutions.

## FOCUS AT THE STATE LEVEL

Soft corruption at the state level has especially negative consequences for the American ideal of representative government. A fundamental fact of political life that most Americans do not understand was enunciated by the late Speaker of the House of Representatives, Tip O'Neill: "All politics is local." He meant politics at the state, county, and municipal levels is more important than national politics in influencing the behavior of government officials, including those serving in federal office. Public officials are creatures of their political environment; they look to the local political infrastructure for election, reelection, appointments, and even policy formulation—indeed, for their own political survival. Patronage, the lifeblood of most political organizations, is primarily administered locally. Virtually all patronage jobs are in state, county, and local government, and local political machinery handles appointments to these jobs. Politics feeds on relationships; in most cases local relationships are strongest.

Despite the local roots of politics, followers of the news tend to pay more attention to politics and government stories about national issues and personalities, and indeed these account for the preponderance of political stories. State and local government are often described as "invisible government." Polls continually show that voters have some knowledge of who represents them at the top of the food chain—their U.S. senators, U.S. representatives, and governors. But ask random voters who represents them in the state legislature, on their county board, and on their municipal governing bodies, and they have a hard time naming any, except perhaps the local mayor. If local officials are less visible, it stands to reason that they are more susceptible to ethical transgressions and political manipulation—which are also under the radar—than the more visible officeholders.

Political reform must begin at the state level because that is the most critical place to do it. The largest body of substantive laws affecting the everyday lives of people is state and local law. Political columnist David Broder remarked in 2000: "Except for Social Security and Medicare, federal spending is smaller than that of state and local governments." He also noted that "only 13 percent of public employees are on the federal payroll."[13] The clear implication is that clamping down on soft corruption must be directed at the state and lower levels of government. This means reforming the systems used by the states to address campaign financing, lobbying, conflicts of interest, patronage, and the electoral process.

Reform will not be easy. Will officials who have overlooked, tolerated, or used soft corruption to their advantage ever have the independence and moral rectitude to do what is right? What will force an attitude change? Can citizens ever be sufficiently motivated and organized to elect officials who represent them honestly and with integrity? For reform to happen, voters will have to be so unhappy with the ethics lapses of their elected officials that they will no longer stand for it and will engage in a broad-scale public rebellion to take back their government.

We can do better. We must do better.

# 2 ▸ CAMPAIGN FINANCING

## How It Works

"There are two things that are important in politics. The first is money—and I can't remember the second."

— MARK HANNA of Ohio, national GOP chairman, 1896–1904, and Republican kingmaker

MONEY'S MOST IMPORTANT function in politics is to win elections. Money buys media exposure, direct mail, consulting services, and foot soldiers for getting out the vote on Election Day, all of which are key to electoral success. Outspending the opponent does not guarantee victory, but it is impossible to be competitive without substantial resources. Unfortunately, money in the political process is the overriding stimulus for and cause of corruption. A river of it runs through New Jersey's politics and government, millions of dollars at the disposal of political officials in the form of honest and dishonest graft. All too often, money corrupts the process.

In addition to spending on campaigns for elective office, the term "campaign financing" encompasses donations that finance the operations of political parties, political action committees (PACs), expenditures between elections, the soft money used by independent sources to influence a political or governmental result[1]—in short, any activity financed by direct and indirect donations to a campaign or political party.

Campaign financing refers to both the solicitation of and donation to a campaign and the spending of that money on behalf of the recipient. The exorbitant sums of political money flowing through New Jersey and the barely concealed motives of the givers and receivers amount to a system of "honest graft" when it follows the law, which it usually does. Examples are local officials running for election who solicit contributions from the same lawyers and engineers who are paid handsomely for professional services by the governing body on which the elected officials serve, and when state lawmakers receive contributions from a trade organization that wants the legislature to enact a measure beneficial to practitioners of that trade. A recently published study of legislatures in all fifty states by the political scientist Lynda Powell uses empirical correlation analysis to show the connection between campaign money and lawmakers' decisions. Powell asserts: "Campaign contributions do influence the behavior of individual legislators and, consequently, influence the policy choices of legislative institutions."[2] Does this mean that policy choices of legislatures influenced by campaign contributions have negative results for the people? Powell suggests the answer is yes, as she concludes from her studies that "the more money a legislator raises, the more the interests of constituents are traded off against those of donors."[3]

## DISCLOSURE

Various strategies have been used over the years to regulate campaign financing in order to protect the electoral process from corrupting uses of money. Requiring disclosure of campaign contributions and expenditures is the most basic regulation, found almost universally at state and federal levels. Laws relating to disclosure generally stipulate that the treasurer of the entity that is receiving contributions, whether a campaign, a political party, or a political action committee, must identify the source of contributions above a specific dollar amount and must report this information, together with all expenditures, in a timely manner.

Disclosure provides transparency so that citizens have some knowledge of the special interests that support the election efforts of candidates and their political parties. Disclosure also has a chilling effect on contributions when the donor or recipient would be politically embarrassed if his or her identity were revealed. In its 1972–1973 session, the New Jersey legislature was considering a campaign finance reform bill. The governor, William T. Cahill, was not enthusiastic about the measure and tried to set the disclosure threshold—that is, the minimum amount requiring disclosure of the donor's identity—at $500. This was considerably higher than the $100 recommended in the legislation. In support of his recommendations, Cahill claimed, for example, that local merchants were accustomed to making substantial donations—as much as $500—to both sides in mayoral contests. For obvious reasons, these merchants did not want their bet hedging to become known. The governor reasoned that contributions would dry up if the merchants had to limit their contributions to smaller amounts to avoid disclosure.

He wasn't imagining the deterrent effects of disclosure. One year before, an earlier version of the same campaign financing bill proposed $50 as the threshold for reporting. Although no law required me to do so, I wanted to set an example indicating my agreement with the bill by disclosing the identities of donors to my campaign. As a matter of fairness, we notified all donors and sought their approval before releasing their names to the press.

An early contributor of $50 was Mary Roebling, a prominent business and civic leader in the state who chaired and owned controlling interest in one of the largest banks in Trenton. Twenty minutes after her office was notified that I planned to disclose her contribution, an official from Roebling's bank was in my office asking that the money be returned. This was a serious matter; he had to return with the $50 or he said he would be looking for a new job. I complied. Even though Roebling had made the contribution from her personal account, she probably thought her bank, which did considerable business with the State of New Jersey, would be subjected to criticism. Or perhaps she just wanted her contribution kept secret from the Democrats in whose good offices she wanted to remain, because they occupied powerful elected positions in Trenton and surrounding Mercer County.

Candidates and political parties do not want to be required to disclose contributions from certain sources, such as organized crime figures, convicted felons, controversial public figures, and the like. In June 1994, a political action committee (PAC) operating on behalf of Republicans in the New Jersey General Assembly held a fund-raiser and received a check for $5,000 from the Coalition for the Preservation of the First Amendment. Three months later, an enterprising reporter revealed the coalition represented adult bookstores in the state. The Republicans quickly returned the $5,000.[4]

Since disclosure is intended to inform the public about the sources of a candidate's support, it is important to make this information available in a timely manner. The New Jersey campaign finance law requires reports be filed twenty-nine days and again eleven days before an election, and twenty days after. Details of contributions of $1,200 and higher received after the eleven-day preelection report must be forwarded within forty-eight hours to the state enforcement agency for publication.

Even so, contributions sent in the last few days of a campaign receive little public notice, and the significance of the information is lost. Many clever donors time their contributions for late arrival. In 1997, a developer-backed conservative running against me in the Republican primary notified the state agency on primary day that he had received the maximum contribution of $1,800 from Hovnanian, a large home-building company. The name Hovnanian was anathema to open-space preservationists. Had this contribution been known earlier, my opponent would have left himself open to serious criticism.

And, of course, there are late filings. Such was the case involving an expenditure of $200,000 for a telephone blitz by the National Rifle Association (NRA) against Democratic governor James Florio in his unsuccessful 1993 reelection bid. By the time the identity of the donor was revealed in a post-deadline filing, the damage had been done. The NRA was fined $7,000, a small price to pay for the objective it had helped to accomplish.[5]

## CONTRIBUTION LIMITS

A more potent component of campaign financing regulation is the contribution limit, the maximum amount a donor can give to a candidate or political entity in an election cycle or calendar year.

Limits apply only to contributions made directly to candidates and political organizations. The U.S. Supreme Court affirmed the constitutionality of imposing limits on campaign contributions in *Buckley v. Valeo* (1976). This ruling came after Congress passed strict campaign financing laws following the Watergate scandal of 1972, and it established the validity of limiting contributions to discourage corruption.

But the Court also found in *Buckley* that limiting campaign *expenditures* would be an unconstitutional restriction of free speech. One important exception is that, if a campaign is publicly financed, the government may impose spending limits as a condition of the candidate's receiving public funds.

When contributions are made to fund independent expenditures to express a political view or to support a candidate's campaign, the Supreme Court found in its 2010 *Citizens United* decision that no limits can be placed on the size of contributions or their source so long as the resulting expenditures are indeed independent, that is, not coordinated with a specific campaign.

Since the ruling in *Citizens United* was handed down, vast amounts of money have entered the electoral system as independent expenditures. Moreover, the special interests that exploit this means of campaign financing have found ways of transmitting contributions so that neither the identities of the donors nor the size of their contributions are publicly disclosed.

The *Citizens United* model of unrestricted contributions for financing major campaign initiatives has recently entered the electoral arena for state and local offices—most notably in a few high-profile gubernatorial contests, where the Republican and Democratic Governors' Associations have served as conduits for independent gubernatorial expenditures. The focus of this book, however, is direct campaign financing, which is specifically regulated by limits on campaign contributions and full disclosure of all activities involving political money.

Table 2.1 provides a comprehensive schedule of the different contribution limits enacted in New Jersey in 1993 that apply to various political entities. The table makes clear the vast amounts of money that inundate the political landscape of the state and the opportunities for a resourceful individual or organization with substantial funds to exploit the system.

TABLE 2.1.    Contribution Limits

| Entities Making Contributions | Candidate committee* | Continuing political committee PAC | Legislative leadership committee | State political party committee | County political party committee | Municipal political party committee |
|---|---|---|---|---|---|---|
| | | | Entities Receiving Contributions | | | |
| Individual (includes corporations, unions, associations, groups) to: | $2,600 per election | $7,200 per year | $25,000 per year | $25,000 per year | $37,000 per year | $7,200 per year |
| Candidate committee to: | $8,200 per election | $7,200 per year | $25,000 per year | $25,000 per year | $37,000 per year | $7,200 per year |
| Continuing political committee PAC to: | $8,200 per election | $7,200 per year | $25,000 per year | $25,000 per year | $37,000 per year | $7,200 per year |
| Legislative leadership committee to: | NO LIMITS | | | | | |
| State political party committee to: | NO LIMITS | | | | | |
| County political party committee to: | NO LIMITS‡ | | | | | |
| Municipal political party committee to: | NO LIMITS | | | | | |
| National political party committee† to: | $8,200 per election | $7,200 per year | $25,000 per year | $72,000 per year | $37,000 per year | $7,200 per year |

SOURCE: New Jersey Election Law Enforcement Commission, Trenton.
NOTE: Public question political committee and Independent expenditure-only committees may receive unlimited contributions.
*THE contribution limit to a gubernatorial candidate is $3,800 per election.
†A "national political party committee" is the principal organization supporting election activities of a state political party committee, which activities include making contributions to that state political party committee pursuant to N.J.S.A. 19:44A–11.4a(2). There shall be no more than a single national political party committee of a political party for each state political party committee.
‡FROM January 1 through June 30 of each year, a county political party committee is prohibited from making a contribution to another country political party committee and a country political party committee is prohibited from accepting a contribution from another county political party committee. A county political party committee is subject to other restrictions; see N.J.A.C., 19:25–11.7.

Some definitions are helpful in understanding the contribution limits in table 2.1. An "individual" is defined broadly as a person, corporation, union, or association acting in an individual capacity to make direct contributions to candidates and political organizations. The law limits the individual donor to a contribution of $2,600 per candidate per election cycle; the primary and general elections are considered separate cycles.

Except for contributions to a gubernatorial candidate, which have a limit of $3,800, the $2,600 amount applies to candidates for all offices, from school board member to municipal council member to county free-holder and state legislator. The limits on contributions by individuals are considerably higher when the donations are made to political groups or committees rather than to candidates.

The "continuing political committee" in table 2.1 is more commonly known as a political action committee, or PAC. A PAC is typically orga-nized by a special interest to raise and spend money over an indefinite period of time for the benefit of its members and supporters. A corpo-rate PAC raises money from the firm's executives and associates; a union PAC raises funds from members; and an association PAC—for example, a group of real estate agents or doctors—gets donations from its mem-bership. The sizable war chests that PACs accumulate allow them to give in even greater amounts to candidates and to the four other types of "no limits" committees listed in table 2.1.

The legislative leadership committees of each party in each house and the state political party committees each can receive contributions of as much as $25,000 per year from any source. The forty-two county politi-cal party committees (of the two parties in twenty-one counties) each can receive a maximum annual donation of $37,000 from a single source; municipal political committees may receive single-source contributions of $7,200. All of these committees can give unlimited amounts to candi-dates and other political entities. An exception prohibits contributions between county political party committees during the first six months of a calendar year.

If one hundred donors, including individuals, corporations, unions, and PACs, give $25,000 each to a single legislative leadership commit-tee, it will have $2.5 million to spend.[6] And if one hundred donors gave $37,000 each to a single county political party committee, it would have a war chest of $3.7 million. Under New Jersey's campaign contribution limits, a wealthy individual who wanted to maximize her influence with one of the two parties in the state could legally make contributions to the twenty-four party committees totaling $852,000 in one year. And that does not even take into account the contributions that person could also make to each candidate from that party.

What do all these committees do with the money they collect? Essentially, they spend it without limit on campaigns of their own choosing.

## WHEELING

These enormous political resources have created the process of wheeling, the transfer of funds from one political party committee to another. Say a heated election campaign is under way in county A, and a wealthy special interest has "maxed out" its contribution to the political party committee there. This special interest can then give another maximum contribution to the party's political committee of county B. The county B party can transfer the same amount to county A, doubling the contributor's donation to be used in county A's crucial election. Wheeling also takes place when several party committees join together to transfer large sums from their treasuries, without limits, to an important campaign.

Wheeling is illegal if the participants conspire to avoid contribution limits by funding transactions in this manner. But in New Jersey's political environment, a conspiratorial agreement, spoken or written, is unnecessary for the players to know where the money should go. Major donors and the political operatives who instruct them are attuned to which campaigns are considered most important, or they simply follow the lead of other known political funders.

An obvious instance of wheeling took place in July 2003, when two high-level Middlesex County Democratic fund-raisers who were real estate developers—Jack Morris and former state senator John Lynch— both wrote checks for $27,000 on the same day from the same address to the Hunterdon County Democratic Committee. Hunterdon is a solidly Republican county. No one would expect a Democrat to win a county election there even with the infusion of three or four times the $54,000 sent by outside sources. Within two months, the Hunterdon Democrats sent two checks of $25,000 each to the Ocean County Democratic Party, which had already received maximum contributions from the same two donors. The $50,000 sent by the Hunterdon Democrats helped elect a mayor, an outcome that was important to the interests of the donors. The Hunterdon Democrats kept $4,000 for their trouble.

In reporting this incident, the *Hunterdon County Democrat* newspaper wrote that it had "learned that the Hunterdon County Democratic Committee (HCDC) accepted two checks for $27,000 each with the understanding that $50,000 would be forwarded to the Ocean County Democratic Committee." Asked about this transaction, a representative of the HCDC stated: "When people make donations, there are no strings attached. We were asked to help out Ocean County, which we did." The party official stressed that there was no collusion regarding the matter, adding that "the request for money came from the Ocean County Democratic Committee."[7]

That same year, business interests connected with Jack Morris of Middlesex, one of the principals in the Hunterdon wheeling case whose firm had been chosen to undertake a massive development of an industrial site in Hamilton Township, sent large amounts of money to the Democratic Party committees of three counties: $25,000 to the committee in Mercer County, where Hamilton is located; $30,000 to the Bergen committee; and $37,000 to the Camden committee. The Bergen and Camden committees each wheeled $25,000 to the Mercer Democratic Committee. During the months leading up to the 2003 general election, the Mercer County Democratic Committee donated $81,000 to the campaign of Democrat Glen Gilmore, who was running for reelection as mayor of Hamilton Township. Gilmore won the election.

When the *Times of Trenton* broke the story about this parade of contributions, representatives of Morris's business interests and the chair of the Mercer Democratic organization—who also served as Gilmore's chief of staff—denied they had engaged in any collusion to circumvent the state's campaign finance laws. A representative of one of Morris's businesses connected to the wheeling said, "All donations made by the company are done to express First Amendment rights and to support the communities in which the company does business." The Mercer Democratic chair denied that any of the contributions were related to the Hamilton mayoral race or were an attempt to influence land-use decisions in Hamilton. He declared, "I am not aware of any connection between the donations." And from the Camden Democrats came this statement: "Camden County Democrats are team players. We regularly provide support to Democratic candidates and organizations, especially when they are engaged in competitive elections."[8]

The race for Bergen County executive in the fall of 2002 gave rise to a classic case of wheeling in three respects: the tremendous amount of money political powers sent to Bergen from other parts of the state; the rapid change in voter preference, from the early favorite to the underdog, who benefited from an avalanche of funds in October; and the stakes—the extraordinary power, in terms of patronage and the ability to award government contracts, wielded by the county executive in the most populous county of the state.

The two candidates vying for county executive were the early favorite, Henry McNamara, a highly respected and popular Republican state senator, and Dennis McNerney, a little-known Democrat. Of the $4 million spent on behalf of McNerney, who won, $3 million came from out-of-county sources in the last stages of the campaign. As one reporter described it, the money was used in "fueling a barrage of virulent campaign ads" against McNamara.[9]

Most of the $3 million wheeled into Bergen County came from three sources, all with significant political clout. The largest contributor was George Norcross of Camden County, who had strong finance and labor connections and who, by all accounts, controlled several South Jersey county Democratic organizations. Norcross and his allies donated almost $500,000 directly to the Bergen campaign and another $960,000 to other Democratic Party organizations, most of it wheeled into the Bergen race, according to the *Star-Ledger*.[10]

The second major player was John Lynch, a former state senator and Democratic leader of Middlesex County with strong ties to developers. The Lynch political machine sent $377,000 from Middlesex sources directly into Bergen and an additional $620,000 to other Democratic committees, which were major funders of the county executive campaign in Bergen.

Finally, Jon S. Corzine, a wealthy former CEO of the Wall Street firm Goldman Sachs who had spent more than $60 million of his own money in winning his U.S. Senate seat in 2000, continued to contribute heavily to Democratic organizations across the state. He made the maximum personal contribution of $37,000 to the Bergen County party and then sent identical amounts to four other Democratic county units, as well as a total of $27,500 to the two leadership PACs of his party. With the four other counties and the leadership PACs giving substantial amounts to Bergen, the lion's share of Corzine's aggregate contribution of $212,500 found its way to the Democrats there.

Wheeling is proof positive that New Jersey has created a smorgasbord of perfectly legal ways for wealthy businesses, individuals, and special interests to buy influence, exact tribute, and destroy the opposition. These conditions add to New Jersey's reputation as one of the states with the most egregious excesses in campaign financing.

Democrats are not the only pols who practice wheeling in New Jersey. During the 2003 campaign, Burlington Republicans, the dominant party in that county, wheeled $500,000 through the Republican State Committee to other GOP campaigns in critical state legislative districts.[11] The record also shows that Jack Morris, the Middlesex County developer who heavily funds Democratic campaigns, also sent more than $64,000 to GOP groups in the four years that ended in 2004.[12]

These wheeling transactions are legal and clearly illustrate the culture of soft corruption in New Jersey politics. Wheeling distorts the normal process of campaign financing, and the public was made well aware of this by the many revelations that appeared after 2000. New Jersey political leaders had made wheeling a fine art, having used the seven years since the state's campaign finance law took effect (in 1993) to figure out how best to exploit its loopholes. By then New Jersey voters had been treated to a steady diet of exposés about wheeling in news stories by the *Star-Ledger*.

Pressure for reform became intense, and the legislature finally acknowledged that something had to be done. A bill, touted as a means of reforming wheeling, worked its way through the Democrat-controlled legislature and was signed into law in December 2004. Yet this measure was flawed—and not unintentionally. Instead of instituting a blanket ban on wheeling, the new law prohibited wheeling only by county political parties and only during the first six months of the year. This would affect county primary elections, which are held in June, but not the general elections in November. This result was a clear response to the concerns of county political bosses, who are paranoid about outside forces influencing primaries in their counties. In New Jersey, the county political parties hold substantial political power, much of it exercised in the selection of candidates who, when elected, will be loyal disciples of their political benefactor. While these power brokers wanted no interference from outside money in their primary contests, they were happy to accept money wheeled in from other counties to help their candidates win in November. It is worth noting the new law would have prevented none of the wheeling examples cited above, because they all took place during general election campaigns.

## DIRECT CORPORATE CONTRIBUTIONS
## AND PAY TO PLAY

Unlike federal law and the laws of a majority of the states, which ban the practice, New Jersey law permits corporations to contribute directly to campaigns. A study of campaign contributions made in New Jersey between 1994 and 1999 found corporations gave more than $32 million, whereas individuals donated only half that amount.[13]

New Jersey does prohibit direct contributions from corporations that are subject to state regulation, such as public utilities, banks, railroads, and insurance companies, a much smaller segment of the corporate universe. This prohibition was part of the Corrupt Practices Act, passed in 1911 at the urging of then-governor Woodrow Wilson. It applied to corporations directly regulated by state agencies, such as the Board of Public Utilities and the Departments of Banking and Insurance. In the modern era, virtually all corporate entities are affected by state regulation and oversight in matters relating to environment, health, taxation, transportation, construction, and more. The question then must be posed: Why not prohibit political contributions from all corporations?

Business interests have vigorously supported the free flow of corporate contributions to political campaigns. These direct contributions facilitate "pay to play," the practice wherein business enterprises make significant contributions to officials who control a government agency and receive a contract from that agency for services or materials. While a campaign contribution given explicitly as a condition for receiving a government contract would be a criminal act, the history in New Jersey of the correlation between making a contribution and getting a contract is so strong that a quid pro quo is suspected every time a major campaign contribution is followed some time later by the award of a big contract to the contributor.

One of the most egregious examples of pay to play in New Jersey involved Parsons Infrastructure and Technology, a large engineering firm from California. Parsons and its related companies donated more than $500,000 to New Jersey candidates, to political committees, and to Republican governor Christie Whitman in the years before 1998,[14] when it landed the $500 million seven-year contract to install and manage the state's auto inspection system.[15]

When Congress amended the Clean Air Act in 1990, New Jersey was said to have the second-worst air pollution of any state; auto emissions were a major cause.[16] The Whitman administration (1994–2001) responded with a privatized auto inspection program designed to meet the federal mandate for clean air in the state. The award of the contract involved behind-the-scenes negotiations and machinations by Parsons and top-level state officials and lobbyists. These activities, revealed in a series of stories by New Jersey's newspapers, climaxed in public hearings held in 2001 by the State Commission of Investigation (SCI) after it had spent fifteen months looking into what had transpired. According to the *Star-Ledger*, the SCI charged in its concluding report that the Parsons contract was "a 'mammoth boondoggle' costing taxpayers $247 million more than a state-run system would, the result of a bidding process corrupted by influence peddling."[17]

The SCI report said in part: "While the contract award was, by law, to have been the result of open, competitive bidding, the process was tainted at key intervals by political considerations and by the granting of favored treatment. Parsons Infrastructure hired consultants with deep ties to the Trenton political establishment to press its case in both the executive and legislative branches of state government." Parsons's monthly bill for the two lobbyist-consultants was $7,500. One was Roger Bodman, whose previous service included a stint as commissioner of the New Jersey Department of Transportation, the agency that oversaw the Division of Motor Vehicles auto inspection program. The other was Frank Holman, former chair of the Republican State

Committee, who was still receiving compensation from the committee as a consultant.[18]

The SCI report continues:

A confidential written agreement between the company and one of New Jersey's most influential lobbying firms called explicitly for the development of a "political strategy" to obtain the contract. . . . Meanwhile, months before Parsons Infrastructure emerged as the sole bidder, company executives met privately and exclusively with senior state officials, including the then-director of the Division of Motor Vehicles, to discuss substantive matters related to the design and timing of the state's RFP (request for proposals, i.e., invitation to bid). . . . Parsons Infrastructure received exclusive information that gave it a head start on the deployment of corporate resources for a bid submission.

The tactics employed in bringing influence to bear on the selection of a vendor created a perception of impropriety and were inconsistent with the public's rightful assumption that the procurement process is, and should be, a "level playing field" for all potential bidders. Once the contract was awarded, a pattern was established in which the state repeatedly granted waivers to Parsons Infrastructure with regard to implementation benchmarks and penalties governing nonperformance—the same stringent timeline and penalties that, in some cases, had caused other firms to decide against submitting competing bids.[19]

According to the SCI, Parsons also obtained inside information about the RFP from a state employee who had worked at both the state Department of Environmental Protection and the Division of Motor Vehicles and was hired by Parsons seven months after it was awarded the contract. The employee denied giving any inside or confidential information to Parsons.[20]

A Parsons strategy memo quoted in the SCI report noted: "We have received constant encouragement behind the scenes and are now extremely well positioned." The memo's author also wrote, according to the SCI, "that Bodman [the lobbyist] further suggested that Parsons Infrastructure 'narrow down' a list of potential subcontractors for the project and that he (Bodman) would 'help select one that will help us win the RFP.'" Among the subcontractors named in Parsons's bid were Anthony Sartor, a substantial contributor to New Jersey Republicans, who ultimately received an engineering contract worth $3.5 million; and Carl Golden, a former communications director for Governor Whitman, picked to manage the $15 million Parsons public relations contract.

The SCI report also emphasized the role of "the nature and timing of political campaign contributions." It found that "during the years bracketing the contract award, substantial sums were contributed to candidates and political committees in New Jersey by entities that make up the Parsons corporate family. In a number of instances, the chief Trenton lobbyist for Parsons served as a fund-raising middleman, personally soliciting corporate donations and passing them to select politicians, and working with Parsons Infrastructure executives to develop a campaign-funding strategy."

One of the lobbyists for Parsons, Frank Holman, had testified before the SCI that he gave this advice to his client: "Every other company that works in New Jersey makes contributions, so I felt they should be doing it too."[21] The other lobbyist, Roger Bodman, commented in criticizing the SCI report, "We played by the rules—rules that almost everyone concedes, and I believe, should be strengthened. Changes are necessary, *but no one broke any laws or rules*" (emphasis added).

Playing by those rules even after a Democrat became governor in early 2002, Parsons continued to make political contributions. Nine Parsons executives paid a total of $4,500 for tickets to newly elected Governor Jim McGreevey's inaugural celebration, and Parsons donated $25,000 to the state Democratic Party in both 2003 and 2004.

Using Parsons as the poster child for banning excessive campaign contributions and vendor influence, reformers set out to stop pay to play. Legislation developed largely by individuals who were members of Common Cause was introduced by senate Republicans in 2003 and was advancing through the legislative process when Governor McGreevey threatened a veto. McGreevey contended that he wanted a more comprehensive reform bill, a tactic many claimed was a stall so the governor and his party could rake in hundreds of thousands of additional pay-to-play donations in the interim. Craig Holman, a campaign finance expert with Public Citizen of Washington, D.C., who helped draft the reform legislation, said of McGreevey, "He is trying to come up with an excuse not to adopt reform while sounding like a reformer. It is exceedingly insincere."[22] The momentum to change pay to play was slowed for more than a year. After McGreevey in mid-2004 declared his intention to resign as governor, he had a change of heart and signed an executive order limiting pay to play in New Jersey. He used the occasion to state, "Political fund-raising and the people's business all happen in the same meetings over the same table."[23]

The ban, which took effect in 2006, prohibited vendors from applying for no-bid state contracts worth more than $17,500 if the vendor had made campaign donations of more than $300 to political entities during the previous eighteen months. Vendors awarded a contract were further banned from making political contributions over $300 for the life of the contract. The prohibition applied to contributions from the firm's principals, employees, and their relatives to state party committees, county party committees, and gubernatorial campaigns. Vendors who violated the law could not seek a state contract for five years. This reform was not greeted enthusiastically in some political quarters. The chair of the state Democratic Party, Assemblyman Joe Cryan, advocated repeal of the ban but was unsuccessful. He claimed that the restrictions were "chasing good people from the process. It's as if we've made participating in the process something wrong, something un-American."[24]

While fewer vendors interested in contracting with the state contributed less money, special interests found many ways to circumvent the reform. Vendors still could contribute to legislative leadership PACs and to municipal party committees. Those funds could then be wheeled to any party organization or campaign. In the first four months of 2007, the ever-resourceful Hudson County Democrats used four municipal party organizations as a conduit to funnel to the county party committee more than $900,000, much of it from state vendors.[25] Hudson politicians could do this because the wheeling ban during the first six months of the year applies only to donations from county political committees, not from municipal committees. The amount was more than the county party committee had received from all municipal organizations combined during the previous eight years. Hudson Democratic insiders put the money to good use, defeating a serious challenge to its candidates in that year's primary election.

Two years later, the legislature extended pay-to-play reforms to prohibit contributions from state vendors to legislative leadership PACs and to municipal party committees. These added restrictions, while helpful, did not stanch the flow of pay-to-play money into the political system. Vendors with state contracts were not restrained from contributing directly to candidates at any level of government—except for governor. Nor were vendors restrained from donating to special interest PACs, which could then wheel the money to the embargoed political committees. Many of these PACs, run by seasoned political operatives, carry such feel-good names as Leadership Horizons, Committee for Responsibility and Trust in Government, Partners for Progress, and the Leaders Fund. In the first two years under the new pay-to-play regulations, the Leaders Fund PAC collected more than $800,000, one-third from firms with state contracts and their employees. In turn, the Leaders Fund channeled the money into the campaigns of Democratic candidates, according to the *Asbury Park Press*.[26] Contributions to PACs are made ostensibly to serve the purpose of the PAC; they cannot be earmarked for a specific race in order to circumvent the law. However, the party pros in New Jersey have pretty good instincts about where the PAC money should go, even without a formal earmark.

Pay-to-play restrictions do not apply to some broad areas of government. The law covers only contracts made with the State of New Jersey while allowing local units of government to remain out of the pay-to-play system by using a "fair and open" process for awarding contracts. "Fair and open" requires only that the contract be advertised, that the criteria for an award be clearly stated, and that approval be made at a public meeting. These are not rigorous standards for competitive bidding and offer little impediment to insider deals for a favored contractor. In the words of former New Jersey state comptroller Matthew Boxer, "Qualifying for the fair and open exception returns the local government entity to the essentially unregulated system of contracting that existed before the pay-to-play law."[27]

In an effort to correct this serious gap in the application of pay to play, a statewide reform organization, the Center for Civic Responsibility, has embarked on a broad initiative aimed at convincing towns and counties to adopt ordinances outlawing pay to play. While this effort, called the Citizens Campaign, has enlisted almost 100 of the state's 565 municipalities and three of the twenty-one counties in a few short years, the most expedient way to make all local governments subject to strict pay-to-play regulations and close the "fair and open" loophole is through state law, a position advocated by the Citizens Campaign.[28]

Laws banning pay to play have the noble intent of reducing the quid pro quo money contributed by vendors who want to do business with government. But these laws apply only to transactions formalized by contract, and not all special interests that use money to seek government largesse are vendors applying for contracts. A much greater volume of political tribute comes from sources that want to influence government policy and administrative decisions on such matters as taxation, land use, financial aid, commercial regulation, and consumer protection. These issue areas attract substantial amounts of campaign and lobbying money, yet laws that curtail pay to play have no effect here because the government decision benefiting the special interest applicant is not consummated by vendor contract. The magnitude of campaign contributions exempt from pay-to-play restrictions was demonstrated by the fact that twenty-seven contributors made state donations of more than $200,000 each in 2003, but only five held government contracts.[29]

A good example of a nonvendor special interest that spent huge sums to influence a government result is EnCap, a North Carolina–based superdeveloper.[30] In 1999, the state chose EnCap to develop several old landfill sites in the Meadowlands section of Bergen County, five miles west of New York City. EnCap planned to transform the landfills into an $850 million planned development of 2,600 residential units and a thirty-six-hole golf course.

This was not a traditional pay-to-play transaction in which a vendor made contributions to officials connected to a government agency and then the agency granted the vendor a government contract. In this case the vendor, EnCap, spent $13 million over several years, mostly in fees to prominent law firms that worked with government agencies, to secure financing and approvals for the EnCap development. Included in that sum was $2 million for Trenton lobbyists and $300,000 in direct campaign contributions to officials and political committees. The law firms both provided services to EnCap and made heavy campaign contributions of their own. Table 2.2 shows the fees paid to the law firms and campaign contributions made by these firms.

TABLE 2.2.   EnCap and Its Five New Jersey Law Firms

| Law firms | Fees received from Encap and as bond counsel | Political contributions, state and federal, made by each law firm and its partners |
|---|---|---|
| DeCotiis, Fitzpatrick | $8,200,000 | $1,330,000 |
| McCarter & English | $1,250,000 | $279,000 |
| McManimon & Scotland | Not recorded | $340,000 |
| Parker, McCay | $400,000 | $938,000 |
| Windels, Marx, Lane | $850,000 | $79,000 |

SOURCE: John Brennan and David Sheingold, "Politicians, Law Firms Have Reaped $13M from EnCap," *Hackensack Record*, April 9, 2007.

Although the law firms contributed to political officials across the state, the *Record* noted: "In some cases, those officials' support has been crucial to help make the ... EnCap project move forward."[31] Eric Wisler, a principal of the DeCotiis, Fitzgerald law firm, engaged a key Trenton lawmaker, State Senator Wayne Bryant, with a secret consulting retainer of $8,000 per month starting in mid-2004, the *Record* reported. According to the newspaper, Bryant "voted yes on legislation favorable to EnCap's $1 billion landfill-to-links project in the Meadowlands" ("links" refers to the golf course). Bryant also served "as a paid point-man for Wisler to turn to in time of need," the newspaper said.[32] After the New Jersey inspector general issued a 2008 report critical of the EnCap development, Bryant and Wisler were indicted in 2010 on federal charges of fraud and bribery in relation to the retainer arrangement. Bryant was acquitted in 2012, and Wisler died before trial.[33]

An example of how EnCap campaign contributions reached even low-level elected officials was the $12,000 donated by EnCap executives, some of whom lived in North Carolina, to the 2001 and 2005 election campaigns of James Guida for mayor of Lyndhurst, home of a landfill proposed for development. The DeCotiis law firm contributed $6,000 to Guida for those campaigns.[34]

Despite $300 million in government loans and financing, EnCap struggled, finally breaking ground on its project in 2004. Cost overruns, environmental problems, defaults on debt payments, and unpaid contractors eventually derailed the project. EnCap filed for bankruptcy protection in 2008. One year later, the Hackensack Meadowlands

Development Commission terminated the agreement under which EnCap was operating. The state suffered a net loss of more than $50 million as a result of the EnCap fiasco.

One result of the debacle was an executive order issued by Governor Jon Corzine in late 2008 imposing pay-to-play restrictions on redevelopment agreements like the one EnCap made with the state. While the executive order is helpful, special interests use money in countless other situations to gain a government benefit or result without need for a written agreement. These remain outside the scope of pay-to-play reform and are perfectly legal.

As noted earlier, one category of campaign contribution to candidates and political organizations allowed under New Jersey law but prohibited in half the other states and in federal elections is the direct corporate contribution. Allowing direct corporate donations encourages pay to play, as seen in a simple comparison of contributions by donors identified as businesses, as reported by the *Asbury Park Press*. In 2003, before the pay-to-play ban, the New Jersey Democratic Party received 70 percent of its contributions from businesses, most of which can be presumed to be corporations. In 2006, the first year pay-to-play reform was in effect, business contributions dropped to 10 percent, although some of this falloff was undoubtedly made up by channeling money through recognized loopholes.[35] If corporate (business) contributions and pay-to-play payments are related, making corporate contributions illegal, as they are in many other states, would help in the battle against pay to play.

## BUNDLING—THE KUSHNER CASE

One of the more bizarre episodes of campaign finance extravagance involved New Jersey real estate tycoon Charles Kushner, whose business empire controlled more than seventy corporations and partnerships that managed more than 24,000 apartments, built as many as 1,000 houses per year, and administered 7.5 million square feet of office, industrial, and retail space. Kushner was a prodigious political contributor (a.k.a. rainmaker), raising more than $5.7 million between 1989 and 2004, mainly for Democratic candidates and party committees. Among the recipients of his generosity during this period were the following:

| | |
|---|---|
| Democratic National Committee | $1,933,635 |
| Democratic Senatorial Campaign Committee | $1,062,750 |
| New Jersey State Democratic Committee | $773,000 |
| N.J. Governor Jim McGreevey | $433,550 |
| U.S. Senator Robert Torricelli (D-NJ) | $242,150 |
| U.S. Senator Frank Lautenberg (D-NJ) | $231,000 |
| U.S. Senator Hillary Clinton (D-NY) | $157,000 |
| U.S. Representative Robert Menendez (D-NJ) | $123,250 |
| U.S. Senator Charles Schumer (D-NY) | $92,500 |
| U.S. Senator Jon Corzine (D-NJ) | $88,000 |
| Rudolph Giuliani, former NYC mayor and U.S. Senate candidate | $61,000 |
| Vice President Al Gore | $56,000 |
| National Republican Senatorial Committee | $42,430 |
| U.S. Senator Bill Bradley (D-NJ) | $38,450[36] |

Campaign finance reports contain a mother lode of information. Jim McGreevey, the Democratic candidate for governor in 2001, had lost by only 25,000 votes to the incumbent, Whitman, in 1997. McGreevey's 2001 early campaign contribution report was an eye-opener. A list of contributors five pages long revealed a clear pattern of relationships among them. All forty-one individuals on the donors list were connected to Kushner through separate real estate partnerships that shared his Florham Park, New Jersey, address, and all made their donations on the same day, August 9, 2000. All but one gave the maximum amount then allowed for individual contributors, $2,100. The final contributor gave $1,050, half the maximum. The aggregate amount was $85,050. Twenty-one of the forty-one contributors were Kushner family members. Charles Kushner himself, as the controlling partner of the real estate empire, had the right to make donations in the names of partners under the "partnership attribution" principle, so long as he received their written consent. It was clear that all $85,050 came from a single source, the Kushner business conglomerate.[37]

This process, which combines contributions from many sources, is known as bundling, and it is legal. When the donations are delivered to the chosen candidate or political organization, the bundler can be said to be extremely influential because she or he is not restricted to the limit for an individual contributor.

Bundling received national attention in the 2000 presidential campaign of George W. Bush. Those who bundled $100,000 in direct contributions to the Bush campaign were honored with the title of Pioneer. Those who collected $200,000 were dubbed Rangers.[38] But bundling for Bush was more orthodox than bundling by Kushner because the Bush effort involved collecting money from friends, relatives, and others who were not necessarily part of the same business entity.

McGreevey also received multiple contributions from Kushner and his associates that were directed to McGreevey's political action committee and other Democratic Party organizations. These contributions were ten to fifteen times the $2,100 limit that New Jersey then applied to individuals making a direct contribution to the gubernatorial race. The party organizations that received these larger donations bundled by Kushner were politically tied to McGreevey, and they clearly had an interest in helping him in his gubernatorial bid. Between 1997 and 2002, the Kushner network donated more than $1.5 million for McGreevey's benefit.[39]

Bundling by partnership attribution is a clever tactic for a wealthy donor to use to circumvent individual contribution limits and maximize the amount of funds going to a campaign. But when Kushner sent bundled contributions totaling $60,000 to two candidates for mayor of New York City in 2001, all but the legal limit of $4,500 per candidate was returned. Rules of the progressive New York City Campaign Finance Board stipulate that a contributor to the city's campaigns must be a "single source," and contributions bundled through entities that the source "establishes, maintains, or controls" are not permitted.

Craig Holman, a nationally recognized expert on campaign finance, commented on the multiple Kushner contributions: "When people start throwing that kind of money into the political process—that's a lot more than access." He said the result of Kushner's spending was "to systematically buy his way into a position of vast influence."[40]

Did lavish campaign spending by Kushner bring him any major governmental benefits? Apparently not, with one exception. McGreevey, the consummate political fund-raiser, wanted to show his gratitude once he became governor and so appointed Kushner to the board of the Port Authority of New York and New Jersey. McGreevey planned to make Kushner chair of the Port Authority when that position opened up.[41] As chair, Kushner would be able to exercise considerable power over regional development issues that conceivably could affect his real estate empire. But Kushner's tenure on the Port Authority board was short-lived (as I explain shortly), and he never became the chair.

Charles Kushner was unlike many political powers in New Jersey who aggressively sought government benefits in the form of zoning approvals, public contracts, legislative concessions, and the like. Instead, it appeared that he merely wanted the personal satisfaction of ensuring that his brand of politician occupied high public office and was in charge of policy in New Jersey and Washington, including former president Bill Clinton, with whom Kushner was on a first-name basis.

## KUSHNER LOSES BIG

In late 2001, after Kushner's disagreements with his sibling business partners led to lawsuits and allegations of misappropriation of business monies for campaign contributions, the brouhaha caught the attention of the U.S. attorney for New Jersey, who initiated an investigation. The Federal Election Commission (FEC) and New Jersey officials also started to examine contributions made by Kushner and his partners. A violation being investigated by the New Jersey attorney general involved Kushner's controlling interest in NorCrown Bank of New Jersey. Under state law, such ownership prohibits him from making political contributions to New Jersey candidates and campaigns because banks are part of a regulated industry to which this prohibition applies.[42]

At the federal level, the FEC revealed that Kushner had made contributions to many campaigns under the partnership attribution system without the approval of the partners. The increasing intensity of criticism directed at his campaign financing practices forced Kushner to resign from the Port Authority in February 2003.[43]

Violation of campaign finance regulations is almost always settled by a fine. Such was the case in early 2004, when Charles Kushner agreed to a state civil penalty of $230,000 for contributions made as owner of Nor-Crown Bank. Later that year, he paid $508,900 to settle with the FEC for making illegal contributions of more than $540,000 to federal candidates in 1999 and 2000 from forty firms and partnerships he controlled.

Kushner's lawyer stressed the $508,900 settlement was made to avoid litigation and was not a penalty. It was the fourth-largest fine ever assessed by the FEC.[44]

Aware that federal prosecutors were still looking into his political financing, Kushner decided to take bold action to prevent incriminating testimony from those involved in his real estate enterprise. The plan he devised crossed the line to criminal. He set out to hire a prostitute to engage in sex with his brother-in-law and use a videotape of this escapade to blackmail family members who might testify against him.

He hired two men to recruit a prostitute, but they failed in their mission. He himself then located and hired a prostitute in New York; the prostitute ultimately fulfilled her mission with Kushner's brother-in-law, and a satisfactory videotape was made. Kushner eventually sent the tape to his sister (wife of the brother-in-law), who then turned it over to the FBI.[45]

On July 13, 2004, Charles Kushner, in handcuffs, was arraigned in federal court on several charges, including conspiracy to promote interstate prostitution. One month later, he pleaded guilty, and in March 2005, he was sentenced to two years in prison and fined $40,000.[46]

The significance of the Kushner episode is not the unique tactic to stifle family dissent, nor is it the inadvertent use of contributions from a regulated financial institution. Rather, it is the ability of someone who possesses great wealth to transmit, under New Jersey's wide-open campaign finance laws, hundreds of thousands—even millions—of dollars into the political arena to serve the personal objectives of the donor.


## LAW FIRMS AND BUNDLING

The Kushner bundling model illustrates two important points: a single source with vast wealth can deliver immense sums of money, and limits on the amounts individuals may donate are easily circumvented through partnership attribution.

The most prolific practitioners of bundling are large law firms, most of which have a substantial number of government entities as clients. Probably the most lucrative of these clients are the independent authorities, which generally have large, stable revenue flows and considerable legal work for outside attorneys. Although the primary reason for a government body to establish an authority is to separate its specific operational purposes from the normal functions of government, the ties between the two remain strong. Elected officials generally appoint political allies to the authority board, and they in turn pick the outside attorneys. Law firms contribute heavily to the campaigns of elected officials who have jurisdiction over the authorities, and these officials, or their political patrons, are in a position to suggest to authority board members which law firms would be best to retain.

Campaign finance records are replete with examples of law firm campaign contributions. At the top of the New Jersey list for years has been the Bergen County firm of DeCotiis, Fitzpatrick, Cole and Wisler, which, according to a series of reports by the *Record*, "billed 128 government entities" almost $26.6 million between January 2001 and June 2003, apparently in no-bid contracts. In roughly the same period, the DeCotiis lawyers donated almost $500,000 yearly to campaigns across the state.[47]

The clout attributed to senior partner M. Robert DeCotiis and his partners in securing government business was not solely related to campaign contributions. In fact, firm members vigorously argued that the awards they received from government agencies were made because of the experience and abilities of the eighty-lawyer staff, not political contributions. There is good reason for this view, because the principal partners have occupied positions of considerable influence in New Jersey:

- In 1992–93, M. Robert DeCotiis, senior partner, was chief counsel to Democratic governor Jim Florio.
- From 1986 to 1989, Michael Cole, managing partner, was chief counsel to Republican governor Tom Kean, after serving as first assistant attorney general of New Jersey. Cole also did a stint as attorney for the New Jersey State Democratic Committee and was married to Jaynee LaVecchia, a justice of the New Jersey Supreme Court. (He died in 2011.)
- In 2003–04, Michael R. DeCotiis, son of M. Robert DeCotiis and former managing partner, served as chief counsel to Democratic governor Jim McGreevey.

The extent of bundling by the DeCotiis lawyers is shown by the following: Among the contributions by the DeCotiis lawyers was $997,000 donated to various officials and political parties in New Jersey's five most populous counties: Essex, Middlesex, Bergen, Union, and Hudson. During this time, the firm received more than $12 million in fees from the government agencies with which these officials were affiliated.[48]

Campaign finance reports showed that from April 2000 to June 2000, Edward Fitzpatrick, a partner in the firm, made eight contributions totaling $8,250 to three different campaign funds in Hudson County. However, Fitzpatrick had died the previous January. The error in making these contributions was generally dismissed as inadvertent. The head of the Center for Responsive Politics in Washington, D.C., wryly observed: "One of the basic principles of any campaign finance system is whether the contributions are made voluntarily. . . . It's a question of how voluntary a contribution from a dead man can be."[49]

Mauro Tucci, a commissioner of Nutley Township in Essex County, received $14,500 from DeCotiis attorneys for his 2004 reelection bid. This had triple implications for the law firm, because Tucci held two other public offices. He chaired the Essex County Utilities Authority when it awarded a $2.3 million no-bid contract to DeCotiis. Tucci also had a full-time job as township administrator for Bloomfield, which paid the law firm $350,000 for services from 2001 to 2003. And Nutley Township, where Tucci served as an elected commissioner, gave the DeCotiis firm a $25,000 retainer to provide legal advice in connection with a local project. When a reporter asked Tucci about his relationship with the DeCotiis firm, he said, "I needed to solicit funds for my campaign and my friend (a DeCotiis partner) stepped in and helped me raise money. What happened afterward—one contract for $25,000 (the Nutley contract). Is that pay to play? In life, when you've got to get something done, you go to your friends. . . . Just because DeCotiis contributes money, does that make him a bad guy?"[50]

Late in 2000, fifteen DeCotiis partners contributed $7,500 to the campaign of Mayor George Spadoro of Edison Township, who expected to face a challenger in the June 2001 primary. One month before the primary, these same partners kicked in another $10,000 to Spadoro's Edison

Township Democratic organization. The DeCotiis firm was municipal attorney for Edison, whose annual budget for legal costs was more than $203,000.[51]

Relationships between law firms and government are not peculiar to those of the Democratic persuasion. Republican government agencies have their favorites, one of which is the Riker Danzig law firm of Morristown, which prospered handsomely when GOP governor Christie Whitman was in office in the 1990s. Under long-term contracts, Riker Danzig collected $3,945,000 in fees from independent state authorities in 1999 while making campaign contributions of $362,600 to Republican candidates and party committees. Four years later, after Democrat Jim McGreevey became governor, fees paid to this firm for state services dropped to $977,000. At the same time, fees paid by state authorities to the DeCotiis firm, which apparently was more highly regarded by Democrats than by Republicans, went from $802,000 in 2001 to $2,730,000 in 2003.[52] This pattern points to the political bias in awarding contracts to law firms.

Bundling of political contributions by most political fund-raisers is not illegal. It is simply an efficient way to bring money into campaigns. But when bundling is performed in an organized manner with the hope of receiving a government benefit, it crosses the line and becomes pay to play. As revelations of presumed pay-to-play episodes increased, the pressure for reform in New Jersey also increased, resulting in the measures that took effect in 2006 and thereafter to restrict pay-to-play political contributions by state vendors.

Governor Corzine's executive order breaking up pay to play between vendors and contracting state agencies also prohibited awarding no-bid contracts to law firms, engineering firms, and other types of partnerships that provide professional services to government agencies. But there was an exemption in the 2006 measure: the prohibition applies only to those members of a professional services firm who own or control more than 10 percent of the firm. Any partner who owns less than 10 percent of the firm can make the current maximum contribution of $2,600 to a candidate (the limit rises to $3,800 for donations to gubernatorial candidates). Partners who own less than 10 percent of the firm can also donate the maximum amount allowed to political committees, as shown in table 2.1, and they also may bundle their contributions with colleagues of similar status.

## DEEP-POCKET CANDIDATES

In New Jersey, the many opportunities to maximize contributions produce a race to obtain as much money as possible to spend in campaigns. Extraordinarily high contribution limits combine with wheeling and bundling to generate ever-increasing sums of money for political treasuries.

Another stimulus that adds even more dollars to political campaigns is the millionaire candidate. As noted earlier, Democrat Jon Corzine, former CEO of Goldman Sachs, spent more than $60 million of his own money to win a U.S. Senate seat from New Jersey in 2000. The phenomenon of the millionaire candidate is familiar in other states, too. Former New York City mayor Michael Bloomberg, who built a financial services empire, self-financed his campaigns, spending more than $100 million to win reelection in 2009. In 2010, Linda McMahon, a Connecticut Republican seeking a U.S. Senate seat, spent more than $40 million, while Republican Meg Whitman, CEO of eBay, invested more than $140 million of her own money in her attempt to win the governorship of California. Both McMahon and Whitman lost.

The political establishment has logical reasons for welcoming millionaire candidates: they relieve the parties and their fund-raising organizations of the chore of collecting the enormous amounts of money required in key races; highly visible campaigns, such as those funded by wealthy candidates, help to elect lower-level candidates on the same ticket; and political leaders can sanctimoniously claim their deep-pocket candidates can't be bought by special-interest money, which of course is absent in these campaigns.

The New Jersey experience of how the super-wealthy candidate influences campaign financing is illuminating. Before 1999, Corzine was a modest contributor to Democratic candidates running statewide. Then, one year before he ran for the U.S. Senate, he started to pump major amounts of money into county Democratic organizations. The support of these organizations was key to producing a majority for Corzine to win the primary in 2000 and again in providing political power for his general election victory in November, when he outspent his opponent by 10 to 1.[53]

When McGreevey resigned as governor, Corzine decided he would rather be governor than U.S. senator. His popularity with the county parties he had financed so handsomely since 1999 paid off when, in 2005, he received the Democratic nomination for governor without a fight.

As table 2.1 shows, the maximum contribution from an individual to a county party committee is $37,000. In 2004, Corzine had maxed out his $37,000 contributions to many county organizations, including Bergen's. But on October 14, 2004, the Bergen Democrats received another perfectly legal $37,000 contribution with the name Corzine on the check. It was from Corzine's mother, a resident of Oak Park, Illinois.[54]

With minimal help from his immediate family, Corzine contributed a total of $4,339,000 to New Jersey's twenty-one county Democratic Party organizations between 1999 and 2008. He gave another $1,155,000 to Democratic legislative leadership PACs and the state party committee, $837,000 to the PAC of South Jersey Democratic power broker George Norcross, and more than $500,000 to individual candidates. Not only did Corzine sprinkle around vast sums of money to various Democratic committees and candidates, he also self-financed his two campaigns for governor—spending nearly $42 million for his 2005 race and $30 million in 2009.[55]

In October 2009, the *Record* published a study of Corzine's contributions to Democratic organizations. After becoming governor in January 2006, Corzine contributed more than $1.45 million to what the newspaper called the "wheeling pool" of Democratic organizations, consisting of county party committees, the state party committee, and the state senate and assembly Democratic leadership PACs. During this period, he was the largest individual contributor to twenty of the twenty-one Democratic county organizations. In two counties, his donations accounted for more than 50 percent of all contributions received from individuals. Corzine claimed he was making the contributions in the interest of bolstering the Democratic Party throughout the state.[56]

Super-wealthy candidates also often establish and fund charitable foundations. The awards made by such foundations to nonprofit organizations can have political implications. In the several years leading up to the 2005 gubernatorial election, the foundation Corzine had set up—and for which he was the sole trustee—gave or loaned more than $5 million to predominantly black churches in North Jersey's metropolitan area and in Camden. Many of these churches and their ministers are politically influential, not least the Reverend Reginald Jackson of Saint Matthew AME Church in the city of Orange. Jackson, who had served as executive director of the Black Ministers Council of New Jersey, with six hundred member congregations, joined fifteen other council leaders in publicly endorsing Corzine for governor two months before the 2005 election.[57]

Jackson's church had received a $50,000 loan from the Corzine foundation in early 2004. After Corzine had set his sights on the governorship following McGreevey's August 2004 decision to resign, Corzine forgave the loan to the church on January 1, 2005, and reclassified it as a gift. This well-timed adjustment meant the foundation did not have to report the $50,000 loan on its 2004 tax return, which would appear as a public record in 2005 and would have been an embarrassment to Corzine during his 2005 run for governor. Instead, the gift became public with the release of the foundation's 2005 tax return in August 2006, well after Corzine had been elected and had taken office.[58]

Jon Corzine used his vast wealth in creative ways to expand and consolidate his political power in order to win election to the highest office in New Jersey. But did spreading this largesse to local party leaders in the name of party building endow Corzine with the leadership to develop a sound record of governing the state? Or was this just another example of how money excesses pervert the principles of sound representative government? In 2007, Leonard Lance, the usually mild-mannered GOP state senate minority leader, summed up the litany of Corzine financial extravagances by saying of the governor, "He is an enabler of our corrupt system."[59]

## PUBLIC FINANCING OF CAMPAIGNS

Under the 1976 U.S. Supreme Court ruling in *Buckley v. Valeo*, no limits can be placed on political spending. But the Court did define a way to constrain spending in a political campaign through the adoption of a system of public financing for candidates. The rationale is straightforward: in exchange for receiving a campaign financing subsidy, the candidate must agree to limit the total funds he or she will spend, as prescribed by law.

In 1974, New Jersey Assemblyman Al Burstein collaborated with then-governor Brendan Byrne to shepherd a public financing law for gubernatorial campaigns through the legislature. Its rudiments are simple: a candidate for governor who opts to enter the public financing program must raise from private sources at least $380,000 in individual contributions no greater than $3,800 each to qualify. The candidate is then eligible to receive two dollars in state money for every dollar raised from private sources, with an overall spending limit in the gubernatorial campaign of $5 million for the primary and $10.9 million for the general election.

The New Jersey program for subsidizing races for governor worked reasonably well in keeping excessive special interest money out of these campaigns. Of course, the special interests can still direct their donations to legislative leadership PACs and to county and state political parties, where they can expect a sympathetic response, but these contributions cannot be transferred to gubernatorial campaigns.

One fault of the gubernatorial public financing program is that millionaire candidates who do not want to be constrained by limits on their spending do not have to agree to public financing. Such was the case when Corzine ran for governor in 2005 and 2009. His opponent in 2005 was the wealthy Republican Doug Forrester, who also chose not to accept public financing, which would have limited his spending. The same situation occurred in the presidential campaign in 2008. Even though he had previously given his support to the principle of public financing, then-candidate Barack Obama decided against participating in the program because he was convinced that his campaign could raise more than the maximum limit under public financing and he was fearful that the Republicans were capable of raising even more. However, his opponent, Republican John McCain, accepted public financing and the limits on spending that go with it.[60]

## PERCENTAGE OF PEOPLE WHO CONTRIBUTE

With such enormous sums pouring into the war chests of candidates and political parties, one might assume the money comes from a vast multitude of sources. Actually, the opposite is true. A relatively small percentage of the U.S. population contributes to political campaigns.

In a current study of federal campaign contributions, only one-third of one percent of all Americans make political donations of amounts exceeding $200 (which is the minimum amount in federal elections required for reporting).[61] But even more startling is the concentration of the enormous magnitude of all national contributions made as independent expenditures by only a minuscule number of super wealthy donors as a result of the *Citizens United* decisions. As reported by the Campaign Legal Center, a mere 1,587 donors were responsible for over $760 million (89 percent) of super PAC contributions in 2012. At a fund-raiser that year, President Obama told a group of Seattle multimillionaires, "You now have the potential of 200 people deciding who ends up being president every single time."[62]

Studies tallying the number of political contributions made at all levels of government, including those below the threshold for reporting as well as contributions to PACs, find that, at most, 4 to 6 percent of Americans make political contributions.[63] In its analysis of the 2006 elections, the Campaign Finance Institute showed that only 0.49 percent of New York State's voting age population made reportable contributions to gubernatorial or state legislative candidates. The study found that Rhode Island is the state with the highest percentage of campaign donors at 5.44 percent.[64]

The *Star-Ledger* reported on October 21, 2001, that of all contributions made in New Jersey in 2000, only 26 percent came from individual voters. The rest were from businesses, unions, political groups, and professional interests. In ten of the state's largest municipalities, two-thirds of the contributions for local candidates came from persons and businesses located elsewhere.[65] These data demonstrate the inordinate influence and power that relatively few sources of special interest money have on our system of government and politics.

Why is the percentage of citizen contributors so small? Is it because only those attuned to the inner workings of politics are willing to make an investment? Or are so many so frustrated by political conditions that there is little motivation to show any kind of support for those operating our government?

## INDEPENDENT EXPENDITURES

The most egregious loophole in campaign finance regulations is the independent expenditure made in support of a candidate or campaign. Such an expenditure is unregulated and unlimited. The only restrictions are that the decision about how that money is spent is made independently of the candidate and the campaign, and none of it goes directly to either one. In many cases, donors who provide the money for independent expenditures are not constrained by disclosure requirements. A donor can give the largest sum permissible under the law directly to a candidate and still give thousands more to an organization that makes independent expenditures, also known as a super PAC, on behalf of that candidate or against that candidate's opponent. And if the donor is seeking government business, the donor's contributions that pay for these independent expenditures are not subject to pay-to-play restrictions.

The issue of independent expenditures received a major stimulus in January 2010, when the U.S. Supreme Court, in its ruling in *Citizens United v. Federal Election Commission,* found that no restrictions may be placed on the spending of independent funds. Before the decision, federal law prohibited independent expenditures from being used for express advocacy—urging support for or against a named candidate—within thirty days of a primary and sixty days of a general election. But with the ruling in *Citizens United,* individuals, corporations, unions, and all other groups are now free to contribute to an independent group that finances electioneering messages, including the use of a candidate's name, at any time. Despite this change, the Court reaffirmed the right of government to impose regulations on direct contributions to candidates and political entities, as well as to require disclosure of the sources of independent funds.

It is difficult to know who bankrolls super PACs. They are registered under federal law as nonprofit organizations, and their income is not taxable. Some super PACs registered under a certain section of federal law (known as 527 PACs) must report to election enforcement agencies; others, which are registered under a different federal IRS code, have irregular reporting requirements. Super PACs tend to operate under wholesome, patriotic titles: Americans for Job Security, Club for Growth, American Crossroads, American Future Fund, Americans for Prosperity, and more. Still others make no attempt to disguise their self-interest and register their PACs in their own name: U.S. Chamber of Commerce, National Education Association, AFL-CIO, National Rifle Association, Planned Parenthood. Also considered as independent expenditures, or soft money, are funds from charitable organizations financed by wealthy candidates or officeholders that are used indirectly for political purposes. One source of such donations in New Jersey has been Jon Corzine's personal charitable trust, described earlier in this chapter.

The level of independent expenditures has grown dramatically in recent years.[66]

The estimated total of nonparty independent spending by super PACs and nonprofit entities in the national election of 2012 reached $1 billion. This was more than a threefold increase over independent expenditures spent on federal elections two years earlier. Of this amount, $311 million came from sources where disclosure was not required. An extreme example of the inordinate amount of independent expenditures was the estimated $150 million spent on federal candidates (mostly Republican) in 2012 by one donor, billionaire Sheldon Adelson.

The *Citizens United* impact on political campaign spending has reached down into the state and local levels. In 2013, when the governor and entire legislature stood for election in New Jersey, independent expenditures of nearly $39 million were made on these races. This was almost triple the $14.1 million of spending in the comparable election of 2009. Even local elections have been affected by this trend. Over $5 million of independent spending was pumped into the Newark city election of 2014, and in 2013 the low-level Elizabeth Board of Education election had a super PAC infusion of $180,000 to defeat two school board incumbents.[67]

Although these numbers illustrate high-profile independent spending following *Citizens United*, there have always been soft money campaigns in New Jersey where candidates for the office of governor have spent independently from regular campaign accounts. In early 2000, State Senate President Donald DiFrancesco, a Republican, was gearing up to run for governor the following year. He formed Solutions for a New Century, an independent issues committee that existed outside any formal campaign financing structure. Solutions for a New Century raised money and spent it without having to disclose its donors or the amounts they donated. The purpose of the group, according to DiFrancesco, who served as its chair, was to promote a legislative agenda. In the words of his political adviser: "It's an opportunity for [DiFrancesco] to reach out to people outside of government to get their thoughts on how to solve some of New Jersey's problems."[68] But the Solutions group was separate and distinct from his legislative leadership PAC and his state senate campaign committee, which of course were subject to strict reporting requirements.

At the time, DiFrancesco had not officially become a candidate for governor, but mailings by Solutions publicizing his achievements were essentially political advertisements intended to increase his name recognition and favorability ratings. These are basic strategies for anyone contemplating a statewide run for office. The glossy mailing included a response card to make it easy for interested people to join the Solutions group, a political device for building a corps of campaign followers. Despite appearances of an impending campaign, DiFrancesco protested: "I'm not a candidate. If you look at the ad, it has nothing to do with running for Governor, nothing to foster me as a candidate in any way."[69]

Two other New Jersey Republicans, both potential primary opponents of DiFrancesco for governor, also formed independent committees in 2000. One was Assembly Speaker Jack Collins, who dubbed his committee Leadership for New Jersey's Future; the other was Jersey City mayor Bret Schundler, who used the name Empower the People. Of the three, only Schundler was able to sustain his effort, and he ended up as the Republican candidate for governor.[70]

Similarly, allies of GOP governor Chris Christie established a PAC in 2010 called Reform Jersey Now to make independent expenditures to build support for the governor's programs. Registered under the federal tax code as a nonprofit, Reform Jersey Now was permitted to receive contributions of any amount, and these were not subject to pay-to-play restrictions, two points clearly spelled out in its solicitation materials.

Although its registration as a nonprofit group under the IRS code did not require that the names of donors be disclosed, the group's leaders claimed they would publish names of contributors at the end of the year. An editorial in the *Star-Ledger* cynically commented that the timing of the disclosure of donors was chosen in the hope that "the bad buzz will last just one day during Christmas week."[71]

Reform Jersey Now had sponsored events, featuring Christie as the speaker, with a ticket price of $25,000. This means that business executives could attend one of these events confident that their $25,000 donation will not disqualify their firm from landing a state contract under pay-to-play regulations. In its first few months, Reform Jersey Now received $624,000 from 244 donors. The organization spent the proceeds on ads to promote the governor's agenda. The group released the names of its donors on December 29, 2010. The list included "contractors paid hundreds of millions of dollars by state agencies," according to the *Star-Ledger.* Two days after releasing these names, Reform Jersey Now announced it was going out of business.[72]

# 3 ▸ CAMPAIGN FINANCING
## The New Jersey Version

"Politics is all about money in New Jersey."
—SHERRY SYLVESTER, New Jersey journalist

How NEW JERSEY first came to have any campaign contribution limits at all is a tale worth telling, both because it is a great political story and because it explains how the state's political powers ensure that New Jersey's campaign financing laws always have loopholes.

## A MAJOR SCANDAL AND ITS REPERCUSSIONS

On September 21, 1989, four high-ranking Democratic assemblymen gathered for a secret meeting at the Trenton Contemporary Club across the street from the statehouse. They invited twenty of the top lobbyists, who were brought into the meeting one at a time to hear a pitch for campaign contributions to help the Democrats win a majority in the assembly in the upcoming election. A new governor would be elected, and all seats in the eighty-member state assembly, then held by forty-one Republicans and thirty-nine Democrats, were at stake. The state senate's seats were not up for election and would continue under Democratic control.

On the surface, the circumstances surrounding the Democrats' meeting were not so unusual that they raised any eyebrows—but after the election, all hell broke loose. One lobbyist was so offended at what went on at the meeting that she made the public allegation that the assemblymen were conducting a blatant shakedown for money.[1] Making the charge was Karen Kotvas, a well-respected representative of the trial lawyers of New Jersey.

Kotvas said she was told the Democrats wanted suggestions from lobbyists for their campaign. When she arrived at the meeting, she found that the assemblymen were far more interested in getting a campaign contribution of $20,000 from the trial lawyers group she represented. The rationale for this request was simple and straightforward: the Democratic candidate for governor, Jim Florio, was ahead in the polls, which meant it was likely his coattails would produce a Democratic majority in the assembly. To ensure this result, the Democratic assembly majority fund-raising committee was making a last-minute drive to raise $200,000 to elect assembly Democrats. Kotvas said one assemblyman pointed out that one of the four legislators at the meeting would become the next assembly Speaker. The clear implication, according to Kotvas, was that if she wanted bills favorable to the trial lawyers posted for a vote in the next assembly session, the Speaker would need to feel kindly toward her group. Kotvas was outraged at the use of this tactic, one that by most standards—if proved—amounts to extortion.[2] She told the assemblymen that her client, Lawyers Encouraging Government and the Law, which went by the acronym LEGAL, did not give large lump-sum contributions to legislative leaders but rather made contributions to individual candidates. LEGAL, a political action committee (PAC), was one of the five most generous such donors in the state, contributing $70,000 to Democratic assembly candidates in the 1989 election cycle.[3]

This entire episode might never have come to light if not for a fortuitous circumstance. The Contemporary Club was being used as neutral ground for the meeting.

Newspaper reporter Chris Mondics of the *Hackensack Record* rented an upstairs room at the club for his personal office. When important legislators and twenty lobbyists started filing into the building, he knew something was up. As they emerged from the session, he quickly interviewed the lobbyists, including Kotvas, who told him everything that had happened at the meeting. However, she did not want to be quoted about what had transpired, and neither did any of the other lobbyists Mondics interviewed.

In early January 1990, Mondics contacted Kotvas again and said no other lobbyists would talk openly about the September 21 meeting. That was when Kotvas agreed to go public. She later explained: "Nobody was going on the record, and I felt that if I was complaining about the system, but not telling the truth about it publicly, I was just as much a symptom of a diseased system as these legislators."[4]

The Democrats had indeed won control of the assembly, 44–36, in the November 1989 election, and they then chose the four assembly members who had called the September meeting to be their party leaders for the coming year: Joe Doria as Speaker, Wayne Bryant as majority leader, Willie Brown as Speaker pro tem, and John Paul Doyle as deputy majority leader.

Mondics and Patrick McGeehan broke the story on January 7, the day before the new assembly was to be sworn in. The four Democrats immediately held a news conference and vigorously denied shaking down the lobbyists. Their comments, however, had a hollow ring. Bryant said he had invited Kotvas to the meeting to provide suggestions for the Democrats' election campaign strategy. Doria acknowledged having asked for money, saying, "We had a goal of $200,000 and wanted them [the lobbyists] to help us with it." Bryant acknowledged having said one of the four members at the meeting would be the next Speaker. Kotvas said Doyle had given the figure of $20,000 for the contribution the four expected, and she further added that Willie Brown had raised the possibility that the next Speaker might not be eager to bring her client's measures to a vote. All four men denied anyone had suggested a quid pro quo, but everyone familiar with legislative procedure in Trenton understands the assembly Speaker's power to control the legislative agenda. The mere mention that one of the four was likely to become Speaker was enough to suggest to the lobbyists what the consequences might be if their clients failed to pony up.

Asserting their innocence, Doria and Brown said they would take a lie detector test to disprove the charges. Doyle and Bryant said they would not submit to such a test, the latter protesting that he was offended by the suggestion that he do so.[5]

Stories about the press conference noted that the lobbyist for the New Jersey Chiropractic Society had acknowledged having attended the meeting at the Contemporary Club but said he could not recall much of the conversation. But five days after the meeting, the assembly Democrats received $10,000 from the chiropractors' political action committee. In fact, after the September 21 meeting, the assembly Democratic fund-raising group received contributions of more than $167,000.[6]

During the early weeks of 1990, the Kotvas revelations were topic A in the halls of the statehouse. On the day after the story broke, Nancy Becker, a highly respected Trenton lobbyist, confided her belief that Kotvas had acted foolishly and probably had killed her career. However, Becker had no doubt that Kotvas's account was accurate.[7] Several days later, another top lobbyist, Hazel Gluck, echoed Becker's opinion.[8] Two days after the story broke, Kotvas told the *Star-Ledger* a half-dozen lobbyists who also attended the Contemporary Club meeting had expressed their agreement with her story. She said they had congratulated her on taking a stand but made clear their words of support "can't be on the record."[9]

During a television interview a week after Mondics and McGeehan's story ran, Michael Aron, moderator of the New Jersey Network show *On the Record*, asked the premier Trenton lobbyist, Joe Katz, about the September 21 meeting. Katz said he "knew what the meeting was about when I got the invitation," and, prodded by Aron, Katz added he had brought a check with him to the Contemporary Club.[10]

As Becker and Gluck predicted, Karen Kotvas became a pariah in her profession. One lobbyist remarked, "K is for Kamikaze."[11] Her employer was not happy with her stand, because she had embarrassed powerful legislators and would lose her effectiveness. When she told the trustees of LEGAL what had happened, they demanded to know: "Why did you have to tell the truth [to the reporter]?" Eventually, she was terminated, ostensibly because LEGAL was being absorbed by the American Trial Lawyers Association and her job no longer existed. Kotvas believed this was simply a means of avoiding a lawsuit alleging unjust dismissal.[12]

The shakedown scandal would not go away. Common Cause, other reform groups, and newspaper editorial boards called for a thorough airing of the matter. By late February, the FBI and the state had begun investigations.[13] The legislature finally responded on March 27, two months after the story broke, by establishing a commission to study and make recommendations about campaign financing, legislative ethics, and lobbying. A week later, on April 4, the New Jersey attorney general, Democrat Robert Del Tufo, said his office and the FBI had not found enough evidence of wrongdoing to warrant convening a grand jury. As a result, Del Tufo ruled out criminal charges.[14] He also called for campaign finance reform to restore public confidence in the legislature, offering this cryptic observation: "This episode illustrates that permissible action can also lead to unacceptable appearances."[15]

## THE LEGISLATURE RESPONDS

The legislature's bipartisan commission was called the Ad Hoc Commission on Legislative Ethics and Campaign Finance. It soon became known as the Rosenthal Commission, after its chair, Alan Rosenthal, director of the Eagleton Institute of Politics, a prestigious graduate program at Rutgers University. A prolific author on state politics, Rosenthal was an adviser to legislatures in many states. Among the other eight commissioners were four legislators who were serving, or had served, in leadership positions in their houses.[16] On October 22, 1990, the Rosenthal Commission issued its report, which included twenty-nine recommendations for reform in the areas of campaign financing, lobbying, and legislative ethics.[17] The most significant recommendations for campaign financing should be familiar to readers of chapter 2:

- Set limits on contributions. Candidate committees should be permitted to accept no more than $1,500 from individuals and $5,000 from PACs. In 1990, New Jersey had no contribution limits.
- Raise the threshold for contributions subject to reporting from $100 to $200 and require that contributors disclose their occupations and employers.
- Allow for the formation of four legislative leadership committees to help elect members of the two major parties to the state legislature and to engage in "party building."

- Limit all candidates to a single committee for raising money and paying campaign expenses instead of multiple committees for one candidate, a condition that makes it difficult to trace campaign money.
- Limit to $10,000 per year the amount any source may contribute to a county political committee, and limit to $5,000 the amount any source may contribute to a municipal political committee.
- Allow contributions of as much as $25,000 from any source to state political parties and to the proposed legislative leadership committees while permitting these entities, together with county and municipal parties, to make unlimited contributions to candidates and other political committees.

Permitting large contributions to and from the leadership committees, as well as county and municipal parties, was deemed necessary for them to accomplish their goals. As stated in its report, "The Commission believes that the role of the party in legislative elections should be strengthened and that increased party unity and centralization is desirable." But the argument that legislative leadership committees would strengthen the role of the parties was countered by reform interests and in testimony before the Rosenthal Commission by Dr. Herbert Alexander, director of the Citizens' Research Foundation.[18] Alexander, who had been a member of President John F. Kennedy's Commission on Campaign Costs in 1961 and 1962, later served as a consultant to the Election Law Enforcement Commission (ELEC). Alexander opposed the legislative leadership PACs in the form proposed by the Rosenthal Commission, warning that "leadership of the party in the Legislature [will be] raising money in [the leader's] name, not in the name of the party"—and will create "a cult of personality." But this and other public commentary against legislative leadership committees did not prevail. As a result, New Jersey legislative leaders, Democrat and Republican alike, must have been salivating at the prospect of leadership committees constituted in the format recommended by the commission. Indeed, the establishment of these committees would cause major changes in the dynamics of legislative power and policy formation.

The Rosenthal recommendations proposed to formalize the comprehensive political financing structure for contributions and expenditures as outlined in table 2.1 and the six points listed above. Other suggestions in the Rosenthal report for reforming lobbying and legislative ethics generally met the expectations of reform advocates. Because the New Jersey legislature meets infrequently during the fall, action on the Rosenthal suggestions would not be taken up until 1991.

## IMPLEMENTING THE ROSENTHAL RECOMMENDATIONS

At the beginning of 1991, with the Democrats in control of both houses of the New Jersey legislature, Republicans saw an opportunity to gain political advantage by supporting the Rosenthal recommendations, which the public strongly favored. Legislation unanimously endorsed by the Republican minority was introduced in the state senate on June 10, 1991.[19] This put Republicans on the side of the angels, and they did not hesitate to promote this image in public pronouncements. But the senate's Democratic majority had no intention of giving the Republicans an advantage by bringing the bills to a vote. The matter was stalemated for the rest of the year.

That fall, all seats in both houses were up for election. Democratic governor Florio would not face reelection until 1993, but his first two years in office were marked by legislative turmoil and voter discontent with his championing of sales and income tax increases. In November 1991, New Jersey voters expressed their disapproval of Florio by electing overwhelming Republican majorities to both the state senate and assembly. Donald DiFrancesco and Garabed "Chuck" Haytaian, both of whom had served on the Rosenthal Commission, became senate president and assembly Speaker, respectively.

Now Republicans had the opportunity to enact programs they had championed the year before. They even had enough votes to override a Florio veto if he rejected any of their initiatives. New Jersey voters can be forgiven for assuming that campaign financing and other Rosenthal reforms would now be a priority. The Republicans' love affair with reform issues had by now turned sour, however, and the 1992 Republican state senate declined to advance, or even support, the campaign-financing reforms it had pushed only a year earlier. This was a classic case of legislative duplicity. When they were the minority party, Republicans had nothing to lose by enthusiastically supporting a reform agenda that would curtail political power. Now in the majority, they were relying on that power to maintain their dominance.

Instead of leading their caucuses to enact the Rosenthal reforms, DiFrancesco and Haytaian got busy raising money for the next legislative election in 1993. In late fall 1992, DiFrancesco held a $1,000-a-ticket fund-raising cruise on the Hudson River, and Haytaian held a fund-raising dinner, charging a mere $500 a plate.[20]

But because of the Kotvas revelations and the attention given to the Rosenthal Commission's work, the issue of campaign-financing reform would not go away. Public pressure was such that the legislature had to do something. Certainly, the prospect that the Rosenthal reform program would establish legislative leadership committees with their extraordinary powers was incentive enough for the legislative leaders to move forward—which they did in early 1993.

The emerging reform package imposed limits on contributions, required more comprehensive disclosure, and tied up other loose ends. Contrary to the Rosenthal recommendations, which said leadership committees should be subject to the control of party caucuses in each house, the GOP proposal gave control to four identified legislators: the senate president, senate minority leader, assembly Speaker, and assembly minority leader. The bills would permit each to "establish, authorize the establishment of, or designate" a continuing political committee to help elect any individual or individuals in any election. The measure made the senate president and the assembly Speaker especially powerful, because they determine the legislative agenda, which puts them in a position to raise hundreds of thousands of dollars from special interests seeking advantage in Trenton.

The Republican campaign-financing legislation made another major departure from the Rosenthal recommendations. Instead of limiting contributions to county political parties to $10,000, the GOP version increased the limit to $25,000. This increase, further raised to $37,000 in 2001, was a clear concession to the power of county political leaders in their role as managers of political money.

In addition to encouraging leadership PACs to spend from their treasuries to help reelect legislators, the law allows the legislative leaders to wheel money to county party committees, which has the collateral effect of enhancing the statewide power and prestige of these leaders.

Would legislators elected with the help of this money be beholden to the leaders who supplied it? Would they also be inclined to vote for their benefactors to continue in leadership positions? The answer, of course, is yes, and the proof is the longevity in office the leaders have enjoyed since 1993.

The Republican-dominated legislature approved the bill and sent it to Governor Florio for his signature. The Election Law Enforcement Commission (ELEC), the agency that would be responsible for implementing and enforcing the new law, had paid close attention to the legislation's various incarnations as it wended its way through the statehouse. Agencies in the executive branch that are affected by proposed legislation regularly send comments to the governor before a bill is signed into law. What was unusual was the vehemence with which ELEC expressed to the governor its objections to the creation of legislative leadership PACs.

In a letter to Florio one week after the senate gave final approval to the bill, ELEC observed, "The provision dealing with legislative leadership committees would drastically change the system of democratic government traditional in New Jersey in that this provision would endow legislative leaders with enormous fundraising ability, out of proportion to all other legislators and the established political parties. ELEC has repeatedly called for strengthening the two-party system and the leadership committees created by [this bill] tend to weaken our two-party system."[21]

ELEC urged the governor to conditionally veto the bill and to have the legislature address the problems the agency had identified. Under the New Jersey Constitution, the governor may reject or modify specific provisions of a bill by issuing a conditional veto spelling out the changes that, if approved by the legislature, would make the legislation acceptable. In this case, Florio ignored ELEC's advice and signed the bill into law in April 1993.

## LEADERSHIP PACS CHANGE THE LEGISLATIVE LANDSCAPE

The Office of Legislative Services, a nonpartisan agency, soon called the constitutionality of the legislative leadership PACs into question because it favored the two major parties and would "deny the use of such a committee to an established third party or an individual member of the Legislature."[22] Legislative leaders ignored this admonition, and the leadership committees became the fund-raising goliaths of New Jersey politics.

After the 1993 election, when all the campaigns had reported their donations to ELEC, the math showed that the new leadership committees, together with the state party committees, accounted for $9 million in new spending, increasing the total outlay for legislative races by 60 percent since the previous election cycle two years earlier. This prompted the Center for Analysis of Public Issues, an independent nonprofit research organization based in Princeton, to declare the 1993 campaign-financing measure a flop. The center concluded: "By giving enormous sums to party leaders who control the Legislature's agenda, special interests are now more influential in Trenton than ever before."[23]

As the leadership committees continued to raise increasingly large amounts of money, reform groups clamored for restraints on these entities. Common Cause, the Citizens Lobby, and the New Jersey Public Interest Research Group urged that leadership PACs be abolished.[24] In its annual report for 1995, ELEC recommended that the maximum contribution to a leadership committee be reduced to $10,000.[25] Three years later, the New Jersey Conservative Party, with a minor political presence in the state, sued legislative leaders over these committees, citing the same lack of constitutionality the Office of Legislative Services had claimed earlier.[26] The suit was dismissed December 22, 1999.

DiFrancesco, his staff, and other politicos staunchly defended leadership PACs, reasoning that they fostered the Rosenthal Commission's goal of "increased party unity and centralization," but never addressing the obvious nexus of campaign contributions to committees led by the very people who set the legislative agenda.[27]

During the next several years, the real functions of these PACs became apparent: they circumvent the limits (then $1,500) on individual contributions to personal campaign accounts, they facilitate the wheeling of funds to campaigns throughout the state, they hide the identities of donors, and they aid the political fortunes of the legislative leaders who make the donations.

In 1995, DiFrancesco transferred more than $100,000 from his senate leadership committee to his own senate campaign account, a move that was perfectly legal. This not only got around the limits on individual contributions but also identified as the donor the senate president's PAC, which was not the original source of the money. DiFrancesco claimed transferring the money was easier than holding separate fund-raisers for his own campaign.[28]

In a moment of candor, Democratic state senate leader Richard Codey, who donated $60,000 from his PAC to his legislative cohorts in 1997, referred to the role of leadership PACs as the "legalized laundering" of money. Codey offered another criticism of these PACs when he added, "When someone can give you $250,000 or $300,000 for a campaign, you owe them. When an important vote comes up, do you vote your conscience, or do you do what the leadership wants? No one wants to admit it, but it's a simple fact of life. You've got a close race and you need the dough."[29]

A starker example of the laundering of campaign contributions by the new leadership PACs was brought to light at a 1995 forum at the Eagleton Institute. One of the forum participants was Charles "Chip" Stapleton, executive director of the senate Republicans. The discussion zeroed in on the influence of tobacco money in Trenton and on GOP state senator Jack Sinagra, who had proposed legislation to reduce the power that tobacco interests had on the New Jersey legislative process. One of his proposals would prohibit tobacco companies from making campaign contributions. He was quoted in the press as saying: "The tobacco industry is the No. 1 contributor to political campaigns. As long as they are able to continue using their financial resources to influence policy, we'll have a hard time protecting the public." There was pure irony in this statement, because Philip Morris had given more than $100,000 to the GOP leadership PACs and the state party, helping to gain a Republican senate majority in the previous election. Philip Morris also gave $66,000 to Democratic leadership PACs.[30]

Panel member Stapleton's response to Senator Sinagra's concern was both direct and telling: "Tobacco money elected Jack Sinagra."[31] His point was that candidates don't necessarily know the sources of the campaign money they receive in large chunks from leadership PACs, which often serve as a laundering mechanism to conceal sources of the money coming from tobacco and other undesirable interests. ELEC records show that the Republican senate leadership PAC, having received $80,000 from Philip Morris in the next election cycle, donated $161,000 to Sinagra's 1997 reelection campaign.

In 2000, DiFrancesco once more appeared to use his leadership PAC money for his own political purposes. By then, he clearly was positioning himself to run for governor the next year. In September 2000, the *Trentonian* commented, "Some New Jersey Republicans are quietly fuming about Senate President Donald DiFrancesco using most of the $2.1 million in a GOP campaign fund [the Senate President's leadership PAC] to advance his bid for governor, shortchanging next year's Senate candidates." The claim was that the senate president's PAC had spent $1.8 million of its $2.1 million in cash-on-hand mostly on donations to county Republican committees, not to Republican senate candidates. Having the support of county political committees is crucial in winning a party's gubernatorial nomination in the primary election. DiFrancesco denied that this was his purpose.[32]

Among the recipients of the largesse of the senate leadership PAC was the Burlington County Republican Committee, which received $60,000. And in August of 2000, the Burlington Committee unanimously endorsed DiFrancesco in his run for governor the next year, notwithstanding that former assembly Speaker Jack Collins, a South Jersey neighbor of Burlington, was also running for governor.[33]

Legislative leadership PACs have affected New Jersey politics in yet another way. Before 1993, the custom was that the senate president and assembly Speaker served for only one or two years. With the advent of leadership PACs, this changed. Campaign money supplied by legislative leaders earns the gratitude of members, who reciprocate by continually reelecting them to their offices. In the months leading up to the 1997 election, the four leadership committees contributed $4.6 million in the aggregate to legislative candidates, more than from any other single source.[34] The incumbent senate president and assembly Speaker, Republicans Donald DiFrancesco and Jack Collins, were responsible for donating $2.8 million of this sum, and they were easily reelected to the top legislative posts after the GOP won both houses that year. Both

DiFrancesco and Collins served continuously in the top posts until January 2002, when the Democrats took control of the legislature.

On the Democratic side, in 1997, Joe Roberts, then the assembly's assistant minority leader, had his eye on his party's top position. Seeking backers, he made contributions totaling $25,000 from his personal campaign committee to a number of his party's candidates. But assembly minority leader Joe Doria met Roberts's $25,000 and raised it by $420,000, using his leadership PAC to give $445,000 to assembly candidates. Doria was easily reelected as his party's assembly leader.[35]

In the more than twenty years since leadership PACs were created, they have become an integral part of New Jersey's premier fund-raising triumvirate, along with the county and state political party committees. Since 2001, the contribution limits permitted for these behemoths have remained constant: $25,000 for leadership PACs and state party committees, and $37,000 for the county political committees. Funds accumulated in the treasuries of these three groups can be strategically deployed to affect key races in New Jersey.

Efforts to reduce the political power of leadership PACs have proved fruitless. Although the pay-to-play reforms of 2005 and 2008 have to some extent reduced the flow of money from special interests to these PACs, they, along with the state and county political parties, still receive enough special interest money from other sources to dominate the political financing landscape of New Jersey.

## THE PENSION BOND DEBACLE

Early in 1997, Republican governor Christie Whitman came up with a novel and highly controversial plan to finance the state's annual pension payment in order to ease the strain on the current and future state budgets. The New Jersey pension system, which the state finances with yearly contributions from the general fund, covers retirees from local and state government as well as public school teachers and administrators. The fund is structured to produce enough earnings from its investments to pay all pension benefits in current and future years. However, if the state defers its annual contribution, as has often happened in tight financial times, the system will accrue actuarial deficits—yet the mandated payments to retirees continue.

Whitman proposed to float a $2.8 billion bond issue, with the proceeds going into the pension fund to satisfy the accrued deficits, provide sufficient investment capital to ensure that future earnings at least match future pension payouts, and make the interest payments on the bonds. The plan allowed the state to suspend its current pension fund payment of $590 million in order to balance its budget for the upcoming fiscal year. Democrats howled that the bond sale would increase state debt by one-third—to $12 billion—and complained that the bonds would be sold by a semiautonomous state agency, thereby circumventing the state's constitutional requirement of a public vote on any increase in state debt.

Meanwhile, the bond-rating agencies questioned the administration's expectation of an 8.75 percent return on pension investments, and Standard & Poor's said the bond sale would jeopardize the state's double A-plus credit rating. Public opinion polls showed New Jersey residents were against the bond issue, as were most newspaper editorial boards in the state.[36]

But the governor's biggest problem was that even Republican senators were not exactly enamored of her idea. She needed a twenty-one-vote majority for passage, and all sixteen Democrats were opposed. As many as ten of the twenty-four Republican members disapproved of the plan during early discussions. As the showdown vote loomed, this number was whittled to six holdouts who were extremely unlikely to change their minds: Henry McNamara, Robert Littell, John Scott, Dick LaRossa, Joe Bubba, and me. But Whitman needed three senators to do just that.

The leadership scheduled a vote for early June, right after the primary election, and pressure on all state senators was building. Newspapers speculated that one holdout, Joe Bubba, a Republican from Passaic County who had lost his primary race, had been offered a state job in return for his vote. Bubba denied the charge.[37]

Horse-trading for votes had been going on all spring and lasted right up to the vote on June 5. That day, Republican senators streamed into the governor's office to either seek or be offered special benefits for voting yes on the bond issue. After floor debate on the bill concluded at

9 P.M., senate president DiFrancesco called for a vote. The initial vote count on the tote board settled in at eighteen green lights and twenty-one red (one Democratic senator was absent). DiFrancesco then visited the desks of the Republican holdouts, trying to convince three to change their minds. After an animated discussion, Bubba caved and put up a green light. Next came Dick LaRossa, of Trenton, who also changed his vote. At this point the tally was 20–19, and the tension was extreme. DiFrancesco gave Bergen County's John Scott, the final target, the full treatment. Thirty-six minutes after the vote was called, Scott flipped the green switch, and the bond issue passed, 21–18. The assembly easily approved the measure later in the evening, and Whitman signed it into law shortly thereafter.

Among the stories regarding the pension bond vote, a *Star-Ledger* reporter offered an interesting perspective of one participant when he wrote: "A wistful Sen. Henry McNamara, who voted no, looked back at the power politics that whirled around him for months, and sighed, 'The deals I could have cut.'"[38]

After all the campaign-financing reports for 1997 were filed, it turned out that DiFrancesco's leadership PAC gave a total of more than $480,000 to the campaigns of the three senators who cast the crucial yes votes, LaRossa, Bubba, and Scott. This amounted to more than 42 percent of what the three spent on their reelection bids.[39] (Bubba had received the money for his primary contest.)

All three were defeated in their contests for reelection—but within two months of leaving office at the end of 1997, all landed jobs in the Whitman administration at salaries of approximately $85,000 each.[40] After three years, their newly improved earnings would wind up tripling their monthly state pension benefits.

Postscript: the Whitman $2.8 billion bond issue did not stem the flow of red ink from the pension system, because the state subsequently missed making payments into the system, which also saw shortfalls in expected earnings. As of 2014, New Jersey's unfunded liability for the state and local pension systems stood at more than $54 billion.[41]

## CAMPAIGN SPENDING SKYROCKETS

When the Center for Analysis of Public Issues concluded in early 1994 that the then-new legislative PACs would make "special interests . . . more influential in Trenton than ever before," the Princeton research organization was more than prescient.[42]

Only three years later, New Jersey candidates for the legislature were fairly swimming in money. Twenty years earlier, a legislative candidate spent an average of $16,440 for a campaign, with a total of $3.9 million spent on all statehouse elections. By 1997, average spending per candidate was $100,965, with the statehouse races costing $20.7 million statewide.[43] Money raised by the "big six" committees (the two state party committees and four leadership PACs) increased rapidly. In the three years from 2001 to 2003, the big six collected $66 million, almost double the $38 million they raised in all of the previous eight years.[44] Ten years after their creation in 1993, leadership PACs showed an increase of 325 percent in their donations to legislative candidates.[45]

One of the most expensive New Jersey legislative campaigns was waged in 2003 in District 4 (south of Camden), where Democrat Fred Madden spent more than $4 million to win his senate seat by 63 votes. The cost to Madden was $212 per vote. This compares to the $100 per vote spent by Michael Bloomberg to become mayor of New York City in 2001, and the $43 per vote spent by Jon Corzine to win his U.S. Senate seat in 2000.[46] The $4.4 million donated to Madden and his assembly running mates came from the traditional party organizations in South Jersey; by law the organizations are allowed to donate unlimited amounts to a candidate. Camden County Democrats gave Madden more than $2.1 million. The Republicans were not nearly as good as the Democrats at raising campaign funds, collecting only slightly more than $1 million to finance Madden's opponent, George Geist, who was regarded as having a decent chance of beating Madden.[47]

Enormous sums of money channeled into targeted districts helped not only Madden but also other Democratic senate candidates, producing a majority for their party in the state senate in 2004. Another example in the same year was the contest for state senate in District 36 of Bergen County, won by Democrat Paul Sarlo. Of the $1.66 million spent on Sarlo's election, more than $1 million came from sources outside his district, including $744,000 from the two Democratic leadership PACs.[48] Again, the Republicans fell short in the fund-raising competition for this senate seat. Their candidate spent $591,000, of which $389,000 came from the GOP senate leadership PAC and $124,000 from the party's state committee.[49]

A white paper issued by ELEC in 2004 stated: "The legislative election in New Jersey in 2003 set all kinds of financial records. It also marked the culmination of a trend begun in the 1990s which has altered the electoral landscape from being one that was candidate-centered to one that is party-oriented." The commission went on to say: "The 1993 campaign finance reform law in New Jersey . . . truly paved the way toward political party dominance in giving the advantage to political party entities in terms of fundraising as well as an unfettered ability to contribute as much money as desired to candidates and other party entities."[50]

But only a year later, campaign money injected into New Jersey's political system through large contributions allowed by the 1993 law started to subside. Fund-raising for legislative races in years when seats in both houses were contested increased by 32 percent from 1997 to 2001, by 35 percent from 2001 to 2003, but by only 5 percent from 2003 to 2007.[51]

Contributions slowed because, starting in 2005, New Jersey enacted long-sought pay-to-play reforms. This (and a deep recession) resulted in a 12 percent reduction in the amounts of money spent on legislative campaigns between 2007 and 2011.[52] The contractors had to do something with the money they usually earmarked for campaign contributions, and they soon found alternative avenues through which to channel their money in the customary large quantities, thereby maintaining their influence. These other exempt avenues included direct contributions to campaigns of all candidates (except for governor), as well as special interest PACs, and certain other organizations not subject to state pay-to-play restrictions, including the Democratic and Republican Governors' Associations as well as super PACs and issue groups registered as nonprofits.

Special interest PACs are among the more blessed beneficiaries of the contractors' money, as these PACs are not subject to pay-to-play laws. Today, they perform a much larger role in political fund-raising than they did several years ago, particularly for county and municipal campaigns. A

2012 *Star-Ledger* report showed that ten PACs in the Middlesex County area had received total contributions of more than $2 million since 2008 from the region's contractors. These PACs then doled out campaign money to help elect local officials whose party organizations, because of pay to play, would be barred from receiving campaign funds directly from the contractors. And lo and behold, the contractors hired by the local governments were those who gave money—albeit indirectly—to the election campaigns of these same local officials. The executive director of ELEC told a reporter he saw "a very definite connection between the increase in the number of PACs and contributions to PACs" after the pay-to-play laws were enacted.[53]

The creation of legislative leadership PACs has clearly had a major impact on political money in New Jersey. Defenders of these PACs claim they help a party achieve its policy goals by electing enough of its members to form a ruling majority. Without question, funneling money into the PACs makes the system more efficient by focusing on the locus and exercise of power. But is efficiency at the expense of transparency, due process, and representativeness a worthy goal of the self-government on which this country was founded? Are we being transformed from a bottom-up to a top-down version of representative government?

## POLITICAL MONEY AND GOVERNMENT RESULTS IN NEW JERSEY

In New Jersey, the raising and spending of campaign money for legislative candidates is not an equal opportunity exercise. Although the efforts of the major parties to win control of the Legislature are intense, attention is focused on only half a dozen competitive districts (out of forty) to swing the balance of power. These districts receive the lion's share of campaign money, millions of dollars wheeled in from legislative leadership PACs, the state and county parties, and the abundant treasuries of incumbent legislators in safe districts. Examples have already been noted in the Madden and Sarlo elections of 2003. This concentration of political money is facilitated by New Jersey's campaign finance laws.

Meanwhile, campaigns in the noncompetitive districts are not as heated and require considerably less financial support.

The key question is: Does all this money influence government outcomes for the benefit of the donors? This can be answered by the simplistic follow-up question: Would the money keep flowing from the special interests in the same amounts if it didn't produce favorable results?

Some defenders of the system contend that campaign money is not sinister; it merely buys access. But access is not benign; it has value. And under New Jersey's system, access is not divided equally. It is more available to the big spenders who use it to get the attention of lawmakers. John and Jane Q. Public do not enjoy the same access. Under these conditions, it is easy to see how campaign spending influences government results.

Special interests have different methods of investing in lawmakers. Some, such as the New Jersey Business and Industry Association, sprinkle their money on probable winners in both parties, seeking bipartisan support for their key issues. Others pour their money into the campaign coffers of the party they feel best meets the donors' philosophy and objectives, hoping that it will be in power.

A classic case of diverse interests using campaign money in an attempt to influence a legislative outcome took place in New Jersey's 2003 election and the subsequent struggle in the statehouse between lawyers and doctors. The doctors wanted to roll back the state's tort laws, which allow generous malpractice awards. Their contributions to legislative candidates, primarily to Republicans, amounted to nearly $900,000, triple what doctors had given in years past. The president of the New Jersey Medical Society gave this pragmatic explanation: "In order to move the political process in your favor, the way to talk to them . . . you have to give them donations."[54]

The trial lawyers who regularly provided moderate campaign support donated $280,000 to legislative races that year, mostly to Democrats. The representative for the lawyers rejected the idea that contributions buy influence. He argued that donors merely gain access, which enables them to educate legislators, and commented: "I don't think I've been able to persuade someone to vote a different way because I wrote them a check. We educate them about things they may be unaware of."[55]

Although the doctors gave three times as much money as the trial lawyers to legislative campaigns, they did not gain tort reform; they had bet on the wrong horse. Democrats won majorities in both the senate and assembly, and in 2004 they used their newfound power to beat back the doctors' attempt at tort reform. The president of the Medical Society admitted his group was naïve in its strategy and "should have concentrated on fewer races." In other words, they should have contributed to a few key Democratic legislators, hoping they would break ranks, instead of placing total reliance on one party, the Republicans, to gain control of the legislature.

One special alliance that has developed over the years between a political party and an interest group is the alliance between labor and the Democratic Party. Unions donate big bucks to the Democratic candidates and party organizations. Lawmakers elected with this backing are strong advocates for issues such as public employee pensions and health benefits, workplace standards, prevailing wage laws, public works construction, and more. Union political action committees have dominated New Jersey legislative campaign contributions in recent years. Labor unions accounted for four of the ten largest PAC donors in the 2005 and 2007 legislative elections. In 2009, unions represented nine of the top ten, and 82 percent of union contributions went to Democrats.[56] Total giving to all campaigns and parties in 2013 by the top ten special interest groups was $149 million. Six of the ten were unions, and they spent $129 million, or 83 percent of this amount—and nearly all of it on Democratic candidates and parties.[57]

There is, of course, a substantial amount of money donated to candidates and parties that does not come from PACs or special interests. These are the contributions from the candidates themselves, from their relatives and friends, and from followers of government whose principal interest is to see that the policies and positions of the recipient candidates prevail. These donations are *not* soft corruption. Only when political contributions are given in connection with a specific government outcome or to solidify alliances with sympathetic lawmakers can this process be tainted as soft corruption.

## CAMPAIGN MONEY BUYS RESULTS

In understanding the significance of the campaign contribution in New Jersey's political culture, consider a few examples from the past twenty-five years. These examples confirm the perception, if not the fact, of a correlation between campaign contributions and government benefits.

- In the legislative campaign of 1991, the New Jersey Optometric Association was raising money from its members in an attempt to broaden the law covering medical procedures the profession could be allowed to perform. In its letter to members, the association pleaded for money, saying its proposed legislation would not be adopted "on the cheap . . . unless each of us digs into our wallet, so deep it hurts, we're not going to get the bill. Hard work and tons of bucks WILL give us this bill this year. . . . If YOU want it, YOU have to pay for it. It's that simple. I am looking forward to receiving YOUR pledge in the mail." This appeal apparently paid off. With more than $88,000 in contributions spread among both Republican and Democratic legislators, the bill passed both the senate and assembly by bare margins, and was signed into law by Governor Florio.[58]
- There have been occasions when lawmakers will even concede that campaign contributions influence their vote. Late in 1990, Republican assembly caucus members were discussing a controversial measure involving statewide mandatory site design standards for municipalities. Developers, who were always heavy campaign contributors, were pushing the bill. Local mayors and the state League of Municipalities (which does not make political campaign contributions) strenuously objected. After hearing vigorous arguments supporting the position of mayors and their state organization, the assemblyman from Somerset bluntly responded: "I never get a check from the League of Municipalities." He voted yes, and the bill passed.[59]
- Republican senator Gerald Cardinale, a dentist by profession, has always been an outspoken advocate for conservative causes and a legislator who is not afraid to "tell it like it is." At the state Medical Society convention in 2003, Cardinale addressed the group, saying that money can indeed buy votes. Suggesting that each New Jersey doctor should make a political contribution of $500, he said: "Legislators would trip over themselves to support your cause." Cardinale then introduced his wife, who was in the back of the audience, and invited doctors to buy tickets to his golf outing from her. "I hate the system,"

he said, "but it is the system." Although Cardinale said that contributions do not influence his votes, it was noted in the press that his wife sold a handful of tickets at the event.[60]

- In early 2011, a contentious issue involving Mountain Creek of Sussex County, New Jersey's largest ski resort, was resolved. Operators of ski facilities across the country are concerned about head injuries to skiers who use their slopes. In an effort to address this problem, Republican senator Anthony Bucco of Morris County had for many years sponsored a measure to require skiers younger than eighteen to wear protective helmets while on New Jersey slopes. But the bill always got stuck in committee because it held ski resorts responsible for enforcing the helmet law. Bucco got around that problem by substituting a new bill with the following provision: "Nothing in this act shall be construed to extend liability to the ski area operator." This version delegated responsibility for enforcing the law to parents of young skiers as well as local law enforcement agencies, not the ski slope operator.[61]

  As a result of the change, the legislature quickly passed the bill and sent it to the governor for final approval. As the bill awaited the signature of GOP governor Christie, seven investors in Mountain Creek each donated $25,000 to the state Republican Party. Of the seven, three listed addresses in New York and one in Florida. According to Election Law Enforcement Commission records, only three of the donors had ever made reportable political contributions in New Jersey before, two of them having donated $25,000 to the Democratic Party. The owner of the ski resort explained that the contributions were made to support the election of a Republican legislature to help the governor.[62]

- A more troubling example of the connection between campaign contributions and government contracts was captured in testimony during the September 2011 federal corruption trial of a Newark official accused of taking illegal payments for steering demolition work to a favored contractor, Mazzocchi Wrecking Company. The owner of the company, Nicholas Mazzocchi, had become an informant for the FBI and testified in court that for companies that seek contracts from municipalities in New Jersey, the only difference between a bribe and a campaign contribution is that the latter is legal. He stated: "I make political contributions because I learned over the years, that not making them, I lost tens of millions of dollars."[63]

Lobbyists recognize that it is not enough to try to use the power of persuasion to convince lawmakers of the worthiness of their clients' causes. Money is a much more effective persuader, and lobbyists contribute heavily to candidates and political committees. They also manage fund-raising events for legislators at which their clients and other special interest groups get tapped for contributions. When Trenton lobbyist Kyle Keiderling was asked at a local political meeting, "Why do lobbyists keep giving so much money to the candidates and campaigns?" his reply was simple: "We have to."[64]

With equal frankness, Alan Marcus, a high-profile veteran lobbyist, declared in 2004: "In New Jersey, you contribute money not for access but results. Anyone who doesn't admit that is lying."[65]

The close relationship between money and legislative power is not a new phenomenon. Even before leadership PACs were officially created in 1993, statehouse leaders were attuned to the connection between campaign money and the desire of special interests to influence the legislative agenda. Former assembly Speaker Chuck Hardwick, a Republican, summarized this situation: "You've got to bring something to the table if you want to influence the legislative process. You either bring some votes because you're a labor union, or you bring the ability to get media. You can bring volunteers for campaigns that will multiply into votes, like Right to Life, or you bring money. And money is sometimes the easiest thing to bring."[66]

Such candor is rare in legislators, who are much more likely to offer the stock answer that Senator Ray Zane gave at a 1997 state senate committee hearing. In a discussion about whether large amounts of money in political campaigns buy government results, committee member Zane said, "I don't think the system is that sinister. I object to the suggestion that [legislation] is influenced by money." However, hard evidence contradicts Zane. Several years earlier, the state senate's Natural Resources and Agriculture Committee, which Zane chaired, was considering a land preservation bill. After a state environmental official testified in favor of the bill, Zane informed the official that the committee would not move the bill to a vote until it received a letter saying the New Jersey Builders Association was not opposed. Campaign finance records show that Zane received more than $28,000 from the builders and real estate interests in his campaigns from 1987 through 2001, a significant amount for his rural South Jersey district.[67]

If a specific quid pro quo arrangement exists in the giving of political money and the receiving of an official benefit, the transaction crosses the line into criminality. But the system of money and rewards is so complex, so sophisticated, and so embedded in New Jersey's political culture that no verbal or written quid pro quo is necessary. It is unspoken—not even a wink or a nod is needed. This unspoken understanding is at the core of soft corruption.

Are excesses of money in the political arena a minor and necessary nuisance to make government work? Common sense says they harm the public. In the first instance, campaign contributions can influence government officials to accept a bid for services or products that is more costly than a bid offered by competitors. And in the case of awards meted out by government without bidding, vendors can be expected to add the amount of campaign contributions into their pricing, thereby driving up the cost of government.

But even more fundamental is the unfavorable impact that political money has on how government is run. Whether the money buys access, influences policy, provides a hedge against unfavorable actions, or, as in so many cases, blatantly buys results, it can all be summed up in one word—*tribute*. Society loses when tribute, rather than service to the people, is allowed to have such a dominant role in governing.

# 4 ▸ LOBBYING

"If you can't eat [lobbyists'] food, drink their booze, screw their women, and then vote against them, you have no business being up here."

—JESSE UNRUH, addressing newly elected legislators

Had Unruh, FORMER Speaker of the California legislature, said "If you can't eat [lobbyists'] food, drink their booze, accept their campaign contributions and political help, and then vote against them, you have no business being up here," he would have come a little closer to the mark in describing the more common ways lobbyists influence lawmakers in New Jersey.

Lobbying in its pure sense is not venal; it is communication. Transmitting information about a vast array of issues to legislators and government officials is essential to the functioning of government. Most who are elected to public office thirst for such information. A lobbyist who is knowledgeable, trustworthy, and fair will be both effective for clients and highly regarded by those being lobbied.

So why is the reputation of this profession so negative? A 1977 statement from a New Jersey think tank provides an interesting explanation: "In lobbying, those who know about it won't talk, and those who talk generally don't know."[1]

Are the villains those who lobby or is the system at fault? Do law-makers become overly beholden to lobbyists when they pressure these agents for campaign contributions to fund their next election? Many people conclude that, regardless of the merits of lobbying, the huge amounts of special interest money paid to lobbyists—and, in turn, spent by lobbyists—are crucial to their relationship with lawmakers and have a major influence over government decisions.

## HISTORICAL CONTEXT

Revelations of excessive influence and insider deals that demonstrate the power wielded by lobbyists in the government decision-making process have given the profession of lobbying a bad name—one developed over a long time.

One of the more notorious New Jersey episodes occurred in 1855, when a bank in the town of Mount Holly sought to have the legislature renew its charter. Bank representatives offered the state senator from Sussex County $1,000 for his vote, an offer that he declined and reported to the press. A different tactic was used on a state senator from Salem County who planned to vote against the charter. The bank's people abducted him from the statehouse on the day of the vote and put him on a train to Philadelphia, thereby denying him the chance to vote. Public indignation stirred by these and similar events led to adoption of a strict law against the use of bribes and other devious methods meant to influence the vote on legislation.[2]

By the late nineteenth century, railroads had become the dominant economic force in New Jersey. Their lobbyists were somewhat more restrained, but still openly cultivated members of the legislature with campaign money and other payoffs to ensure that no one would monkey with the railroads' tax concessions and monopoly. By the 1960s, when railroads were no longer major players, lobbying was lower-key and more tolerable, albeit somewhat clandestine. New Jersey still had no effective laws or regulations to govern the activities of lobbyists, except in cases of outright criminal fraud. Lobbyists patrolled the halls of the statehouse in Trenton, had access to the floors of both the assembly and the senate, entertained legislators lavishly with gifts, junkets, and tickets to events, and provided campaign money and assistance when needed.

A prominent lobbyist of that era, Herman Kluxen, wore several hats: one as the representative of the alcoholic beverage industry, another as an aide of a state senator, and a third as an activist in the state Republican Party. Kluxen's presence was clearly felt on the floor of the senate or assembly whenever legislation affecting the liquor industry was being considered.[3]

A seemingly innocuous incident that showed tolerance for lobbyists at the time occurred one day during a recess in assembly proceedings when a prominent lobbyist paid cash for a ticket to a Republican dinner from a member sitting at his desk in the assembly chambers. This is no longer possible since a bill was passed several years later that prohibits soliciting and paying campaign contributions on state property.

When the first comprehensive law regulating lobbyists was enacted in 1971, it required lobbyists to register and to disclose the money they and their clients spent to influence legislation. It also prohibited lobbyists from being on the staff of legislators and required lobbyists to wear identification badges when they were plying their trade in the halls of the statehouse. Badges were necessary so that lawmakers could distinguish between paid agents and other participants when engaged in boisterous discussions over legislative proposals. Anyone lobbying pro se was obviously not being paid to do so and therefore was not subject to the registration and reporting requirements for lobbyists.

Lobbying is much more expansive than a simple one-on-one contact between a paid advocate and a lawmaker. It more often entails a group of individuals or entities with a common affiliation working in concert to achieve a favorable result. Dentists, real estate brokers, banks, retail merchants, and the like will join together as an association to advance their group's objectives. Under New Jersey law, lobbying has been defined over the years in two distinct classifications: The "government affairs agent" is a single individual who is paid to represent a client in an effort to influence government decisions. Also regarded as a lobbyist is the client, or "represented entity," which can be a person, a business, or a group with a common affiliation. Both classifications participate in lobbying, but the represented entity must designate a government affairs agent to do its direct contact lobbying. The government affairs agent, a freelance individual, or someone who works in partnership with others, hires out under contract to lobby for the client. Or, the government affairs agent can be part of the "represented entity" (client) group.

## LOBBYING EVENTS

Powerful business-related lobbies often sponsor lavish entertainment events to which they invite legislators and other government officials. The relationships that take place at these venues are cozy and often clandestine. Opportunities are afforded lobbyists to gain the favor of and consummate deals with government lawmakers, deals that are both good and bad.

The most prominent of these events in New Jersey is the annual State Chamber of Commerce "Walk to Washington" train excursion. A fourteen-car passenger train departing from Newark with stops in Trenton and Philadelphia carries as many as two thousand lobbyists, legislators, public officials, politicos, reporters, and business executives to Washington, D.C., where they stay in a five-star hotel and attend a dinner honoring the state's congressional delegation. Food and drink are plentiful at each point of departure, on the train, and in the many hospitality suites at the hotel hosted by business and other special interests. The trip has been called the "Walk to Washington" because most passengers try to muscle their way through the crowded aisles of all fourteen cars to greet and schmooze with political pals and acquaintances.

For many years, the Chamber paid for legislators' train fare as well as their hotel and banquet accommodations. But reform groups became increasingly offended by the way the Washington trip exploited a captive audience in an effort to influence government decisions with virtually no transparency or accountability. One representative of the reform group Citizen Action described the train trip: "It's a big love fest of money and power. . . . I doubt there is a lot of talk about reform of government on that train."[4] The Chamber relented and stopped subsidizing this excursion, after which legislators and other government officials were asked to pay their own way—which they have done willingly.

Atlantic City is a popular spot for special interest groups to hold conventions well attended by government types. The largest of these is the four-day League of Municipalities convention in November, which attracts more than twenty thousand local officials. The many hotels in Atlantic City have hospitality suites set up by banks, engineering firms, and other service providers who use food, drink, and entertainment to convince local and county officials to do business with them.

As with campaign financing, lobbying in New Jersey has had its share of outrages. One of the more brazen episodes involved a series of intimate soirées in 2002 sponsored by the Democratic State Committee. Lobbyists were invited to bring their clients—and $25,000—to meet privately with Governor Jim McGreevey. The $25,000 could be a single contribution or multiple contributions totaling the full amount. This had all the signs of a shakedown. One lobbyist confided that a client who was establishing a business in New Jersey wanted face time with the governor. The governor's office told the lobbyist that the Democratic State Committee was handling the arrangements. The lobbyist received an invitation for a private meeting that noted the contribution requirement, to which the client agreed. A meeting with the governor followed.[5]

In the *Record* story that gave this scheme a thorough airing, reporters conducted separate interviews with six of Trenton's top lobbyists. All said Stephanie Babek, finance chair of the Democratic State Committee, had told them the governor would attend small meetings with them and their clients if they brought money. One lobbyist told the newspaper, "The price was $25,000. I was floored. They were asking for a command performance. The governor was involved. It's awfully hard to say 'no' to something like that." None of the lobbyists would permit the newspaper to identify them. One commented: "I can't be identified in any way [with this story] or I'm dead meat. My clients will be shut down in a second."

The governor's office, which acknowledged that the governor had "attended three or four small events in recent weeks," countered with the timeworn rationale that this was party building. A spokesman for the Democratic State Committee told a *Record* reporter: "Jim McGreevey resurrected this party on his shoulders. He's got the political responsibility to keep it strong." The governor's press secretary tried to turn the story around by saying, "These lobbyists who are complaining are the ones in the influence peddling business, not us."

The lobbyists further claimed that, as part of the overall Democratic fund-raising initiative, they were subjected to an even more blatant outrage, namely to reduce the amount of money their firms gave to Republicans, the minority party in the legislature at the time. The effort seemed to have succeeded. Campaign finance reports for 2002 showed the Democratic State Committee raised $8.3 million compared to the GOP's $3 million.[6]

The National Republican Congressional Committee (NRCC) used this same tactic on the federal level in 2000, telling special interest PACs that if they wanted Republican support on matters before Congress, they would have to ensure that no less than 75 percent of their contributions went to the GOP. The NRCC formalized this initiative by creating the 75 Percent Club and held fund-raising events in the club's name.[7]

Former Republican governors Thomas Kean and Christine Todd Whitman had participated in their party's "Governor's Club," which hosted contributors of $25,000 at special VIP dinners.[8] While the Democrats tried to claim that the GOP soirées were the same as the McGreevey events, there were distinct differences. Republicans made their appeals to individual contributors, not to lobbyists and their clients, and they made their solicitations through the party, without direction from the governor's office. Further, the GOP events were highly publicized and did not involve private "sit-downs" with the governor.

When told of the McGreevey tête-à-têtes, a senior fellow at the Washington-based Center for Responsive Politics, Larry Makinson, remarked: "People in New Jersey have got to be asking themselves who is really making the laws. The only reason lobbyists exist is to influence policy. By promising access at a specific dollar price, the party is sending an unmistakable message that government in New Jersey is for sale. That is a terrible message to send."[9]

After 2003, when the Democrats had gained the majority in both the senate and assembly, the party continued its effort to raise funds for the next assembly election in 2005. On the day the new legislature took office in January 2004, the *Star-Ledger* reported that the party had assigned many of the chairs of the Democratic assembly committees a quota of twenty-five tickets to sell at $1,000 each for a fund-raising event in Trenton the following month. Lobbyists were solicited and one was quoted as saying: "The requests are just a lot larger. I raised a record amount last year, and they want more this year."[10] A new cycle had begun.

One of the more bizarre lobbying episodes illustrates the extent to which a special interest will go to achieve a personal objective. J. Seward Johnson Sr., the son of a founder of the Johnson & Johnson medical products company, had established a trust for his heirs in 1961. By 1996, the trust was valued at $350 million and was scheduled to be distributed the following year. Johnson's son, J. Seward Johnson Jr., was a beneficiary of the trust. He brought suit in an effort to prevent another heir, Jenia Johnson, from receiving her allotment of $10 million from the trust. Seward Jr. had divorced his wife in 1965, and in the settlement acknowledged Jenia Johnson was his daughter.[11]

But Seward Jr.'s suit questioned Jenia's paternity, claiming the child was the product of an extramarital affair by his former wife. The suit, which asked the court to require Jenia to undergo a DNA test to verify her paternity, went all the way to the state supreme court, which rejected Seward's request in early 2001. The U.S. Supreme Court declined to hear the case.

Undaunted, Seward Johnson Jr. decided to try to change New Jersey law in 2001 to allow for DNA testing when questions of paternity arise. He hired a lobbyist, who convinced legislators in both houses to introduce a bill to effect the change. Johnson, a well-known sculptor, was a prolific contributor to New Jersey political parties and public officials. He and his then-wife donated more than $160,000 during the five years the suit was being litigated, and he gave $119,000 more in 2001 when the special legislation was under consideration.

Although the Senate Judiciary Committee approved the bill in late December of 2001, it died after Jenia Johnson's lawyer, Robert Del Tufo, a former state attorney general and U.S. attorney, convinced legislators that the measure had "enormous—and negative—public policy implications" and accused the Johnsons of seeking "unwarranted advantages in legislation." When the matter started to attract adverse publicity, the sponsor of the bill in the state senate, Republican Robert Singer, who had received $4,400 in campaign contributions from Seward Jr., claimed he had been misled by the lobbyist.

The bill was reintroduced the next year by other sponsors but was never approved by both houses of the legislature. It subsequently died.

## LOBBYING: THE PROCESS AND HOW IT OPERATES

It is often said there is a revolving door between government service and positions with lobbying firms. The ranks of lobbyists are full of former legislators and high-level government officials who gravitate to the field after leaving their government posts. New Jersey, like thirty-one other states, imposes a one-year hiatus between government service and lobbying. Fifteen states have no cooling-off period. In Illinois, for example, after pushing through a bill making it easier for electric utilities to get rate increases, a state representative immediately resigned from the legislature, set up his own lobbying firm, and signed Commonwealth Edison as one of his first clients. Other states have hybrid arrangements: Florida prohibits former lawmakers from lobbying the legislature for two years but allows them to lobby the executive branch without any waiting period. Unlike New Jersey, many states, including those with a cooling-off period, have no prohibitions preventing former legislators from representing clients on matters over which they had jurisdiction while serving in government.[12]

The major New Jersey lobbying firms, located on West State Street across from the statehouse in Trenton, have many former senators and assembly members in their stables. In 2013 the firm Martin, Bontempo employed seventeen government affairs agents, six of whom had served in the legislature. Sometimes the vote of one former colleague is all it takes to win the day on a crucial issue. Clearly, the value of that one lobbyist to the client is enormous.

Experienced lobbyists rely on several techniques for their success. First and foremost is a solid relationship with the leaders of both houses of the legislature who determine the legislative agenda—those bills that will be considered and those that will be buried, and whether to assign a bill to a sympathetic committee or a hostile one. To successfully guide a proposal into law, seasoned lobbyists use their thorough familiarity with all legislators to create a lobbying strategy. This strategy often involves convincing legislators' political allies and constituents to contact their representatives directly to gain support for the lobbyist's proposal.

There have been occasions when lobbyists used tactics of questionable virtue to advance their own interests. One such charade engaged in by some lobbyists was to have a friendly legislator introduce a bill that was particularly harmful to a business or group, but that the legislator had no intention of pushing. The lobbyist behind this plot would then seek to be hired by the organizations that would be adversely affected, claiming that he would be able to block passage of the bill. The lobbyist, of course, would be successful, receiving the gratitude and a big fee from the client. This method of soft corruption was so blatant that it was brought to an abrupt halt by an amendment to the lobby law passed in 1977.[13]

Another contentious lobbying issue was the contingency fee. This was the arrangement with the client that a fee would be paid based on the lobbyist's success in achieving a governmental objective. This practice was outlawed in New Jersey in 2004 because of the inappropriateness of using incentives to get government results.[14] Forty-three states have now imposed total prohibitions on contingency fees to pay lobbyists.[15]

Sometimes lobbyists team up to achieve an objective. In 1999 and 2000, the legislature was debating an electrical energy deregulation bill. The state's largest utility, Public Service Electric and Gas, retained a government affairs agent from each of the top six lobbying firms. This tactic meant that these six firms could not represent any other energy supplier without the consent of Public Service, which thereby had more clout in influencing the provisions of the legislation being considered.[16]

Lobbyists often have a back-up plan that will provide the client group with some measure of success even though the lobbyists cannot deliver on the group's objective. Such was the case in 2004, when legislation was being considered to preserve open space to protect the water supply in the New Jersey Highlands, a large multicounty region in the northern part of the state. Development and construction interests lobbied vigorously against the Highlands measure because it would severely restrict development of thousands of acres. One such interest, the New Jersey Builders Association, spent more than $575,000 on lobbying alone that year. When the Highlands preservation bill passed, all was not lost; the developers had tied it to passage of a companion bill for which they had vigorously lobbied. This second bill allowed fast-tracking of environmental permits for projects in all parts of the state, a measure helpful to developers. The second bill passed with ease, and as explained by the executive director of the New Jersey Environmental Federation, "Highlands was the excuse for 'fast-track'; it wasn't the reason."[17]

Many bills in the legislative hopper at any one time are introduced at the behest of lobbyists. Successful lobbyists spend time, effort, and money to cultivate a strong personal relationship with key legislators on whom they can call to sponsor their clients' bills. Of course, the campaign contribution is probably the most important weapon in the lobbyist's arsenal. This was certainly indicated in obtaining sponsorship for the DNA bill intended to break the Seward Johnson trust.

There is often a direct connection between lobbying and making political donations. The invitation to a 2010 fund-raiser for newly elected assembly Speaker Sheila Oliver asked for a $1,500 contribution payable to the Committee to Elect Sheila Oliver. The invitation to the breakfast reception sent a clear message to lobbyists who were invited with this comment from Oliver: "It is my sincere hope that you will spend the morning with me and discuss any issues that are important to you and/ or your clients."[18]

Another potent weapon a lobbyist can offer a legislator is electoral help in the form of endorsements from client groups that have a favorable public image with his or her constituency. Among these groups are the New Jersey Education Association (teachers), New Jersey Business and Industry Association (businesses), and the Sierra Club (environmentalists).

Some lobbyists have at their disposal significant political power to influence government. Such is the case with Dale Florio, who runs Princeton Public Affairs Group, the top lobbying firm in the state with more than $9 million in yearly billing from its 200 clients.[19]

The power and effectiveness of Florio's lobbying efforts have been enhanced by his service as chair of the Somerset County Republican Party. While Florio is careful to be nonpartisan in his lobbying and is highly regarded for his integrity, it is impossible to ignore the political power he has wielded as chair of one of the strongest GOP organizations in the state. Somerset County produced Christie Whitman, two-term Republican governor (1994–2001). And Somerset County's freeholder board and legislative delegation are 100 percent Republican.[20] Certainly, the county chair's power in selecting candidates, raising money, and managing election campaigns is not lost on these politicians.

As a member of Commerce Bank's regional board for central New Jersey in the early 2000s, Florio's close affiliation with the bank gave him a strong power base among Democrats as well. One principal of this politically influential bank is the undisputed Democratic boss of South Jersey, George Norcross. As a client, Commerce paid Princeton Public Affairs more than $120,000 in fees in 2006 alone.[21]

It has already been shown that the Karen Kotvas incident in 1990 alleging a shakedown of lobbyists for campaign contributions (see chapter 3) so traumatized the political establishment in New Jersey that major changes in campaign financing were adopted. These changes were generated through the Rosenthal Commission, whose report also recommended stronger lobbying regulations. One such regulation was to remove the "expressly" modifier when expenditures are made by lobbyists courting legislators. The term had been surreptitiously inserted into the law so that lobbyists would not have to report any expenditures at entertainment events for legislators unless legislation was "expressly" discussed. Such discussions could easily be avoided, a godsend to legislators, who could continue to receive these benefits without the embarrassment of having them publicly disclosed. This transparency loophole was removed by statute in 1991.[22]

The original law regulating lobbying covered only matters before the legislature. The whole body of regulations promulgated by the executive departments of state government as part of the New Jersey Administrative Code were excluded. This condition gave lobbyists a clear opportunity to influence the formulation and impact of the vast array of administrative regulations. Legislation also passed in 1991 removed this exclusion by also including actions to influence the administrative code under the lobby law.

But there were still government activities outside of legislation and the administrative code that were subject to influence by lobbyists without being covered by regulation and disclosure. These included executive orders, rate setting, purchasing, contracting, issuing permits, awarding grants, and rendering other administrative determinations. A *Star-Ledger* exposé in 2003 revealed that several political heavyweights who worked in Trenton's most influential lobbying and government consulting firms and did not lobby on legislation or administrative regulations had ongoing relationships with legislators and were not registered as lobbyists. Among these were: Jack Collins, former GOP assembly Speaker, who was part of Dale Florio's Princeton Public Affairs Group; James Kennedy, former Rahway mayor and personal friend of Governor McGreevey, who was a principal of State Street Partners; Jeff Michaels, former aide to acting Governor DiFrancesco, who co-owned Public Affairs Management Group, which counted Commerce Bank as one of its clients; and Chip Stapleton, a partner in Public Affairs Management and former senate aide to DiFrancesco. These individuals clearly give the appearance of "shadow lobbyists."[23]

When interviewed, all four denied engaging in the narrow definition of lobbying on legislation or government regulations. But their government relations work, which included roaming the halls of the statehouse on legislative days, implied involvement in other weighty government matters where their influence would be a factor. Indeed, they were helping clients on policy as well as on the procedural issues of permits, contracting, grant awards, and administrative functions. These activities were classified as government process issues and were made part of lobby regulation in an amendatory law of 2004.[24]

"Grassroots lobbying" is a technique developed in recent years by special interests to achieve government outcomes. This process— defined by the New Jersey Election Law Enforcement Commission as "communication with the general public"[25]—usually entails a media campaign designed to convince people to contact their elected representatives about specific legislation. For example, when "no fault" auto insurance was a major issue in New Jersey in the 1990s, insurance companies fought hard for legislation to establish a system to avoid costly litigation when settling auto insurance claims. If passed, the new system would mean monetary benefits for both the insurance companies and the claimants. As a result, auto insurers advertised heavily in newspapers and on the radio urging people to ask their legislators to vote in favor of the legislation. Because communication purchased to influence a government decision is lobbying, it was appropriate to bring grassroots lobbying under the purview of New Jersey's lobby laws, which the Legislature did in 2004.

Interestingly, New Jersey Common Cause took exception to the term because of the implication that it was spontaneous citizen action truly generated at the grassroots. Ed McCool, executive director of Common Cause, preferred to call it "Astroturf lobbying" because it was not a natural grassroots phenomenon; it was artificial.

New Jersey has always required lobbyists to report how much they spend entertaining lawmakers. Entertainment expenses are considered gifts, and the process is referred to as benefit passing. Any single expenditure greater than $25, or in the aggregate exceeding $250 per year per legislator, has to be shown on the lobbyist's reporting forms. In past years, mere disclosure of these benefits did not deter many legislators from accepting this largesse, particularly when it paid for junkets at plush resorts.[26] Legislators traveled, often with their spouses, to Ireland, Tokyo, Hawaii, Bermuda, and other destinations. Senator Gerald Cardinale, ranking Republican on the Commerce Committee, was a frequent guest of the New Jersey Bankers Association at its conventions in Bermuda and Florida. One such excursion in 2004 cost its sponsor $6,000. Cardinale was criticized by his opponent in his 2007 reelection bid for having taken "banking industry freebies" of $27,000 over the previous decade.[27]

Responding to a reporter's criticism of a trip to Florida paid by the bankers, Assemblyman Garabed "Chuck" Haytaian once said: "I'd rather them [the bankers] pay for the trip than the taxpayers do it."[28] Of course, Haytaian was silent regarding the possibility of incurring an obligation between a special interest and a legislator by such a transaction.

Benefit passing from lobbyists to government officials is not unlike when businesses in the private sector spend money to entertain their customers. In giving something of value, the expectation is that the recipient will return the favor. When dealing with taxpayer money, however, the public has a right to expect objective decision making by its representatives rather than decisions influenced by enticements. The benefit-passing provision of the New Jersey lobby law was amended to take effect in 2005. It stipulated that a legislator can receive no more than $250 per year in gifts from a lobbyist, and payments for out-of-state travel cannot exceed $500.[29] This change accelerated the decline in gift giving, as shown in table 4.1.[30]

TABLE 4.1.    Lobbyists' Gifts to Legislators, 1992–2015

| Year | Total spent on legislative benefit passing |
|------|--------------------------------------------|
| 1992 | $163,375 |
| 2001 | 115,442 |
| 2002 | 95,871 |
| 2003 | 83,094 |
| 2004 | 62,931 |
| 2005 | 43,627 |
| 2006 | 45,508 |
| 2007 | 31,630 |
| 2008 | 22,360 |
| 2009 | 9,642 |
| 2010 | 7,476 |
| 2011 | 5,687 |
| 2012 | 5,652 |
| 2013 | 4,022 |
| 2014 | 3,283 |
| 2015 | 2,439 |

SOURCE: New Jersey Election Law Enforcement Commission, Trenton; ELEC news release, March 3, 2016.

New Jersey has done much to reform lobby gift-giving laws and dramatically reduce the amount legislators receive annually from lobbyists. This is of little consequence to legislators, because they really don't need lobbyists to pay for junkets, entertainment, or special favors, particularly since these payments will produce adverse publicity. They can still use their political war chests to finance normal officeholder expenses, out-of-state legislative travel, and other benefits. But they want no impediments to raising campaign funds to maintain their political prominence and finance their next election. Accordingly, New Jersey legislators have done nothing to curtail what lobbyists and their clients give to candidates and political parties as campaign contributions.

Several other states do restrict political contributions from the lobby fraternity. Four states have outright bans on contributions from lobbyists; other states have low limits on the amounts that can be contributed from this source. Connecticut, for example, has imposed a top contribution limit of $100 from any lobbyist with an aggregate maximum of $15,000 that a lobbyist can give to all candidates in an election campaign.[31]

Lobbying in New Jersey is no small enterprise. The ranks of registered lobbyists have grown from 70 when reporting started in 1971 to 484 in 1987 to a high of 1,043 in 2008. There are currently 937 registered government affairs agents, more than seven for every legislator. These lobbyists serve 2,010 clients.[32]

Lobbying is a lucrative profession, as evidenced by salaries drawn by its premier performers. A 2014 analysis of the ten highest-paid lobbyists showed an average salary of more than $493,000 per year. Dale Florio topped the list at $599,519. Twenty-eight lobbyists reported making more than $200,000, while only seven made that much in 1999.[33]

These salary figures, however, don't tell the whole story. Lobbyists belong to firms that generally identify themselves as government affairs consultants. In this role, the principals of the firm, when not wearing their lobbying hats, will work with business clients on activities such as strategic planning, market studies, and general public relations, activities that are not reportable under lobby regulations. Moneys paid for performing these functions are not included in the salaries shown above.

Total spending by lobbyists has grown rapidly since reporting began in the 1970s. With a modest $2.5 million in reported lobbying expenses in 1982, the amount expanded to more than $70 million in both 2011 and 2015, as shown in figure 4.1.

The most dramatic jump in lobby expenditures, more than 90 percent between 2005 and 2006, can be attributed to the 2004 changes in the law when grassroots lobbying and government process issues were added to lobby reporting requirements. Also contributing to the increase was a trend whereby other government entities—local and county governments, public colleges, independent authorities—began to hire lobbyists to intercede with the state on their behalf. In 2009, such government entities spent $2 million on lobbying, although this number was cut in half the next year when Governor Chris Christie banned state authorities and commissions from hiring lobbyists.[34]

## LOBBYISTS AS INFLUENCE PEDDLERS

The Parsons contract for managing New Jersey's motor vehicle inspection and emissions testing program (see chapter 2) is a prime example of

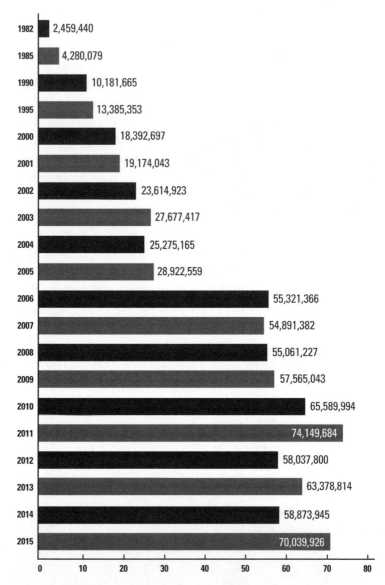

| | |
|---|---|
| 1982 | 2,459,440 |
| 1985 | 4,280,079 |
| 1990 | 10,181,665 |
| 1995 | 13,385,353 |
| 2000 | 18,392,697 |
| 2001 | 19,174,043 |
| 2002 | 23,614,923 |
| 2003 | 27,677,417 |
| 2004 | 25,275,165 |
| 2005 | 28,922,559 |
| 2006 | 55,321,366 |
| 2007 | 54,891,382 |
| 2008 | 55,061,227 |
| 2009 | 57,565,043 |
| 2010 | 65,589,994 |
| 2011 | 74,149,684 |
| 2012 | 58,037,800 |
| 2013 | 63,378,814 |
| 2014 | 58,873,945 |
| 2015 | 70,039,926 |

FIGURE 4.1. Annual Lobbying Financial Expenditure Summary, 1982–2015
Source: New Jersey Election Law Reform Commission, Trenton, news release,
March 6, 2016.

how former government officials become powerful lobbyists and work wonders for a client in securing a lucrative state contract.

This was not the only case of lobbying extravagance in New Jersey in recent years. In the 2009 gubernatorial election, former U.S. Attorney Chris Christie was the Republican candidate and Jon Corzine was the Democratic incumbent. Each campaign engaged the services of three of Trenton's top lobbyists, who acted as both paid and unpaid consultants—and fund-raisers. In a system that is virtually unregulated, the lobbyists were free to continue representing their firms' clients during the campaign and, of course, after the election. Key lobbyists helping the candidates were Roger Bodman and Dale Florio for Christie and Jamie Fox for Corzine. It doesn't take a cynic to recognize that this relationship is a formula by which special interests get favorable government treatment.[35]

In October 2012, superstorm Sandy devastated New Jersey's coastline, creating the need for a massive clean-up. New Jersey was unprepared for the work of removing post-storm debris, because it had no contracts in place to address such a circumstance. Two days after Sandy hit, Governor Christie hired AshBritt, a large company from Florida, on a no-bid contract to dispose of refuse and debris from fifty-three towns at a cost of $150 million. AshBritt proceeded to hire New Jersey lobbyists to persuade the affected towns to participate in the state's contract, but some towns claimed that AshBritt's charges were excessive and chose to use local disposal contractors at lower cost.[36]

The AshBritt deal drew the attention of the press and many of Christie's Democratic critics because it resulted, in part, from the recommendation of former Mississippi governor Haley Barbour, who had played a key role as a political supporter in Christie's successful campaign for governor. Christie's relationship with Barbour was captured in his comments from an earlier interview: "If it wasn't for Haley Barbour, I wouldn't be governor . . . you remain incredibly indebted to somebody like that."[37]

Barbour was a cofounder of the lobbying firm that represented AshBritt, and he actively lobbied for AshBritt in the nation's capital. In early 2013, the head of the lobbying firm, BRG Group, planned to have a fund-raiser for Christie's reelection at his estate in Virginia. The governor of Virginia, Bob McDonnell, would be the ceremonial host. This sequence of events drew the following comment from campaign finance specialist Craig Holman: "The fundraising event by Haley Barbour's [firm] not only violates the spirit of the pay-to-play law, it's outrageous to think that a government contractor can hire a lobby firm to represent itself and then do fundraising for the same candidate who awards the contract."

Clearly, it is in the best interests of lobbyists to build up relationships with powerful lawmakers through political help and campaign contributions. In New Jersey and most other states, lobbyists are free to assume any role in a candidate's fund-raising and campaign activity, even the role of campaign treasurer. Evidence of the political establishment's high regard for lobbyists is seen in the fact that of the 937 lobbyists currently registered, 160 serve as appointees on public boards, authorities, and commissions throughout the state.[38]

Operating in this culture, lobbyists can maximize their ability to attract high-paying clients. Whether one calls this influence peddling or merely soft corruption, the relationship between lobbyists, their clients, and public officials results in the inequitable distribution of government power and benefits. Clearly, the relationship does not endow the participants with the highest degree of professional integrity we might expect in our representative democracy.

We have seen that special interest money has two principal avenues for entering New Jersey's political system: one is through campaign contributions and the other is in payments for lobbying. Campaign spending on legislative races alone approximates the $70 million plus spent in 2011 and 2015 on lobbying as shown in figure 4.1. With both exceeding this level of spending per year, they clearly demonstrate the very real threat of special interest money buying government results.[39]

# 5 ▸ CONFLICT OF INTEREST

"Jersey is a business man's state; business men and their lawyers have ruled it always, and the laws they have made permit a business man to hold office and engage in private business, almost any office and any business."
—LINCOLN STEFFENS, *McClure's Magazine*, 1905

MANY OFFICEHOLDERS BEHAVE as if their positions entitle them to receive government benefits not usually available to the general public. Common Cause reported a classic case about a Maryland state senator who was in the business of selling alcoholic beverages. In 1973, the Maryland legislature was considering a bill mandating an increase in liquor prices, and someone suggested that the aggressiveness with which the senator pushed for passage might reflect a personal interest on his part. He responded indignantly: "There is no conflict with *my* interest!"[1]

Conflict of interest occurs when a public official is faced with taking action on a government matter that affects, or could affect, the personal and business interests of the official, members of the official's family, friends, and/or business associates. The American public wants its government representatives to be honest and to be guided by a high standard of ethical conduct. Too often, these officials have come up short and are found to have been using their positions for personal gain. As a result, most states now have laws that require elected and appointed officials to disclose their personal finances and prohibit specific practices that constitute conflicts of interest. Full and total disclosure is key to ending corruption in government.

And, of course, controlling conflicts of interest is not possible without alert reporters who seek out information on officials' personal financial disclosure forms, campaign contribution records, and performance as a public official, all of which give them the information to expose ethics violations.

New Jersey's conflict of interest law, enacted in 1971, spells out the various do's and don'ts that govern the behavior of public officials.[2] Among the proscribed activities are:

- representing any person or interest other than the state before a state agency, with a few exceptions;[3]
- having an interest, financial or otherwise, in a business, investment, transaction, or professional activity that is in substantial conflict with the discharge of the official's duties. When such a conflict exists, the official must not participate in making a decision relating to that interest. In addition, public officials cannot have any interest, direct or indirect, in a casino;
- using one's official position to secure unwarranted privileges or advantages;
- using government facilities or equipment for personal benefit;
- accepting any gift, favor, service, employment, or other thing of value when there is reason to believe that the gift is offered with the intent to influence the performance of the official's public duties;[4]
- contracting with a government agency unless the contract is awarded through a publicly advertised competitive bidding process;
- releasing confidential information; and
- participating, postemployment, in matters in which the official was directly involved while in state service.

In addition, a catch-all provision in the conflict of interest law covers those situations in which a state official's actions give the perception of impropriety, declaring that no such official "should knowingly act in any

way that might reasonably be expected to create an impression or sus-
picion among the public having knowledge of his acts that he may be
engaged in activity violative of his trust."[5]

Even with the new conflict-of-interest law in 1972, the New Jersey
legislature was not ready to give up its old habits. The chairman of the
Assembly Transportation Committee was engaged as a consultant to a
national containerized freight company on May 3, 1973, at $10,000 per
year. When this became public later that month, adverse publicity—
and the new law—forced the assemblyman to terminate his consulting
arrangement, and he returned all fees paid to him, notwithstanding the
fact that the legislator had received clearance from the Joint Legislative Committee on Ethical Standards for this activity.[6] But in the days
following, when he was campaigning for a senate seat, he accepted the
largest contribution given by the Motor Truck Association for that
election ($1,000), amounting to 10 percent of the funds he raised in
the campaign. After election to the senate, he sponsored and helped
pass a bill increasing the allowable gross weight of trucks using New
Jersey highways.[7]

Governors frequently fill their cabinet with supporters who were
instrumental in helping them get elected. The Reverend William Watley,
pastor at Saint James AME Church in Newark and an active supporter of
Jim McGreevey for governor in 2001, was selected for the cabinet post
of secretary of the Commerce and Economic Growth Commission.
This appointment was controversial among New Jersey business executives, who expected one of their own to get the post. Watley supporters countered that Saint James Church, with its affiliated educational
and community services divisions, operated essentially as a $24 mil-
lion business enterprise in the urban areas of northern New Jersey. To
accept the appointment, Watley had to forgo his church salary of more
than $100,000, but he continued his ministry while living in the church-
owned $500,000 residence.[8]

After he took the cabinet position, it became clear that Watley would
still head Saint James's community development programs. His chief
assistant at the church, Lesly Devereaux, followed him to the state to
become chief of staff of the Commerce and Economic Growth Commission. At the same time that Saint James was actively seeking funding from Jersey City for a proposed housing development, Jersey City

was applying for grants from a state authority that Watley chaired. One Jersey City councilman described Watley's active lobbying of council members on the Saint James project as "outrageous." It was reported that Watley also attempted to make a campaign contribution to the Jersey City Council president during the permit review process.[9] Nevertheless, Saint James received approval of the housing project as well as $870,000 in funding from Jersey City—and was donated the land. Jersey City subsequently received $4.3 million of state money from the Watley-chaired, state-run Urban Enterprise Authority. Other projects sponsored by Saint James received favorable treatment from local government agencies that were simultaneously applying to the state for funding.

Despite holding her state job, Devereaux did not relinquish her position as president of Saint James development interests, where she actively advocated for the church's programs. Saint James II LLC, an affiliate of the Saint James AME Church and in partnership with for-profit developers, had applied to the New Jersey Housing and Mortgage Finance Agency (HMFA) for an $11.5 million loan to finance affordable and market rate housing on land leased from the City of Newark. The HMFA, a board on which four of Watley's fellow cabinet officers served, originally approved the loan but later rescinded it because of concerns over conflict of interest and an ongoing criminal investigation of Devereaux. The Devereaux probe uncovered $200,000 in questionable travel expenses by the commission and spending of more than $9 million, almost 60 percent of its budget, without approval of the commission comptroller. Devereaux had retained out-of-state relatives as paid consultants for services that didn't exist. This scandal, which ultimately resulted in Devereaux's indictment and conviction, was too much for Watley, who resigned his cabinet post in 2004.

Unlike the Watley/Devereaux case, where engaging in governmental conflict of interest was clear and actionable, it is not always easy to identify and guard against conflict of interest in the public sector. United States Supreme Court Justice Potter Stewart famously observed in trying to define hard-core pornography: "perhaps I could never succeed in intelligibly doing so. But *I know it when I see it*" (emphasis in original).[10] Defining conflict of interest is similarly difficult; it is both abstract and subjective.

One reason conflict of interest is so imprecise, so hard to grasp, is that it is the one corrupt practice that does not always rely on a conspiracy of two or more people.

A single public official, acting alone, can engage in a situation in which there is a conflict of interest. If the official has a personal interest in a matter that comes before his or her government agency, and if that interest is not disclosed, private gain can drive the official's action and no one will be the wiser. One Trenton journalist labeled this activity "pay-off solitaire."[11] Therefore, full financial disclosure is the most crucial component of any government ethics code that addresses conflicts of interest.

Government service and politics are all about relationships—with friends, allies, family, adversaries, the press, public officials, and those seeking government assistance. These relationships almost inevitably lead to conflicts of interest when public officials are motivated by self-interest rather than the public good.

Attitudes have not changed all that much since the conflict-of-interest law was passed in the early 1970s. This was evident in 2002, when Republican state senator Robert Littell of Sussex County worked to further the economic interests of Intrawest Corp., a resort developer that had large land holdings in Sussex County and was hoping to create a huge tourist/recreation destination. As chair of the appropriations committee, Littell was instrumental in arranging a state subsidy of $7 million that allowed Intrawest to proceed with its project, Mountain Creek.[12] Bringing the economic benefits of this development to his district was completely legitimate and certainly justified Littell's efforts.

But during the same period, Intrawest hired Virginia Littell, the state senator's wife, as a paid consultant. Virginia Littell claimed that her clients' interests—and Intrawest's in particular—had nothing to do with her husband (he made the same claim) and that there was "nothing inappropriate" about her representing the developer. "It's nothing more than making a living, and that's the American way," she declared. Among Virginia Littell's duties as consultant to Intrawest was introducing her client to local officials, whose approval was important for the project to move forward.

When questioned about the potential conflict of interest, legislative counsel in the nonpartisan Office of Legislative Services declared that unless an elected official's spouse tried to directly influence the official on behalf of the client, no conflict existed, adding, "You have to assume the independence of spouses."[13]

## QUESTIONABLE BEHAVIOR

Public officials who are influential in determining government policy and making official decisions must be careful not to expose themselves to conflicts of interest—including in the professions they hold outside government. State legislators, who serve part-time, frequently hold other full-time jobs. Their positions often create situations in which the legislators' private interest is in conflict with their legislative duties. This is particularly true for lawyers, who are often called upon to advocate for clients before government entities.

There remains a shortcoming in the 1971 conflicts law. Although legislators may not represent private interests before state courts and agencies when the interests of the client are adverse to that of the state, the law does not prohibit a legislator or state official from appearing before local government entities on behalf of a private interest. Yet this can be just as great a breach of ethical conduct. For example, when a private interest pays a lawyer-legislator to appear before a local board or agency in an adversarial proceeding, the legislator implicitly carries the political power of his or her office and may very well be asked to advocate an outcome that is against the will of the legislator's constituents.

This very situation led to exposés in 2003 and 2007 of Democratic state senator Bob Smith's appearances as a lawyer before local government boards. Smith, one of thirty-four lawyers in the legislature at the time, represented more than fifty private clients before the planning and zoning boards of Piscataway Township during the five-year period preceding 2007. Smith lived in Piscataway, which was part of his legislative district. He had been the town mayor a few years earlier. Forty-nine of Smith's clients won approval from the town; a fiftieth case was withdrawn, and several others were still pending when the story ran in the *Star-Ledger*.[14]

Piscataway is located in Middlesex County; both are solidly Democratic. Smith was former chair of his county party organization, and his wife had chaired the party in Piscataway. Most of Smith's clients were seeking land-use permits from boards whose members were appointed by Piscataway's municipal governing body, historically composed of Democratic members. Sitting on the planning board were two members of the council and two of the town's Democratic county committee members. The zoning board had four members who also served on the Democratic county committee. The law firm serving as counsel to the town's planning board donated $3,000 to Smith's 2001 election campaign.

The Piscataway planning and zoning boards clearly are part of the political hierarchy of both the county and the town. How likely would they be to oppose a permit application urged by their powerful state senator? Would opposition hurt a board member's future chances to run for elective office as a Democrat? Would turning down an application cause the state senator to be less enthusiastic in his efforts to obtain future state aid for Piscataway? These considerations are unspoken, but in the political world they are real.

This case raises questions about the ethics of representing private interests before local government entities, a representation that is not allowed before a state agency. Whenever Smith asked nonpartisan legislative counsel to rule if he had a conflict of interest in these cases, he was always told there is no law prohibiting such representations before local boards.[15]

## DISCLOSURE IS KEY

Those who believe in the words of Thomas Jefferson, "When a man assumes a public trust he should consider himself as public property,"[16] scrupulously avoid using their office for personal advantage. Just as there is no such thing as being a little bit pregnant, the honest lawmaker believes that in government there is no such thing as being a little bit dishonest. However, the ethical compass that guides many public officials, in New Jersey and elsewhere, does not always direct them away from conflicts of interest. So it has become the job of government to establish and administer codes of ethics.

Conflict-of-interest laws and regulations set standards of conduct for government officials, both elected and appointed. These laws do not cover obvious criminal behavior, such as bribery and extortion; that's the job of criminal law. Part of New Jersey's structure governing ethical conduct is the requirement that all government officials in management, supervisory, and other high-level positions file personal financial disclosure forms. The positions requiring financial disclosure are spelled out by executive order.[17] This requirement applies to officials at all levels of government: elected and appointed; part-time and full-time; and those serving on independent authorities. Officeholders must annually list outside occupations (if any), sources of income, real estate holdings, liabilities, and directorships and executive positions held in private entities. Reporting income from a source is required only when the income exceeds $1,000 per year. While the precise amount of income from a source does not have to be reported, lawmakers must disclose where, within a given set of ranges, the income falls. These ranges are: less than $10,000; $10,000 to $25,000; $25,000 to $50,000; and more than $50,000. Disclosure must include the same information for officeholders' spouses.

Officials are not required to disclose assets (other than real estate holdings) and their value, but if an asset produces more than $1,000 in income, the identity of that asset, of course, becomes known as part of the disclosure filing. Some contend that the principle of disclosure is better served by publishing all assets and their exact dollar valuations held by a public official. New Jersey has not adopted this approach, on the basis that such a system does not respect legitimate privacy concerns of officeholders. Showing exact dollar figures could expose public officials to threats to their personal safety and security while satisfying only the voyeuristic proclivities of the media and the public.

When disclosure of a relationship between a public official and a private interest on an impending government matter is likely to signal a conflict of interest, the official might very well refrain from becoming involved. But when officials ignore potential conflicts and engage in a prohibited activity anyway, the appropriate enforcement agency has the responsibility to investigate and impose sanctions as warranted.

Disclosure of a specific financial holding by a public official does not always signal that a conflict exists. If a legislator has an interest in a specific piece of real estate zoned for commercial development, and if legislation is being considered that will affect all similarly zoned property in the state, the legislator is not required to refrain from voting on the measure or participating in the debate. In this instance, the legislator is deemed to have no personal conflict because the code of ethics recognizes that "no benefit or detriment could reasonably be expected to accrue to him, or a member of his immediate family, as a member of a business, profession, occupation or group, to any greater extent than any such benefit or detriment could reasonably be expected to accrue to any other member of such business, profession, occupation or group."[18]

But if legislation is introduced proposing that the state purchase the legislator's specific property for a major public project, then ownership of the property is unique to the legislator who has a personal interest in it and so he or she must refrain from any involvement.

The benefits of financial disclosure to the public weal are obvious, but they bear repeating. Making the business associations and financial interests of government officials public gives voters information as to whether government officials attend to their constituents' well-being or to their own. Voters should know how elected officials who are associated with the development community in private life vote on environmental preservation measures; or how lawyer-legislators vote on tort reform in matters involving medical malpractice; or how members affiliated with unions vote on measures to expand public employee benefit programs; or how officials with business backgrounds approach corporate tax breaks. Financial disclosure brings these relationships into the open so that citizens can make the ultimate decision through the ballot box.

Despite conflict of interest and financial disclosure laws, some major governmental transgressions were detected only through the exceptional work of investigative journalism. A case in point was the exposure of a questionable business deal between 2000 and 2003 that involved Assembly Majority Leader Joe Roberts. Roberts and South Jersey Democratic political boss George Norcross had consummated a $33 million arrangement to take over U.S. Vision, an eyewear manufacturing company with a chain of six hundred optometry outlets. Norcross became president and Roberts vice president. When the transaction took place, Roberts's holding in the company was 350,000 shares worth $1.4 million. Commerce Bank, a politically connected financial powerhouse with ties to Roberts and Norcross, provided a loan of $32 million to facilitate the takeover; directors of Commerce as well as Norcross and his lawyer/lobbyist brother were investors in the enterprise.[19]

At the same time, Assemblyman Roberts introduced legislation to change the law to allow optometrists to perform laser eye surgery, a change that would have been a boon to the business of U.S. Vision. This entire matter did not come to light through Roberts's financial disclosure; at the time, he was not required to report this type of investment, because he received no income from it.[20] It was only through the diligence of resourceful newspaper reporters who found information from other sources that the U.S. Vision business matter came into public view. Reacting to intense negative publicity, Roberts soon withdrew his bill. He also sold his interest in U.S. Vision.

One of the more difficult times for preventing conflict of interest occurs when the government official has an indirect connection with a special interest—a connection that doesn't have to be disclosed on the official's personal financial statement. Examples of these include unknown clients of lawmakers who have legal, business, or consulting relationships on matters involving government actions. Senator Littell's wife, who was a consultant for a developer receiving benefits from the senator's legislative efforts, did not show in her financial disclosure that she received income from the developer. Rather, she reported receipts of income from her consulting business composed of fees paid by the developer.[21]

A similar situation occurred in the case of Assemblyman Gerald Green, who received income of more than $50,000 in 2006 from his consulting firm, Jerry Green Enterprises, but showed none of the clients for whom he provided services. At the same time, Green was vice president for local affairs of the Alman Group, a lobbying and government consulting firm. In the legislature, Green served as chair of the assembly committee that had jurisdiction over housing issues, which of course would be of concern to Alman's developer clients. The connection with Green appeared on the Alman website, not on the assemblyman's disclosure filing. Green insisted that the projects on which he consulted involved no lobbying or state contracts. Nonpartisan legislative counsel ruled in 2006 that Green's work at Alman violates no ethics code as long as it is unrelated to his "official duties." But wouldn't it be more reassuring to the public if Green were compelled to disclose his major clients, whether through Alman or Jerry Green Enterprises, as well as affirm that his relationships with these clients did not conflict with his official duties? After an *Asbury Park Press* article raised this question,[22] his subsequent financial disclosure statement showed a decline in income from Jerry Green Enterprises to zero in 2009.[23]

In contrast to many legislators who take steps to conceal the identity of major clients, Republican assemblyman Francis Bodine was not reticent in disclosing that he earned $71,000 per year from two businesses, an insurance agency and an engineering firm. The service he provided these businesses was to "make introductions" to potential government clients. When criticized by his opponents and the press about this activity, Bodine responded: "You guys want to deprive everybody of a way of life. I mean, good Lord, can't we go out and make an honest living?"

If Bodine wanted to conceal his connection with the two companies, he could have formed a personal consulting business and disclosed only the income range he received from this business without identifying clients, a legal but unethical subterfuge. When he tried in 2007 to run for the vacant senate seat in his district, the GOP dumped him from the ticket. He then switched parties and ran for senate as a Democrat. Ironically, the Republicans campaigned against him, citing his past ethical misconduct as "trying to use his position to personally profit," which, of course, he was doing when he was representing their party. He lost his bid for the senate seat.[24]

## DIFRANCESCO GOES DOWN

If a New Jersey official engages in a conflict of interest and the matter becomes public, serious political consequences can ensue. He or she can be fined or severely rebuked. Even if legal sanctions are not called for, citizen reaction to this type of ethical misbehavior can be just as damaging. Such disclosures can inflict the ultimate penalty: the official becomes unelectable. What happened to Republican state senate president and acting New Jersey governor Donald DiFrancesco in 2001 proved this point.

First elected to the senate in 1979, DiFrancesco gradually rose into the ranks of legislative leadership. In 1992, and for each succeeding two-year legislative session through 2001, he was elected president of the senate. This position gave him an excellent opportunity to succeed Christie Whitman when her two terms as governor were due to end after 2001. Even more fortuitous was Whitman's resignation as governor in January 2001 to accept a position in the cabinet of President George W. Bush. Under New Jersey law, this meant the senate president, DiFrancesco, would assume the post of acting governor for the remainder of her term, giving him invaluable statewide exposure. Most observers believed he had a lock on the GOP nomination to run for New Jersey governor in 2001.[25]

DiFrancesco had already been making all the right moves in preparation for his gubernatorial run. From the $1.1 million in his campaign treasury, he used a large portion to pay for political consultants, mailings, and newspaper advertisements directed at a statewide audience. In addition, he contributed $310,000 to other Republican candidates and party organizations, a strategy clearly intended to curry favor with his party in advance of a run for governor.[26]

As early as January 2000, DiFrancesco formed a nonprofit issues organization called Solutions for the Next Century to raise money and provide publicity that would not be subject to restrictions on direct campaign fundraising and expenditures. To collect money for this effort, he recruited many of the state GOP fund-raising heavyweights. In six months, Solutions had raised $1.3 million. Forming such an organization is standard procedure for someone planning to vie for the office of governor. In the words of political scientist Alan Rosenthal: "Front-ending a political campaign is quite important . . . building name identification . . . putting people together who will help a campaign. . . . It's to a political campaign what foreplay is to lovemaking."[27]

During the 1990s, however, some of Senator DiFrancesco's personal financial dealings, bordering on conflict of interest, would form a cloud over his role as a government leader. An attorney, DiFrancesco was the principal of a firm with thirty-three lawyers and an extensive practice representing local towns and government entities throughout central New Jersey.[28] He also had been the longtime municipal attorney for his hometown of Scotch Plains. A litany of damaging revelations came into public view in 2000 and 2001:

- In 1993, DiFrancesco had been in default on a $1 million personal loan to finance a commercial property in neighboring Chatham. Among the friends and associates who helped bail out DiFrancesco was fellow Scotch Plains resident Anthony Sartor, who advanced $150,000. Sartor was the principal of an engineering firm that was a major contractor of state work, including a $3.5 million subcontract awarded in 1998 in the Parsons auto emissions project.[29] Sartor had been appointed to the prestigious board of the Sports and Exposition Authority in 1992 on the recommendation of DiFrancesco, and in 1999 he was appointed as a director of the Port Authority of New York and New Jersey.[30] A subsequent review by the Joint Legislative Committee on Ethical Standards on the loan and its repayment exonerated DiFrancesco of any violations of the legislative ethics code. Clearly, however, Sartor's involvement in the loan repayment did not pass the smell test.[31]

- A parcel of land in Scotch Plains owned by DiFrancesco family members became the source of further embarrassment for Senator DiFrancesco. Family members attempted to get zoning approval to locate a supermarket at the site, a move that was not popular with local residents. The effort failed. The DiFrancescos then defaulted on the loan that had been financing ownership of the property, and the holder of the loan proceeded to sue family members as well as Senator DiFrancesco to recover his money. Meanwhile, the state's largest home builder, K. Hovnanian, became interested in the parcel for potential development and advanced Senator DiFrancesco $225,000 to help settle the outstanding debt. The matter took an ominous turn when the town initiated foreclosure action for nonpayment of taxes, thereby taking title to the property and leaving Hovnanian out $225,000. The DiFrancescos, including Donald, the town's municipal attorney, took legal action against Scotch Plains to overturn the foreclosure. In a sworn statement, accusing town officials of bad faith, Donald DiFrancesco supported the position of the property owners, thereby placing him at odds with his client, the Township of Scotch Plains. Attempts to rescind the foreclosure failed.[32]

- The fate of DiFrancesco had been further damaged in the eyes of the public when in late March 2001 he decided to bare everything relating to his personal finances. Included was a revelation that DiFrancesco and his wife had made a profit of $135,000 in two years on returns from initial public offering (IPO) transactions. Of thirty-eight IPOs, the DiFrancescos made profits on thirty-four, half of which were held no longer than one day. The package of investments, lucrative yet legal, was managed by a brokerage executive with strong financial ties to the state GOP.[33]

- The coup de grâce came in a scathing *New York Times* news story on April 17, 2001, unveiling a confidential letter signed in June 1998 by two attorneys retained by Scotch Plains, one a Democrat and the other a Republican, recommending to the Township Council that DiFrancesco be dismissed as municipal attorney. "Mr. DiFrancesco's acceptance of the money [from Hovnanian] and failure to advise Council of same was an egregious ethical breach," they wrote. "The reason for the payment from Hovnanian to Mr. DiFrancesco is obvious. The payment was made at a time when Hovnanian had an interest in three (3) separate parcels in Scotch Plains, two of which were before land use boards." [34]

Although the Republican-controlled Scotch Plains council did not remove DiFrancesco from his post as its legal counsel, one of the members expressed the belief that he would not be reappointed after his term expired at the end of 1998 because, despite his denials of a conflict of interest, he had not given a satisfactory response to the lawyers' charges. It became a moot point, as Democrats took control of Scotch Plains after the November 1998 election and replaced DiFrancesco. When Republicans regained control one year later, they did not choose DiFrancesco to fill his old position.

These negative stories built to a crescendo of bad publicity against the leading Republican gubernatorial hopeful. On April 25, 2001, DiFrancesco withdrew his candidacy for the governorship.[35]

The DiFrancesco cautionary tale demonstrates how conflict of interest is unique among all the five conditions of soft corruption. Engaging in one of the other four—unethical manipulation of campaign financing, patronage, lobbyist influence, and exploitation of the electoral process—will seldom result in the loss of office. On the other hand, conflict of interest, when uncovered, is often the cause of self-inflicted punishment.

## DUAL OFFICE HOLDING

New Jersey's conflict-of-interest laws do not expressly prohibit the practice of holding more than one public office at one time. Dual office holding takes several different forms. Some elected officials hold a second elective office; other elected officials hold one or more appointed offices; still other appointed officials hold a second appointment, usually on a part-time basis; and some elected officials, primarily lawyer-legislators, hold professional positions with government entities—as municipal attorney, local prosecutor, planning board attorney—that are, in effect, second government jobs.

Dual office holding contributes to ethical misconduct, that is, soft corruption, by public officials in two respects: it creates conflicts of interest, and it generates many of the evils associated with patronage.

The phenomenon of dual office holding is especially prevalent in New Jersey—the state with the highest percentage of its public officials engaged in double-dipping of all fifty states.[36] By contrast, the constitutions of eleven states explicitly prohibit their officials from holding more than one public office.

Legislators who also serve as county freeholders (aka county supervisors in most states) or elected municipal officials defend dual office holding by arguing that experience in local office gives them unique insight into issues that are frequently debated at higher levels of government. This premise is certainly true, but it does not mean that both offices have to be held simultaneously.

Officials who hold two elective offices at the same time also use the rationale that the voters approved their dual positions. This reasoning, of course, presumes that the voters had a real choice, which is not necessarily true in those jurisdictions where one party is dominant and dictates the selection of candidates.

A fundamental conflict of interest occurs in these situations because, as an ethical matter, the dual officeholder cannot always serve two masters at the same time. Consider the role of a mayor who also serves in the assembly representing ten towns in a district, one of which is the mayor's own town. Innumerable issues will come before the legislature that might affect the mayor's town differently than the other nine municipalities in the district. Among these are: highway alignment;

water supply; state grants; land preservation; affordable housing; location of state facilities; commercial development; sewage treatment; and on and on. What position is the representative going to take on an initiative that benefits the mayor's town but has an adverse impact on several of the other towns in the legislative district? Clearly, the individual who holds two offices at the same time can be exposed to multiple conflicts of interest.

In addition, when an elected official also holds an appointed position, performance in the appointed job is often compromised, as the elected official is unable to devote sufficient time and attention to the appointive role, commonly referred to as a "low show" job. New Jersey law actually facilitates a legislator's absences from these appointed municipal, county, and agency positions by allowing the legislator time off, without loss of pay, "when he or she attends sessions of the Legislature and hearings or meetings of legislative committees or commissions."[37]

Counties and municipalities dominated by one party already make it difficult for public-spirited citizens with political ambitions to advance. An analysis of the twenty legislators who held a second elective office in 2004 (five Republicans and fifteen Democrats) showed they were all in "safe" districts.[38] As observed by government policy consultant Tom O'Neill in his extensive studies on dual office holding: "There is not a single dual elected office holder in New Jersey who represents a competitive district. This only flourishes in non-competitive districts where they are not going to be attacked for their dual office holding by a well-funded opponent."[39]

Dual office holding in these single-party bastions clearly limits opportunities for citizens to seek public office. Double-dippers are usually incumbents who enjoy twice the visibility of a single office representative, thereby reinforcing their chances for reelection. This in turn enhances their ability to turn on the spigots of campaign funding. As a result, the strong get stronger and potential challengers remain weak. A truly competitive political environment, one that allows the more talented candidates to filter to the top, does not exist.

By 2007, revelations of the abuses associated with dual office holding were too much for the legislature to ignore, so it passed a half-baked reform bill prohibiting any elected official from holding a second elective office after January 2008, while grandfathering in all those who at the time held another elective office. It did not address holding an elective and appointive office at the same time, or the question of professional service appointments as dual offices. Many reformers considered this measure woefully inadequate, but Governor Jon Corzine signed it into law with no attempt to remove the grandfather clause—or to extend the reach of the law to appointive office.

Perhaps even more troubling, because there is not even the pretense of voter control, are elected officials who also hold an appointive office, which can carry the same conflicts of interest. Take, for example, a lawyer-legislator who also serves as a municipal attorney. This is serving the interests of two jurisdictions just as much as a nonlawyer who is both a legislator and a local elected official. The town a legislator represents as an attorney could have a legal issue with the state, putting the municipality's interests at odds with other towns in the legislator's district. How can this individual pursue both interests with the same intensity, objectivity, and integrity?

In New Jersey, it is not unusual for lawyer-legislators to represent local units of government. Democratic state senator Bob Smith of Piscataway in Middlesex County, already cited earlier in this chapter as representing private clients before his township's planning and zoning boards, also enjoyed appointments as solicitor on local boards outside of Piscataway. Among these were: zoning board attorney for New Brunswick, prosecutor for East Brunswick, and prosecutor for Hillsborough—until Republicans regained control of Hillsborough in 2003. These sinecures earned him almost $75,000. In addition, Smith's law firm, Bob Smith and Associates, received more than $36,000 as prosecutor for South Brunswick.[40] Smith's situation is far from unique:

Republican Assemblyman Brian Rumpf was reported in 2007 to have eleven municipal appointments, six as public defender;[41]

Democratic Assemblyman Reed Gusciora held three municipal prosecutor appointments in 2011;[42]

Republican legislator James Holzapfel's firm held thirty-two public contracts and five positions as municipal attorney. In 2007, Holzapfel personally held seven of these positions.[43]

A 2007 study showed fifty-three state legislators (44 percent of the total) and fifty-six county freeholders (41 percent of the total) held another public office, either elective or appointive. The ten largest cities in the state with a total of seventy-two elected officials among them identified thirty-seven (51 percent) who had at least one other government job. Of all the elected officials in New Jersey (state, county, and municipal) almost seven hundred hold another nonelective position in the public sector.[44]

Why is dual office holding so embedded in the political culture of New Jersey? One reason is that elective office is part-time—except for the governor, mayors of the largest cities, and in the five counties that operate under the county executive form of government. The pay for these part-time jobs is modest to low. Legislators earn $49,000 per year, a freeholder's salary averages in the low $20,000s, and the stipends for many municipal officials are in the four-digit range—or even zero. These lawmakers must have other sources of income if they don't already have a private job that pays well. This situation creates a sense of entitlement. It is only natural that they exercise their patronage powers and seek additional compensation by using the influence of their office to secure an appointment to a position in a politically friendly government agency. Besides, "Other lawmakers are doing it. Why shouldn't I?"

As noted earlier, counties with a preponderance of dual office holding are usually single-party strongholds in which incumbents have little or no competition. Hudson County, home to Jersey City, is a Democratic Party bastion where dual office holding—and patronage—thrive. Of the nine state legislators who represented all or parts of Hudson in the 2007 study, seven held other public jobs, including four as mayor. The nine-member Hudson Board of Chosen Freeholders had six members who served in appointed government positions. One had two public jobs. The Jersey City Council has nine members, four of whom worked regular jobs for Hudson County and one for the city.[45] The poster boy for lawmakers who hold multiple public offices is state senator Nicholas Sacco, a Hudson Democrat who is not only mayor of North Bergen but also an assistant superintendent of the regional school district. In 2012, his three salaries provided him an annual income of $309,000.[46]

Essex, which includes the city of Newark, is another county solidly in the Democratic camp. Essex has the distinction of having the highest-profile dual officeholders in the state. Two state senators and the assemblywoman who served as Speaker from 2010 through 2013—Teresa Ruiz, Nia Gill, and Sheila Oliver—have top county jobs under the control of County Executive Joe DiVincenzo. The average compensation for the three is $74,540 per year; and of course this pay continues unabated while they are performing their legislative duties.[47]

Republican-dominated counties are not immune from dual office holding. Three of the five-member Ocean County freeholder board (all Republican) have other public jobs.[48] Ocean is also home to Republican Daniel Van Pelt, who at one point served simultaneously as an assemblyman, mayor of Ocean Township, and business administrator of nearby Lumberton Township, with a combined annual income of $144,800. In 2009, Van Pelt's career as a double-dipper turned from honest graft to dishonest graft when he was caught in a sting by the U.S. attorney for accepting a $10,000 bribe to help a developer obtain permit approvals. Before his arrest, Van Pelt had resigned from the Ocean Township Committee to devote more time to his other posts, a commitment he couldn't keep for long. A week after his arrest, he withdrew from the assembly, and was subsequently fired as business administrator of Lumberton. In May 2010, Van Pelt was convicted of bribery and sent to prison to serve a forty-one-month sentence.[49]

Perhaps the ultimate case of chutzpah involving dual office patronage occurred in Carteret, where Dan Reiman, who was elected mayor in 2002, installed himself as business administrator for the town, a salaried position. Reiman earned the distinction of being the only New Jersey mayor who held a second job working for his own town government.[50]

## ETHICS ENFORCEMENT

All efforts to enact the highest standards of governmental integrity are of little consequence if ethics oversight is ineffective. Oversight bodies must be in place with the power and the will to vigorously monitor compliance, investigate abuses, and enforce all code requirements.

The ethics laws of New Jersey are divided into four domains, according to the type of public office to which they apply: legislators and staff,

all state officials, local (including county) officials, and school employees. A common ethics regulation in all four categories is the principle
of recusal: public officials are required to refrain from voting on or participating in any matter in which they have a personal interest. The act of
recusal is generally stated in advance and acknowledged on the record by
the official, who then abstains from voting on the issue at hand. When
an official does not recuse himself or herself from involvement in such a
matter, and the conflict is made known, the enforcement agency has the
responsibility to intervene and take corrective action. The logic of recusal was captured by journalist and author George Amick, who wrote:
"We would not ask a man to be a judge of a beauty contest in which his
wife was a competitor."[51]

The most vexing enforcement of ethics rules has been in the legislative branch, which is governed by the Joint Legislative Committee on
Ethical Standards. The biggest problem of the twelve-member Joint
Committee in past years was the dominance of legislators who served on
it. Appointment to the committee was partisan. Each of the legislative
leaders (senate president, senate minority leader, assembly Speaker, and
assembly minority leader) selected two members from his own house
and one from the general public. Public members were invariably political allies of the leader making the appointment. To say that the committee had a political taint would be an understatement. Legislators who are
expected to pass judgment on their colleagues create a situation leading
to leniency if not outright bipartisan forgiveness on charges brought
before the committee.

In the thirty-five years of its existence, the Joint Committee has heard
more than one hundred cases of possible conflict of interest and taken
action against offenders in only three. One resulted in a fine of $200 in
1978; two produced reprimands in 1992. In a few other cases, the committee has faulted legislators, but without punishment.[52] One reason for
its weak enforcement is that the committee can only fine or reprimand;
it does not have the power to impose criminal sanctions or to remove a
legislator from office. This power is reserved for the legislature itself by
the state constitution. (By statute, the courts can remove a legislator for
criminal offenses.) Another factor that limits enforcement by the Joint
Committee is that it can consider only signed complaints, not anonymous ones.

An embarrassment for the Joint Committee came in 2003 when its then-chairman, Assemblyman Anthony Impreveduto of Hudson County, declared that matters coming before the committee amounted to nothing more than "donkey dust." Impreveduto himself resigned from the legislature in 2004 after pleading guilty to using campaign funds and legislative payroll for personal use. He subsequently became a lobbyist, patrolling the halls of the statehouse on legislative days.[53]

Efforts to reform the Joint Committee have always been focused on removing the image of legislators judging their own. In 2004, four appointed public members were added to the committee's twelve-member body. But this did not seem to change the committee's tepid approach to ethics enforcement on two high-profile cases. One involved state senator Joseph Coniglio, a $5,500-per-month consultant to the Hackensack University Medical Center, who was accused of improperly steering state grants to the hospital, which was in his district. Although the committee dismissed the complaint, Coniglio was subsequently charged with extortion and convicted in federal court in April 2009.[54]

The second case concerned a complaint accusing Democratic state senator Wayne Bryant of influencing legislative action to benefit his law firm. The committee concluded by a 7–4 vote that it was an issue of legal ethics and referred it to the attorney general's Office of Attorney Ethics. Ethics committee member and former state judge James M. Coleman Jr., who was one of four to vote against relieving the committee of the complaint, objected publicly when he commented: "I'm tired of reading in the paper that this is a toothless committee" and that critics "blame us for not doing anything. All we do is hold the leaky bag." Bryant was later indicted, convicted, and sent to prison for his misdeeds.[55]

As public criticism mounted against the Joint Committee for its leniency toward legislators, the assembly passed a bill requiring that only public members be appointed to the committee. This comported with ethics committees in many other states, which are also made up of non-lawmakers. However, Senate President Richard Codey opposed the assembly measure, arguing: "I'm certainly against a select group of elite people running the ethics committee. I don't think it's wrong to have some legislators on it, who've been there and understand the difficult problems of having to be a legislator and pay college tuitions and earn a living."[56]

Finally, in 2008, the law was passed accepting the assembly version of a reformed Joint Committee that consists of a total of eight members, all of whom are from the public sector. Of the eight, two can be former legislators, but no current or past lobbyist can serve. With all appointments still made by the four legislative leaders and with the legislature's legal staff serving as counsel to the committee, the verdict is still out as to whether the system has been immunized from legislative bias. The restructured body has received more than twenty complaints, with only one rising to the level of adjudication by the committee. This involved Assemblyman Scott Rumana of Passaic County who, as CEO of a not-for-profit energy cogeneration facility, was accused by a political opponent of improperly appearing before state agencies to get approval of his energy enterprise. After lengthy deliberation, the committee rejected the charges by a 4–3 vote in September 2011.[57]

Ethics enforcement involving activities of all other state officials and employees, both full and part time, are handled by the State Ethics Commission (SEC). This body has seven members, all appointed by the governor. Four are members of the public, two from each party, and three from the executive branch of state government. (I served on the commission for six years, appointed by Governor Corzine in 2006, and elevated to vice-chair by Governor Christie in 2010.) With a highly professional staff, the SEC operates efficiently, levying fines that can range from $500 to $10,000 for a single offense, as well as disciplinary penalties. The SEC will consider anonymous complaints, which gives this body a wide-ranging caseload. The record has shown that aggressive enforcement actions by the SEC, including fines, censure, and reprimand, have been effectively administered and appear to have improved the ethics of state government officials.

The SEC has, however, fallen victim to political tampering in recent years. In early 2014, I and two other former commission members asserted that the governor's office had used improper influence in the appointment of two successive executive directors of the commission in 2011 and 2014, thus compromising its integrity and independence.[58]

At the local level, New Jersey suffers from a proliferation of government units: 21 counties, 565 municipalities, and a multitude of other authorities and special districts. This leads to inconsistent and sporadic application of ethics standards. Municipalities and counties are allowed to form their own councils for ethics oversight and enforcement. Only 43 have done so, adopting varying levels of ethical standards in their codes; the ethics of the remaining 543 governments are overseen by the overworked local government services agency in the state Department of Community Affairs.[59]

These haphazard conditions led to the formation of a task force in 2008 to study the problems and recommend a more efficient process for monitoring and enforcing ethical behavior in local government. The one overarching recommendation of the task force was to consolidate ethics administration of all government employees—state, county, and municipal, as well as those employed by authorities, commissions, and special districts—into one state agency, preferably the State Ethics Commission.[60] This would achieve greater uniformity and more consistent enforcement of high ethical standards for all government officials in New Jersey. The task force recommendation has yet to be enacted.

The final government category responsible for its own ethics enforcement is the school sector. While the inner operations of the New Jersey education system are generally less visible to the public than state, county, and municipal government bodies, school boards are indeed political institutions. Board members go through the election process, sometimes in highly contested races; they exercise patronage when making appointments to various administrative positions; and they use taxpayer funds to pay for construction projects, professional services, and supplies. All of these functions call for strong ethical procedures to prevent conflicts of interest and financial skullduggery.

The School Ethics Act adopted in 1991 holds school officials in management positions in New Jersey's education system, specifically elected board of education members and high-level administrators, to an ethics code that mirrors many of the provisions of the state code including financial disclosure, prohibited activities, training requirements, and enforcement procedures.[61]

Ethics regulation for the lower strata of school administrators together with staff personnel is lumped in with teachers and is subject to collective bargaining agreements with the New Jersey Education Association. It is worth noting that New Jersey was the first state to protect teachers from the ravages of patronage when it created the tenure law in 1909; among other features, the system currently allows tenure after four years of service.[62]

The conduct of boards of education in New Jersey is not entirely benign, uncontroversial, or the embodiment of integrity. Most notorious of all school board political machines in the state has been that of the City of Elizabeth, which is covered at some length in chapter 6. In an exposé starting in early 2011, the *Star-Ledger* explained how the Elizabeth school board not only controls the city's education system, but also has built "a relentless political machine fueled by nepotism, patronage, money and favors, using its nearly 4,000 employees as a ready-made fundraising base."[63]

The example of the Elizabeth school board clearly demonstrates the existence of soft corruption—and even criminal corruption—in education governance in New Jersey.

Among the five areas of ethical misconduct analyzed in this book, conflict of interest is unique because it is the only one in which it is always improper for public officials to engage. Conflict of interest represents corruption; it is "bad in its own right." There is no justification or rationale for any vestige of conflict of interest in public service.

On the other hand, the four other areas of potential soft corruption are government functions in which public officials routinely engage and that can be performed in a totally ethical manner. Financing campaigns, receiving input from lobbyists, awarding jobs, and selecting candidates to run for office are perfectly reasonable—and legal—responsibilities that political and governmental officials undertake as normal procedure. It is only when these functions are abused by acts of ethical misconduct that they become soft corruption and go against the public interest.

Acts of conflict of interest can readily be circumscribed by laws requiring disclosure of personal finances and business connections combined with imposition of a strong ethics code spelling out impermissible activities. Enforcing penalties against violations under such a structure can result in fines, reprimands, and other forms of punishment. Even if the enforcement agency levies no forms of punishment against an offender, exposure to the stigma of conflict of interest can destroy a political career.

# 6 ▶ PATRONAGE
## Jobs, Contracts, Perks

"If you live in New Jersey and you're not getting something for nothing, you're not getting your fair share."
— FORMER GOVERNOR BRENDAN BYRNE

IF MONEY IS the mother's milk that nurtures political parties, patronage is what holds them together. The quest for jobs and other perks is a primary factor that attracts people to party organizations, and they in turn provide the political muscle to win elections and maintain power.

The extensive scope of patronage is important to consider when analyzing its effect on government integrity. Patronage is generally recognized as jobs awarded through the political process to the party faithful. But, more broadly, patronage encompasses other government benefits and emoluments, including contracts for goods and services, professional appointments, permit approvals, program funding, and enhanced pensions. Government largesse dispensed as patronage has three basic features: value to the recipient, a decision by someone in government to bestow the award, and recognition of past or future political assistance and loyalty.

Patronage is a natural phenomenon; it is absolutely necessary for the functioning of government. Providing the myriad services for which government is responsible requires the efforts of a lot of people. Patronage is harmful only if it is abused—if unqualified individuals are put on the public payroll, if no one is held accountable for performing the work, or if government dispenses benefits that are not in the public interest. Yet, it is often conceded, even by reform purists, that some patronage excesses are a small price to pay for a system that works.

Political writers Martin Tolchin and Susan Tolchin argue that the "real lesson of patronage politics is that those who control patronage invariably control policy."[1] Jobs and other patronage favors are awarded through the executive powers of public officials who are in policy-making roles—governors, county executives, mayors, and appointed heads of governmental authorities. Of course, the appointed heads are expected to carry out the policies of those who appoint them. Elected officials often delegate to party leaders (aka political bosses) the actual selection and approval of individuals for public jobs. In New Jersey, the county party chairs assume this leadership function by long tradition.

An example of the role of the county political chair in patronage matters was clearly demonstrated in a hard-and-fast rule of the Republican Party, dominant in Somerset County. Lewis "Luke" Gray, the GOP chair of Somerset County from the 1950s to the 1980s, assumed sole power over all patronage that flowed from party representatives elected to county and state offices. In return, these Republican officials would not have to raise their own campaign funds, a chore Gray would handle.[2] Successful New Jersey party bosses amass enormous political influence over government when they combine their role of dispensing patronage with their other basic functions of fund-raising and candidate selection.

Other areas that are ripe for unethical conduct—campaign financing, lobbying, conflicts of interest, and electoral manipulation—all weaken the quality and delivery of government services, but it's patronage that often generates the most citizen outrage and scorn. Voters work hard for their money and find favoritism in hiring, exorbitant salaries, pension padding, and special perks doled out to insiders to be especially offensive.

The history of patronage in New Jersey has been both colorful and sordid. An episode in 1935 showed how awarding patronage jobs was used as a bargaining strategy. New Jersey's Republican governor at the time, Harold Hoffman, was desperate for more state revenue. He wanted the state to adopt a sales tax, but he could not get enough votes in the legislature, so he approached Hudson County Democratic boss Frank Hague for help. The tax was ultimately approved by the legislature when it was reported that "Hoffman made a deal with Hague giving him control of several hundred patronage jobs" in exchange for his help in passing the bill. However, this matter had an unexpected twist. The sales tax was so unpopular with New Jersey citizens that it was repealed later that year—but nothing was done to repeal the patronage jobs.[3]

Until enactment of civil service reforms in the late nineteenth century, virtually all government jobs were awarded through an age-old system: "To the victor belong the spoils."[4] The civil service system, established at the federal level by the Pendleton Act of 1883 and subsequently adopted by state governments (including New Jersey in 1908), requires that positions be filled according to merit as determined by testing and credentials that meet detailed job specifications. Those covered by civil service laws also are protected against arbitrary discharge and changes in their conditions of employment.

George Washington Plunkitt, New York City's fabled Tammany Hall leader, based his power on dispensing government jobs, and he brooked no interference. He proclaimed that civil service was the "curse of the nation" because it denied jobs to those who were "full of patriotism," that is, those who had put in long hours rounding up votes for the Tammany ticket. Plunkitt further lamented: "Most of the Anarchists in this city today [1890s] are men who ran up against civil service examinations."[5]

Although the great majority of state, county, and municipal public employees are today in the civil service system, thousands of positions remain subject to "at will" patronage hiring. Many of these positions are in the higher echelons of management and the people who hold them are more heavily involved in matters of policy. So to fill open positions, it is only natural that the government executive responsible for hiring will look to friends and associates who are loyal and have proven abilities. The executive is building a team that shares political and governmental interests to implement the programs and policies of the administration.

However, civil service, also known as the classified service, is not immune to manipulation for purposes of patronage. An official who wants to appoint a favored individual to a classified position without the bother of the civil service qualifying process can modify the job description so that it is removed from classified status while it awaits the determination and assignment of a new civil service classification. During the hiatus, the favored individual can be hired provisionally.

In New Jersey, when a new government agency is created and hiring begins before civil service specifications can be established for the positions, the agency remains unclassified. Thus the new agency, chock-full of public employees not covered by civil service, can provide a corps of political workers for the party and the appointing official. The master of this stratagem was Chicago mayor Richard Daley, who in 1975 had as many as ten thousand unclassified "temporary" city workers serving as the "core of his political army."[6]

Despite efforts of good-government advocates who attempt to maximize the number of government employees covered by civil service, a substantial number of public positions still are filled by direct appointment. Of the 74,400 persons working directly for the state of New Jersey, approximately 12,650 (17 percent) are not under civil service and therefore are subject to patronage appointment.[7]

## POLITICAL BOSSES, PATRONAGE, AND POWER: THE RISE OF GEORGE NORCROSS

Political leadership in New Jersey generally resides in the office of chair of the county political party. The chairmanship derives its power from fund-raising, choosing candidates, and awarding patronage jobs. By law, voters in even-year primaries choose one man and one woman in each election district to serve as county committee members. One week later, the members gather to elect a county chair, who manages the party's affairs for the next two years. Obviously, to be elected county chair requires the support of the political players in the county. When an incumbent chair seeks reelection, the task is relatively easy. All that is necessary is to corral the votes of the party faithful, those county committee members who have been given jobs or special perks during the chair's tenure.

Leaders of the party that is out of power in a jurisdiction are not lacking for patronage. Many commissions, agencies, and judicial appointments require representation from both major parties. For example, each county election board in New Jersey provides well-paying part-time jobs and benefits to its four members, two Democrats and two Republicans. These officials are appointed by the governor upon recommendation by the county chair of the party. And there are other gubernatorial appointments to agencies, boards, and commissions requiring bipartisanship.

Every county and municipality has many jobs and professional service contracts to award. When the majority of a governing body are members of one party, their party chair usually has enough influence with local elected officials to become the de facto patronage dispenser. Nevertheless, in some cases an elected official—whether county executive, freeholder, or mayor—may choose to exercise that power and may even be selected party chair.

Although patronage per se is not evil, there are occasions when the power of those who use patronage as a political tool is not only absolute, it is excessive. Some political leaders who wield great patronage power have never been elected to office—not by the voters and not by their party's members.

Such is the saga of Democrat George Norcross of Camden County, who undeniably has become the biggest behind-the-scenes political powerhouse in the state.[8] Today, he even has the ear of Governor Chris Christie, a Republican. Norcross attained this status partly on his own but also as a principal of Commerce Bank, where his political abilities and the bank's ambitious expansion plans combined to produce a financial giant.

A college dropout, Norcross spent his early career as a South Jersey union leader. He briefly chaired the Camden County Democratic Party. He then developed a successful insurance business, which he sold to Commerce in 1996, and became one of the major owners of the bank as well as its vice president in charge of insurance operations.

Meanwhile, Norcross leveraged his fund-raising abilities to acquire patronage power to gain the allegiance of government and party officials. The Norcross influence dominates four county governments in southern New Jersey: Camden, Gloucester, Cumberland, and Salem, which together spend more than $500 million in public tax money each year and provide more than 5,800 jobs. And, by virtue of his influence over who is elected, he commands the loyalty of the twenty Democratic legislators who represent South Jersey districts.

Norcross first caught the attention of the New Jersey political establishment in 1991, when he masterminded the election of the Democratic
candidate for state senate, Harvard-educated John Adler, from Camden County's suburban district. Norcross spent $1.9 million, including
$250,000 on network television ads in the waning days of the campaign,
to pull off a stunning upset over incumbent Republican Lee Laskin.
Fueling Norcross's efforts was his anger at Laskin, who had blocked the
appointment of Norcross's father to the state racing commission. Adler
was the only Democrat to beat an incumbent Republican for a seat in the
legislature in a year when the GOP swept the state.

The Norcross influence extends beyond South Jersey. For fifteen
years, beginning in the early 1990s, four of the most powerful members of the legislature were Norcross's political protégés from South
Jersey: assembly majority leader Joe Roberts, who became Speaker in
2005; state senator Wayne Bryant, chair of the powerful Senate Appropriations Committee; Louis Greenwald, chair of the Assembly Appropriations Committee, who became majority leader in 2012; and Adler, chair
of the Senate Judiciary Committee, who served in Congress from 2009
until his death in 2011.

Norcross's ability to raise money has been equally impressive. He
was a top fund-raiser for James McGreevey's successful gubernatorial
campaign in 2001 and became his confidant and adviser. With his strong
ties to legislative leaders, Norcross joined with power broker and former senate president John Lynch of Middlesex County to wheel massive campaign funds into Bergen County in 2002 to help win the county
executive race.

George Norcross started to use the political capital he had accumulated with South Jersey legislators to weigh in on the selection of Democratic legislative leaders. This was especially important because of the
power exercised by these leaders, particularly the senate president and
the assembly Speaker, who influence the policy agenda for the state
and who have the ability to raise huge campaign funds through their
legislative leadership PACs. In addition, these two leaders, who award
committee chairmanships and assignments to party colleagues, are key
dispensers of legislative patronage.

With a Democratic majority in both houses after the 2001 election,
Democratic assemblyman Joe Doria of Hudson County, in North Jersey,

set his sights on becoming Speaker, a position he had held in 1990 and 1991. He was opposed by Norcross protégé Joe Roberts. New Jersey leadership struggles have always been characterized by efforts to achieve a balance between political interests of the northern and the southern parts of the state. In a deal promoted by Norcross with the help of newly elected governor McGreevey, Roberts became assembly majority leader, and Albio Sires, a one-term Hudson assemblyman, was chosen Speaker. Senator Dick Codey, despite his hostility to Norcross, retained his position as Democratic leader of the senate.[9] Doria was frozen out.

Norcross's attention to local politics has been just as intense. He gained influence with local officials in part by providing them with campaign funds. This gave him considerable sway with county political chairs in the selection of candidates who would get the Democratic Party's nod to run for office. The next step was for elected officials to cede to Norcross the power to manage patronage, including deciding which vendors would do business with local governments. Bowing to Norcross's demands was a matter of survival in the minds of many Democratic— and even Republican—elected officials.

In 2000 and 2001, John Gural was a member of the town council of Palmyra and an employee of JCA Associates, a South Jersey engineering firm that did work for many of the municipalities and several counties in the area. Norcross was pressuring Gural to vote against the reappointment of the Palmyra solicitor, a political enemy. Gural also got heat from the owners of JCA, who intimated that his job would be in jeopardy if he didn't take action against the Palmyra solicitor. These men explained that Norcross funneled substantial government work to JCA, saying, "George is too important to business." In a defensive move, Gural decided to tape his conversations with Norcross, JCA, and others. After he presented the tapes to the Division of Criminal Justice in the office of the New Jersey Attorney General, the state decided to wire Gural and initiated its own investigation.[10]

The content of the tapes found its way into the press. They clearly show Norcross's influence on the business fortunes of JCA, his behind-the-scenes political tactics, and his elevated, yet realistic, opinion of his own power. The tapes make general reference to his ability to provide no-show jobs for friends, direct government contracts to campaign contributors, and even get an opponent out of the way by making him a judge. In one of his more colorful moments, Norcross asked Gural to remove the Palmyra municipal attorney, saying, "I want you to fire that [expletive] . . . you need to get rid of this [expletive] . . . for me and teach this [expletive] a lesson." When admonishing South Jersey assembly-man Herb Conaway for being too friendly when jockeying for legislative leadership with Norcross's nemesis Joe Doria, Norcross is heard saying: "I sat him [Conaway] down . . . and said, 'Herb, don't [expletive] with me on this one . . . don't make nice with Joe Doria 'cause you don't want him pissed at you. 'Cause I'll tell you if you ever do that and I catch you one more time doing it, you're going to get your [expletive] cut off.' He got the message." Norcross is also recorded on the tapes as boasting of his power in the state: "In the end, the McGreeveys, the Corzines, they are all going to be with me. Because not that they like me, but because they have no other choice."

Revelations on the tapes led to an investigation by the New Jersey Attorney General's office, and the filing of a federal lawsuit by the municipal attorney Norcross attempted to remove. After joining the investigation, then-United States Attorney Chris Christie sharply criticized the attorney general's efforts as "materially hampered by poor oversight, inexplicable strategic decisions, and a failure to fully develop potential evidence." No charges resulted from the investigation, and the federal case was dismissed.[11]

## COMMERCE BANK: BUSINESS AND POLITICS

The rise of George Norcross as a political leader in South Jersey closely paralleled the emergence of Commerce Bankcorp of Camden County as a banking powerhouse. Both Norcross and the bank knew how to parlay campaign contributions and political clout to get the attention of government officials who would then favor the bank with patronage in the form of government deposits, bond underwriting deals, and insurance contracts.

A one-office bank in 1973, Commerce had 225 branches and 6,800 employees throughout the state thirty years later, and expanded thereafter into metropolitan New York. Vernon Hill, the founder and chair of Commerce, used his chain of forty-two Burger King restaurants as a model for developing a user-friendly bank that was open seven days a week. Its slogan was "America's most convenient bank."

As a generous contributor to candidates of both parties, Hill was also attuned to political reality. Commerce sought to maximize its business with government by showering campaign contributions on candidates in the localities where it had branches—or planned to have them. Although because it is part of a regulated industry under New Jersey law a bank cannot make direct campaign contributions, officers and employees of a bank are allowed to donate to a bank's PAC, which then can legally give to candidates and parties. Commerce formed a political action committee, ComPac, to carry out this campaign financing strategy. Contributions by ComPac to officials and party organizations were several times more generous than political contributions by any other banking source in New Jersey.[12]

Commerce also sought to maximize its government business by recruiting high-profile political and business leaders to serve as board members and top executives. At the top of the list was George Norcross, who owned $88 million in the bank's stock and drew a salary of more than $1 million for running the insurance division. Among others were Joseph Buckelew, Ocean County GOP chair whose insurance business had been acquired by Commerce; John Lynch, the Democratic power of central New Jersey; Dale Florio, Somerset GOP chair and principal in Princeton Public Affairs, to which Commerce paid more than $300,000 for lobbying services from 1999 to 2003; Robert Beck, a partner in the law firm of Parker McCay, whose managing partner was George Norcross's brother Philip and who handled Commerce's municipal bond work; and Republican Donald DiFrancesco, former state senate president and acting governor, who joined the board three months after leaving office. While a state senator, DiFrancesco received campaign contributions from Commerce sources, and his law firm was retained by the bank. The insurance division of Commerce hired Diane DiFrancesco, Donald's wife, while he was senate president.

The patronage payoff to Commerce from its political forays was enormous in terms of government business. Between 1997 and 2003, deposits from private sources increased by 348 percent while deposits from government agencies went up 2,407 percent. The level of government deposits at Commerce was twice the level of government deposits at any other New Jersey bank; by 2003, Commerce had moved into Pennsylvania, New York, and Delaware, and fifteen hundred government entities were using Commerce as their bank.

Also benefiting from Commerce Bankcorp's strategies was the bank's investment banking arm, Commerce Capital Markets, which in 2002 underwrote the sale of more government bonds for New Jersey government entities than any other banking institution. Two-thirds of the long-term bond deals for which Commerce served as lead underwriter were handled under no-bid contracts. One of these was to manage the sale of more than $500 million in bonds for Essex County and its authorities, earning the bank more than $900,000 in fees. At the time, Essex County Executive James Treffinger and his GOP county organization received $42,000 in political contributions from ComPac.

When DiFrancesco was acting governor for eleven months in 2001, Commerce served as lead underwriter for $225 million in bond sales for the state, more than Commerce had handled during the previous seven years of the Whitman administration.

In his dual role as acting governor and senate president, DiFrancesco approved legislation allowing the relatively obscure Burlington County Bridge Commission to expand its scope so that it could issue bonds to finance county economic development projects. This southern New Jersey county was under the solid control of the Republican Party, which received more than $225,000 in contributions from Commerce in the previous five years. With its political connections, Commerce Capital Markets took immediate advantage of the new law, receiving underwriting awards from the Burlington authority, on a no-bid basis, for two bond issues that raised $134 million. This earned the bank a majority share of the $642,000 in fees.

In addition to making money from local governments as a depository for their funds and as a bond underwriter, Commerce sold insurance to government clients through its National Insurance Services division. The insurance arm run by George Norcross earned $5 million annually from government business. In 2002, this division of the bank had insurance contracts with seven counties, several state authorities, 140 municipalities, 100 fire districts and first aid squads, more than 20 local authorities, and 40 school districts.

The May 21, 2003, articles by the *Record* summarized the impact of Commerce Bank and its subsidiaries on New Jersey by saying, "This $17.7 billion-a-year financial powerhouse is run by a corporate syndicate whose members wield an astonishing breadth of influence over New Jersey's elected officials, the public policy they make, and the taxpayer dollars they spend."

Negative reaction to Commerce's use of political connections and campaign contributions to gain market share began to mount, particularly in the financial community. Although the executives of Commerce Capital Markets were prohibited by federal law from making political contributions to government officials whose agencies were prospective bond underwriting clients, other Commerce employees not connected with the Capital Markets division could donate money, thereby circumventing this restriction. In early 2003 Commerce responded to public criticism by suspending ComPac, and stopped making political contributions.

Federal investigators started to look into possible pay-to-play activity between ComPac contributions to public officials and the underwriting of municipal bonds by Commerce Capital Markets.[13] Much of the investigation was focused on the Philadelphia treasurer's office and on attorney Ronald White, Commerce regional board member and paid consultant to the bank at $15,000 per month. White was a prolific fund-raiser for John Street, mayor of Philadelphia. Commerce donated $25,000 to Street's reelection campaign. Over the years, White had been paid more than $1.6 million in legal fees from the City of Philadelphia.

In 2004, White and two executives of the Pennsylvania branch of Commerce Bank were indicted on charges of bribery. The indictment stated that in overseeing the city's finances the Philadelphia treasurer had arranged for a $30 million line of credit with Commerce, moved more than $50 million in deposits to Commerce, and awarded substantial bond work to the bank. White died while on trial, but the two Commerce officials were convicted of bribing a Philadelphia city official. Neither Norcross nor Commerce Bank was involved in the criminal proceeding.

The fortunes of Commerce Bank began to falter. In 2005, the bank paid $600,000 to settle charges by the National Association of Security

Dealers for violating its rules in acquiring municipal bond underwriting business. For the next two years, the Office of the Comptroller of the Currency (OCC) and the Federal Reserve Board investigated real-estate dealings relating to Commerce's expansion. In April 2007, the OCC froze approvals for additional branches. These pressures led the bank's directors to remove Vernon Hill as CEO of Commerce two months later. As a result, Hill sold his interest in Commerce, which was then absorbed into the much larger Toronto Dominion (TD) Bank.[14] As part of the transaction, George Norcross bought back the insurance division, which he continues to operate with Joseph Buckelew.

## NEW JERSEY'S BOSS TRIUMVIRATE

Even without Commerce Bank, Norcross remained a dominant power in New Jersey political circles, as demonstrated by his continuing involvement with top-level state government leaders after the 2009 elections. At the time, no South Jerseyan held either of the top leadership positions in the legislature. Norcross wanted to replace Richard J. Codey, a Democrat representing Morris and Essex Counties, as senate president. Supported by Essex Democratic leaders, with whom he had a close alliance, Norcross succeeded in persuading enough legislators to elevate his South Jersey ally, state senator Stephen Sweeney, to the state senate presidency. Norcross also rounded up the votes to install Sheila Oliver, a three-term assemblywoman from Newark (Essex County), as assembly Speaker for 2010. Norcross was also instrumental in managing the selection of Democratic leadership positions in the legislative elections in 2011 and 2013. After the 2013 election, Democratic power brokers arranged for the replacement of Oliver as assembly Speaker with Vincent Prieto.[15]

The Essex leaders who collaborated with Norcross in the leadership reorganization came into their positions of political power through patronage. Steve Adubato Sr., familiarly known as Big Steve, is the acknowledged Democratic boss of Newark. He is the elected Democratic Party chief of Newark's North Ward, in which he exercises political leadership by selecting the party's candidates and delivering votes on Election Day. He does this not so much through threats and intimidation but rather through the jobs and help he provides Newark residents from his North Ward Center, where he runs a large preschool, a job training center, a day care facility for the elderly, and two charter schools. These community organizations supply Big Steve with political foot soldiers who produce reliable electoral majorities for the Democratic Party.[16]

The electoral prowess of Adubato and his political army was responsible for the emergence of the second Essex boss, Joe DiVincenzo, who was elected county executive in 2002. County executives in New Jersey have a multitude of jobs they can give to their followers. It is the political prominence of some of DiVincenzo's followers that gives him his extraordinary clout. Newark state senator Teresa Ruiz serves in her regular job as deputy chief of staff for DiVincenzo. Assemblywoman Oliver is Essex County administrator. Another Essex senator, Nia Gill, is attorney for DiVincenzo's county improvement authority. These patronage appointees have sided with DiVincenzo and Norcross against their Essex colleague, Senator Richard Codey, in continuing battles over legislative leadership.[17]

The power of these three political bosses was not limited to being kingmakers; it extended into the legislative process. Republican governor Chris Christie was well aware of their influence on all matters political, and in fact visited Adubato personally on his first day as governor.[18] He actively courted their support with the powers of his office—for example, by supplying continuing support for Norcross's Cooper Hospital in Camden. Democrat DiVincenzo, a disciple of Adubato, would later show his allegiance to Christie by endorsing the Republican governor for a second term in 2013. When Christie needed legislative votes from Democrats to pass major policy initiatives, he called on the Norcross-Adubato-DiVincenzo triumvirate for help.

One high-profile example was the pension and health benefits reform of 2011, which called for larger deductions from public employee salaries. Although vigorously opposed by the teachers' union and organized labor, the legislation received support from the three Democratic bosses. It passed, giving Christie a major victory.[19]

## PATRONAGE POOLS

Most of New Jersey's autonomous authorities and agencies were established to provide a specific public service—transportation, public works, sewage disposal, housing, solid waste management, water supply. They are also veritable gold mines for public patronage.

The state has about 350 local authorities, boards, and commissions that rely on patronage to fill most positions.[20] Added to these are nearly thirty state authorities, which provide more than 28,000 public jobs.[21] These amounts are not unlike the expansiveness of authorities in other states.

The rationale for independent authorities is simple: they have their own revenue streams; they can provide a specific public service distinct from the services provided by the governments that formed them; and they can issue bonds to raise money for capital projects without affecting the government's credit rating. To political power brokers, authorities have another purpose: they are a patronage pool. These organizations are anything but politically independent. They are managed by commissioners who are allied with the elected officials who appoint them. The commissioners understand, moreover, that one of their duties is to reward the party faithful with jobs at the agency and to favor the vendors who are reliable campaign contributors.

The poster child of state authorities that fairly oozes with patronage and special benefits has been the Passaic Valley Sewerage Commission (PVSC), an autonomous organization that provides sewer service to 1.3 million North Jerseyans in the metropolitan counties of Essex, Bergen, Hudson, and Passaic. More than eighty of the commission's six hundred employees—13 percent—are paid more than $100,000 a year. The nine commissioners who run it include mayors and the politically connected, some of whom subsequently resign from the PVSC board to take high-paying administrative positions at PVSC. Nepotism involving commissioners and other high-level staff is common.[22]

As structured under the law that created it in 1902, the PVSC is accountable only to its commissioners, who are appointed by the governor and confirmed by the senate. They conduct their business behind closed doors because they are not subject to New Jersey's Open Public

Meetings Act. Commissioners take turns awarding patronage jobs. And unlike other state authorities, the PVSC's decisions cannot be overridden by the governor.

Lobbyists hired by the PVSC to represent it in Trenton were paid more than $500,000 during the 2006–2007 legislative session. A few years later, its lobbyists were busy contacting newly elected Governor Christie, trying to convince him to tone down his criticism of the commission's political excesses. After taking office in 2010, Christie began to expose the extravagances of the PVSC, including exorbitant salaries, massive patronage, no-show jobs, and favoritism in awarding vendor contracts.

The nine-member commission was barely functioning because two of its seats were vacant and four of the remaining seven commissioners served as holdovers after their terms of office had expired. Labeling the authority a "patronage mill filled with political hacks collecting obscene salaries," Christie started to use the power of his office in his crusade to make changes.[23]

The pressure to reform the agency was so great that the PVSC's executive director, whose $313,000 salary was almost twice that of the governor, decided to retire. Leaving office did not result in financial hardship for the executive director. His retirement pension amounted to $140,000 per year, and he received $600,000 in severance pay benefits. The commission had little choice but to accept the governor's pick for a new executive director. Shortly thereafter, New Jersey's attorney general opened a criminal investigation into the PVSC. Ultimately, six of the seven serving commissioners left office under threat that the governor would bring charges against them. In addition, the PVSC's staff was cut by 12 percent, and four of its top managers were indicted, and later convicted, on charges of using PVSC employees to make improvements to the managers' homes. One of these managers had served as the PVSC's chief ethics officer.

Systemic reform of the PVSC, however, has not come about. Legislation to require the authority to conduct its business more openly, to give the governor power to veto the commission's decisions, and even to grant the state Department of Community Affairs oversight over the authority has been introduced in every session since 2002 but has never been approved.[24] The entrenched influence of legislators who are politically connected to the authority appears to hold more sway in Trenton than the exhortations of reformers.

The Delaware River Port Authority (DRPA) is a regional transportation agency that operates four bridges spanning the Delaware River between New Jersey and Pennsylvania, as well as a high-speed rail line from Philadelphia to South Jersey. It is run by sixteen commissioners who are appointed on a 50–50 basis by the New Jersey and Pennsylvania governors. In early 2003, the DRPA made headlines when Republican state senator John Matheussen gave up his $49,000 per year legislative seat to become chief executive officer of the DRPA at $195,000 per year plus multiple perks. Democratic governor Jim McGreevey named Matheussen to the position. The *Philadelphia Inquirer* commented that Democrats had been "wooing" Matheussen for months for the DRPA job because they had their eye on his South Jersey senate seat, and, according to one published story, Norcross arranged for "installing Republican Senator John Matheussen in a $195,000-a-year job as head of DRPA."[25] As it turned out, the Democrats won the seat in the record-setting $5 million battle between Fred Madden and Republican George Geist (see chapter 3) and captured control of the senate. If one connects the dots, one will readily see that this episode has all the trappings of a high-level patronage play.[26]

In 2010, the New Jersey Office of the Comptroller began an investigation of the DRPA, uncovering the multiple benefits and privileges that the DRPA lavished on its commissioners, their families, and political allies. These came not only in the form of jobs but also as perks such as extravagant dinners and conference venues, and exemption from tolls on the DRPA bridges. The authority also had a habit of subsidizing organizations and development unrelated to bridges but with ties to its commissioners. The comptroller's report stated: "We found people who treated the DRPA like a personal ATM, from DRPA commissioners to private vendors to community organizations." Among its many revelations was that George Norcross's insurance agency was paid more than $400,000 as broker for placing the authority's insurance business with other firms.

Until its dissolution in 2013, the University of Medicine and Dentistry of New Jersey (UMDNJ) had a staff of more than eleven thousand workers who provide health care and medical education. Aware that it needed government help to fund its programs, the university responded to the lawmakers who hold the purse strings by becoming a prime source of patronage. Describing UMDNJ in a 2011 editorial, the *Star-Ledger* said: "Over the past fifteen years, this umbrella organization fell prey to New Jersey's culture of corruption. The result was a governor-appointed board that catered to political bosses and a proliferation of no-show jobs."[27]

Charles "Chip" Stapleton, chief of staff for the state senate Republicans during the legislative leadership PAC fight of 1993, formed his own lobbying firm in 1995 after leaving the state senate's employ. UMDNJ hired him as a consultant "to enhance the state recognition and reputation of the university." For the next ten years, he was paid a total of $1 million under a no-bid contract, an assignment that produced not a single report, document, memo, or letter showing he had performed any work.[28] Asked about this, Stapleton said: "I don't have the type of business that requires a lot of stuff in writing." After Democrat Richard Codey became acting governor in late 2004, Stapleton lost the UMDNJ consultancy, only to be replaced by a prominent Democratic lobbyist from Trenton at a monthly fee 25 percent higher than Stapleton's. This second lobbyist, politically connected Harold Hodes, at least supplied UMDNJ with written reports.[29]

Also representing UMDNJ in those years was none other than Ronald White, the Philadelphia attorney who, as a consultant and board member of Commerce Bank, was indicted in 2004 for colluding with bank executives to award much of the city of Philadelphia's banking business to Commerce. Three years earlier, White was a major fund-raiser for the McGreevey gubernatorial campaign. Following McGreevey's election in 2001, UMDNJ hired White at $25,000 per month for three months to serve as liaison between the university and the governor-elect's transition team. UMDNJ records show no evidence of work performed by White, according to the *Star-Ledger*.[30]

Routine job appointments at UMDNJ were not left to chance. The administration developed a patronage scoring system whereby applicants with political clout would receive favored treatment.[31] If a political friend of the university submitted a name for appointment, the application would be marked with a circled number 1 and routed directly to the human resources department for consideration. Others without high-level backing would be relegated to a lower-priority number 2 or 3 and receive less attention.

In 2003, Sen. Wayne Bryant of Camden County was chair of the powerful Senate Budget and Appropriations Committee, which has great influence over what programs and projects are funded. Bryant and the dean of the UMDNJ School of Osteopathic Medicine in Camden struck a deal. The school hired Bryant at a salary of $38,000 as a program support coordinator. On the face of it, nothing was extraordinary about a legislator receiving this perk from a government agency. But in this instance Bryant's influence would help UMDNJ get state money. He would steer millions in state funds to the university after this appointment.[32]

State funding for UMDNJ's School of Osteopathic Medicine rose from $2.7 million in 2003 to $5.83 million one year later. The state contributed $350 million to UMDNJ's annual budget of $1.6 billion, and Bryant was in a position to help maintain this subsidy. Bryant also secured state grants for projects in Camden, his home county, that produced revenue for his law firm.

Bryant's efforts to secure personal benefits from government apparently knew no bounds. In 2005, he and five members of his family held ten public jobs with an aggregate annual income of $685,000. One of these jobs was at the DRPA, which paid Bryant's wife a salary of $135,000.

The financial excesses at UMDNJ attracted the attention of then-U.S. Attorney Chris Christie, who began an investigation. The university was charged with Medicaid fraud in December 2005. Christie appointed a monitor to oversee the UMDNJ operations while the investigation continued. After it became apparent that Bryant was a target of the investigation, he quit his position at UMDNJ and shortly thereafter resigned as chair of the Senate Budget Committee. In March 2007, Bryant was indicted on charges of funneling $11 million in state aid to UMDNJ as a reward for his patronage appointment to the institution. He was also charged with illegally padding his state pension through other low-show appointed positions. Bryant was convicted in 2008 and served forty months in prison.

## GOVERNORS AND PATRONAGE

The New Jersey governor arguably has more power than any of the other forty-nine governors. One source of this power is the New Jersey governor's responsibility for making fifty-two hundred appointments to boards, commissions, judicial posts, and authorities.[33] This number does not include the governor's recommendations for staffing the thousands of state agency jobs.

The pejorative connotation associated with the term *patronage* really should not apply to the vast majority of the governor's appointments; filling positions is part of the statutory responsibility of New Jersey's chief executive. But the negative aspects of patronage are a fact of life within some agencies in state government. One of former governor Thomas Kean's advisors explained that he did not heed advice to reform the patronage-laden Departments of State and Community Affairs because every administration must "find a place to bury your most loyal but least talented supporters."[34]

Under Governor Chris Christie, the very large and prominent Port Authority of New York and New Jersey has attracted public attention as a destination for patronage positions. With its sixty-eight hundred employees, the Port Authority is the largest and most visible government agency in northern New Jersey. Its operations cover airports, rapid transit, seaports, river crossings, and other transportation modes in the vast metroplex surrounding New York City. There is joint governance of this agency between the states of New York and New Jersey.

Public concern about the integrity of this superagency was raised when newspaper exposés in early 2012 showed the Christie administration was making referrals of as many as fifty persons to the Port Authority for jobs, more new hires than were advanced by any recent governor of either party on either side of the Hudson River.[35]

Although Port Authority staffers protested that these were not patronage appointments, the people referred by Christie's office included the former vice chair of the Passaic County GOP, the former director of the state Republican Committee, the son of a former Republican assembly Speaker, eleven people who donated to the Christie campaign for governor or who had an immediate relative who donated, and five more who were in the Christie administration or had worked in his campaign.[36]

In a convoluted political patronage move, the former Democratic sheriff of Passaic County, Jerry Speziale, was appointed as deputy superintendent of the Port Authority police department at a salary of $198,000. Speziale, the most popular Democratic vote-getter in Passaic, had been making $151,000 as sheriff. In the new position, his salary was augmented by a tax-free New York City disability pension of $58,000 per year plus a pension of $32,000 for his accrued time as sheriff. And of course, there was the prospect of a Port Authority pension after five years of service.[37]

Why would a Republican state administration do such a favor for a Democratic sheriff? Speziale's appointment meant his former $530,000 campaign war chest as sheriff would not be available to assist Passaic Democrats in the upcoming 2010 election. According to news reports, the deal was masterminded by the Republican chair of Passaic, Assemblyman Scott Rumana, with assistance from a GOP state senator. A big unanswered question is why Christie allowed this maneuver when it violated his call for more modest public salaries and the elimination of multiple pensions. In the end, the neutralizing of Speziale's $500,000 campaign funds made no difference in the election outcome of 2010. The Passaic Democrats won all county seats, including sheriff.[38]

A bizarre instance of patronage abuse was Governor McGreevey's attempt to appoint Golan Cipel, an Israeli national, as special counsel for homeland security in New Jersey at an annual salary of $110,000. Cipel had no professional experience in security matters and, as a noncitizen, would not have access to classified government documents. The only known rationale for the appointment was his friendship with McGreevey and a minor role as Jewish outreach coordinator in the 2001 gubernatorial campaign, for which he was paid by Charles Kushner. The appointment eventually succumbed to public criticism and was dropped, but the probable reason for attempting to reward Cipel with a cushy job became apparent in 2004, when McGreevey declared that he was gay and was attracted to Cipel.[39]

Patronage is generally thought of as a way to reward friends and political supporters. But reverse patronage, the removal of people from government positions as punishment or reprisal, is not uncommon. When Governor Chris Christie and Democratic state senator Dick Codey got into a public spat over an appointment in late 2011, Codey learned several days later that the state police security detail assigned to him since his days as acting governor, ending in January 2006, had been removed. On the same day, a Codey loyalist was fired from his $107,000 job as deputy director of the Division of Consumer Affairs. This was followed by Codey's cousin's "stepping down" from his $215,000 deputy counsel position with the Port Authority to be replaced by Paula Dow, an appointee of the governor alleged to be a patronage hire.[40]

Micromanaging patronage at more obscure levels of government is not unlike what happened to the executive director of the State Ethics Commission (SEC) in January 2011. She was forced to resign when the governor's office asserted that it wanted its own person in that position and pressured the chairman and members of the SEC to replace her with a designee from the governor's office. This was done despite the fact the SEC is an independent government agency and has always had sole discretion over who occupies the position of its executive director. A much more likely reason for her removal, as the *Star-Ledger* revealed in an exposé three years later, was that the executive director had been investigating a complaint about an ethics violation by one of the governor's staff, and refused to turn the matter over to the Governor's Office for handling.[41]

One of the more contentious cases of gubernatorial patronage involved Democratic governor Jon Corzine and the brother-in-law of his former girlfriend. While he served in the U.S. Senate in 2002, Corzine, the superrich ex-CEO of Goldman Sachs who had divorced his wife, started dating Carla Katz, then-president of the largest state employee union. When this relationship ended two years later, Corzine gave Katz a multimillion-dollar gift, paying off the mortgage on her rural home and financing her acquisition of an upscale Hoboken apartment. Before taking office as governor after the 2005 election, Corzine claimed Katz would receive no more money from him, in order to avoid a conflict of interest, as the two would subsequently engage in collective bargaining over state employee wages and benefits.[42]

Katz's brother-in-law, Rocco Riccio, who had received help from the governor's office in getting his state positions, had been working in the New Jersey Treasury office early in Corzine's tenure as governor. At the end of 2006, he transferred to the New Jersey Turnpike Authority. The press reported claims that Riccio used his position in the Treasury to spy on the tax records of political adversaries, and while these claims proved to be unfounded, they became embarrassing to Corzine. The governor's office pressured Riccio to resign after only two weeks on the Turnpike job with the understanding that Corzine would find him employment in the private sector.

Several months later, Corzine gave Riccio $15,000 to tide him over while he was unemployed. When reporters unearthed what had happened, Republicans asserted that the $15,000 payment violated Corzine's pledge to end all financial help to Katz and her family, and called for an investigation into this transaction. When no job was forthcoming well into 2008, Riccio threatened to sue Corzine for breach of promise. Rather than engage in what would have been protracted litigation, Corzine personally settled with Riccio by paying him $362,500.[43]

Another patronage function of the executive branch—and one that leads to dispensing lucrative benefits—is the awarding of bond underwriting contracts to investment banking firms. The executive branch evaluates and selects the financial institution best suited for an underwriting. While regulations imposed by the Securities and Exchange Commission have greatly curtailed campaign contributions given directly by prospective underwriters to lawmakers and party organizations in an effort to secure underwriting work, investment houses still make use of indirect pay-to-play methods to secure business. The bond houses hire lobbyists and other politically connected consultants to try to steer contracts their way. And, of course, lobbyists and consultants are not constrained from making political donations to gain advantage. Attorney Jack Arseneault, a close associate of Governor McGreevey, received $670,000 in consulting fees from Bear Stearns for his services in 2003 in securing New Jersey's $1.7 billion tobacco settlement bond deal, which reaped $6.4 million in underwriting fees for Bear Stearns. Arseneault, a generous donor to the Democratic Party and its candidates, gave $28,000 to the Hudson County Democrats in 2005 alone.[44] During McGreevey's thirty-four months as governor, Arseneault was paid $995,000 in bonuses and fees in his consultancy with Bear Stearns. Part of this was in the form of a retainer at $10,000 per month. Two weeks after McGreevey left office, the consulting retainer between Arseneault and Bear Stearns was terminated.[45] The Arseneault episode is an example of influence peddling as soft corruption.

But the granddaddy of all New Jersey scandals tinged with patronage took place in 2013, when two of Governor Christie's highly placed political operatives at the Port Authority of New York and New Jersey were implicated in the infamous Bridgegate episode. These two operatives were Bill Baroni, former rising Republican star in the state senate and campaign aide in Christie's election campaign of 2009, appointed by the governor in 2010 as deputy executive director of the Authority at a salary of $290,000 per year,[46] and David Wildstein, who went to high school with Christie and who in recent years had run a New Jersey political blog, appointed as director of interstate capital projects at the Authority with an annual salary of $150,000. Wildstein reported to Baroni in the Port Authority's chain of command.

Wildstein implemented a clandestine plan to sharply curtail highway access to the George Washington Bridge over the streets of Fort Lee for several days in September 2013.[47] This caused massive traffic jams and generated intense anger from motorists trying to cross the bridge and from officials of the town of Fort Lee. Baroni knew about the traffic obstruction, but Patrick Foye, the Authority's executive director, said he did not. When he learned of it after five days, Foye put an abrupt stop to the traffic blockage.

Wildstein and Baroni tried to sell the highway shutdown as a traffic study, but there was published speculation that the real reason was retaliation against the Democratic mayor of Fort Lee for not endorsing Christie for reelection in the 2013 gubernatorial race.

Intense investigation by a New Jersey assembly committee revealed a smoking gun pointing to the source of the scandal: an e-mail from Governor Christie's deputy chief of staff, Bridget Anne Kelly, sent to Wildstein in August 2013 stating that it was "time for some traffic problems in Fort Lee." Christie denied that he had any responsibility for the traffic imbroglio, but it was clear that his high-level staff did. Further investigation by the U.S. Attorney for New Jersey resulted in a guilty plea by Wildstein and indictments for Baroni and Kelly.

Although the final verdict on Bridgegate is not in, it is clear that patronage players who owe loyalty to the sources of their appointments can have a significant impact on the quality and integrity of government, regardless of whether they commit certain acts on their own or with instructions from higher up. Governor Christie has denied knowledge of or involvement in the affair, but he cannot escape the perception of mismanaging the conduct of officials from his office as well as his direct appointees.

## THE LEGISLATURE AND PATRONAGE

Virtually all legislators are products of local politics. They owe their positions to the party organization of their district as well as to the many volunteers who helped in their campaigns. It is only natural, therefore, that legislators are ready and willing to use their influence to reward their followers who seek jobs in government.

The most direct source of patronage for a legislator comes from the money allotted to him or her to hire personal staff. In the 1960s, this was a meager $4,500 per year, which allowed a legislator to pay someone to handle constituent service and correspondence. In those early years, patronage abuses were more common—and open. By 1972, the yearly amount for legislative staff increased to $7,500, producing some creative patronage arrangements. Assemblyman Karl Weidel ran an insurance agency in Trenton and paid his two agency managers $3,250 each, ostensibly to do research and keep track of legislation.[48] When he was criticized for this arrangement by opponents in a subsequent election, Weidel considered suing them for slander—until he was advised by counsel that a lawsuit would probably require his employees to testify about the amount of legislative work they actually performed.

Assemblyman Walter Foran used his staff allowance in a unique way. He paid a local Republican woman $500 for "clipping newspapers." When Democrats objected to this as misuse of taxpayer money, Foran played to the sympathies of the public by pointing out that this woman had to use a wheelchair that was in bad shape, and a new one would cost just about $500. Foran also took liberties with his staff allowance by paying $2,000 to Arthur Johnson, an assistant editor at the largest newspaper in his district, for unspecified general services. A grateful Johnson returned the favor with his wife donating $200 to Foran's reelection campaign.

During the final decades of the twentieth century, the New Jersey legislature adopted many reforms and upgrades in its efforts to become a truly co-equal branch of state government. Professional nonpartisan staff was increased severalfold to improve the quality of the legislature's work. There was a comparable increase in partisan staff working out of the statehouse, and the amount available for individual legislators to hire their own staff rose to its current level of $110,000 per year. The state also pays for a district office for each legislator as well as equipment, supplies, and postage to run his or her office.

Many legislators, as might be expected, populate their staffs with political cohorts whom they trust. But there was a trend among some to use these staff positions as havens for nepotism. Nepotism in the offices of lawmakers, banned in nineteen other states, was legal at the time in New Jersey, where almost 20 percent of legislators engaged in the practice.[49] Hudson County Democratic assemblyman Anthony Impreveduto spent $238,000 of three years' staff allowance to pay his daughter, sister, and other relatives.[50] Senate GOP co-president John Bennett, in a show of family harmony, put both his mother and mother-in-law on his legislative staff payroll.[51]

The straw that broke the camel's back regarding legislative nepotism was the report made public in 2003 that Assemblyman Gary Guear had hired his wife at $55,000 per year to run his legislative office. But the two-term assemblyman paid the price later that year, when he was blasted by his Republican opponent on this issue, resulting in the distinction of being the only Democratic legislator in the state to be defeated for reelection.[52] After the Guear defeat, in order to avoid any further self-inflicted embarrassments, legislative leaders outlawed nepotism on legislative staffs.

Nepotism is not confined to situations where a lawmaker is the one who gives a government job in his own office to a family member. Nepotism takes place even more frequently, and more insidiously, when a third party, usually the county or local boss, appoints a legislator's relative to a public position. This happened in 2003, when the wife of Democratic state senator Joe Coniglio of Bergen County received a political job in county government at a salary of $71,000.[53] At the time, the Democratic chair of Bergen was Joseph Ferriero, who had the reputation of micromanaging all things political in his Democrat-controlled county. Consider how this affects the state senator if he gets a call from the county chair asking him to vote a certain way on a bill in Trenton or to endorse one of the chair's anointed candidates. Nepotism is a potent weapon in the hands of a political boss.

Politicians are always on the lookout for ways to increase the number of patronage appointments at their disposal. When McGreevey was governor, he decided to appoint a Democrat to the Morris County tax board in 2004, replacing the Republican incumbent whose term had just expired. With an odd number on the board, the majority is always held by the party that controls the appointments, the party of the governor. But the ousted Republican, who really appreciated the perks that went with the job—$18,000 in salary for minimal work, pension and health benefits, conventions at posh destinations—collaborated with his GOP ally, state senator Tony Bucco, to fix the problem.

Bucco introduced a bill to increase all county tax boards by two members on the premise that the boards were seeing so many tax appeals that having larger boards would expedite the appeals process. In sixteen counties, this meant going from three to five members; in five larger counties, from five members to seven. Recognizing the patronage benefits, legislators happily bought into the plan and passed the bill. And that's how the ex-board member in Morris County got his job back.[54]

Shortly thereafter, a report revealed that the number of tax appeals across the state had actually dropped by more than 80 percent from the previous ten years when boards had fewer members. An embarrassed Bucco and his colleagues made an about-face and introduced legislation to rescind the increase in tax board members. But legislators were not enthusiastic about giving up patronage, and the rescission bill has languished in committee ever since.[55]

For many years, the legislature's most serious patronage activity was the secretive annual insertion of line items in the state budget to pay for pet projects and programs of members of the majority party. Individual legislators would privately negotiate their requests with party leaders outside the normal budget process. The leaders set aside in the budget a lump sum, often in excess of $100 million, to cover all the requests for this purpose, usually under the heading Property Tax Assistance and Community Development Grant Program. When this process is used by members of Congress, it is referred to in the pejorative as earmarking. In New Jersey parlance it was the Christmas tree, analogous to gifts traditionally placed under the holiday tree. In 2001, the last year in a decade of Republican control of the legislature, leaders allotted $149 million for Christmas tree items. Projects and programs funded under this system included schools, the arts, medical facilities, athletic leagues, historic sites, and even religious groups. These objectives were not necessarily against the public interest, but the process by which they were achieved was fraught with political machinations, and the "winners" were chosen not on merit or need but on whom they had influence with in Trenton.

In more recent years when Democrats were in the majority, their leaders gave themselves specific dollar amounts for spending on Christmas tree items: the senate president, $12 million; the senate appropriations committee chairman, $4 million; the senate majority leader, $4 million; the assembly Democrats had $20 million to divvy up.[56]

The Christmas tree program sometimes made questionable awards. In 2005, state senate president Dick Codey invited party boss George Norcross, who was not a legislator, to participate in distributing $350,000 worth of goodwill. Norcross and Codey were political rivals, but Codey was considering a run for governor, and offering an olive branch to Norcross made good sense. Other Christmas tree earmarks did not meet even reasonable ethical standards, including the $200,000 earmarked by appropriations chair senator Wayne Bryant for a nonprofit health care group run by his brother.

Clearly, earmarking fails the test of good government in both accountability and due process. Ideally, the budget and appropriations function of government requires that all spending priorities be determined under a prescribed format administered by a representative group of legislators. The ability of some lawmakers to make side deals defeats the objective of a unified budget approach and fragments legislative leadership's control of the process.

After much criticism of New Jersey's Christmas tree system from reformers and editorial writers, Governor Jon Corzine made changes in the budget process in 2006 that required legislators to disclose their names as sponsors of any special earmark, as well as the purpose of the funding, at least fourteen days before consideration by the full budget committee. Although this modification did not stem the tide of special requests, it made the process transparent and accountable. More important, the direct patronage aspects of the Christmas tree earmarks were eliminated. They were transformed into the legitimate legislative function of resource allocation.


## SENATORIAL COURTESY

While the majority of gubernatorial patronage positions are direct appointments, some must be confirmed by the state senate. The advice-and-consent process applies to those gubernatorial nominations specified by the constitution and by law—including judges, cabinet officers, and members of many high-level boards and commissions. Once announced by the governor, these nominations are sent to the Senate Judiciary Committee for approval or rejection. If approved by the committee, the nomination goes to the full state senate for a confirmation vote.

In practice, however, the system known as senatorial courtesy thwarts the process by requiring that the nomination first be approved by one or more state senators living in the same county or representing the legislative district in which the nominee resides. If these elected officials do not sign off on the nominee, it never gets to the Judiciary Committee. In other words, the nomination is in limbo—it is dead, either temporarily or permanently. Senatorial courtesy gives a single senator the power to unilaterally and secretly deny the right of a nominee to come before the state senate for a vote without so much as stating a reason. It is personal blackball and one of the most pernicious forms of soft corruption. It can force governors to settle for their second or third choice, and it can make highly qualified people reluctant to be nominated in the first place and thus avoid a process that can become degrading and embarrassing.

Senatorial courtesy is an unwritten, informal tradition that is not sanctioned in law, in state senate rules, or in the state constitution. The constitutionality of senatorial courtesy was challenged in legal action in 1993 before the New Jersey Supreme Court, which deadlocked in a 3–3 decision, leaving the practice in place and producing the declaration that the matter is "nonjudiciable."[37]

How does senatorial courtesy change the dynamic of gubernatorial appointments? Very simply it gives each senator absolute power to influence, change, or block any appointment from his or her district. Before announcing a prospective appointment, the governor usually checks with the senator, or senators, who come from that jurisdiction. If they do not object, the nomination is made and allowed to proceed to the Judiciary Committee.

But the process becomes sticky if a state senator objects to a proposed nomination. Meetings are held with the governor's office in an effort to work out any problems. Sometimes a state senator will ask the governor to appoint a political ally, friend, or business associate to another position in exchange for the senator's consent to the nomination. Or the state senator will ask for support of a legislative measure or funding for a pet project to benefit the legislator's district. The senator's ability to place an absolute block on the nomination—a block that the state senator's colleagues will uphold—smacks of extortion. When a nomination becomes stalemated in negotiations, the governor might decide to go ahead and make the nomination in the hope that pressure from adverse publicity will force the objecting state senator to cave and sign off on it. Or the state senator holds out until the name is withdrawn and another nominee is submitted.

Senatorial courtesy had its origin in the old 21 Club of the state senate before the mid-1960s, when malapportioned legislative districts were allowed. Each of New Jersey's twenty-one counties had its own state senator regardless of the county's population. Operating as a feudal lord over a county, the senator would not tolerate appointment of a judge or other official who did not pass his or her personal political muster. It was in this environment that the senators concocted senatorial courtesy to assure that they would control all appointments of county residents to important positions in state government. Often collaborating with the party chair, the state senator became the de facto political boss of the county.

After the U.S. Supreme Court handed down its decisions on one-person-one-vote in the early 1960s, the 21 Club no longer existed.[58] The number of legislative districts increased from twenty-one to forty, with one state senator representing each district. Yet senatorial courtesy continued with even more complicated effects on the appointment process. New legislative districts, formed to meet equal population standards, seldom aligned with county boundaries. Some counties with large populations would contain multiple districts and, therefore, multiple senators—each with the power under senatorial courtesy to block a nominee residing in that particular county.

The political outrages perpetrated under senatorial courtesy are many and varied. Sometimes they apply to the most important appointment a governor can make, such as former governor Robert Meyner's nominee in the 1950s for state attorney general, Grover Richmond of Burlington County. This was during the 21 Club days. Richmond was blocked through senatorial courtesy by Burlington state senator Al McCay, who stood up on the senate floor, as was required in those days, and declared the nomination to be personally objectionable. Although McCay had the courage to publicly take responsibility for rejecting the governor's choice, there was retribution. Constituents defeated him at the next election.[59]

More recently, one of Essex's five senators, Ron Rice, blocked Christopher Cerf, Governor Christie's choice as New Jersey education commissioner, a situation that created interesting side issues. In what appeared to be retaliation, Christie refused to appoint eleven judges to fill vacancies in Essex County, thereby creating a crisis, overloading and backing up the court system. The stalemate lasted more than a year, while Cerf served in an acting capacity. Finally, Cerf, a resident of Montclair in Essex County, took action to break the standoff by moving to an apartment in Somerset County, where he received an immediate sign-off from the GOP senator of that district. Cerf was officially approved as education commissioner in July 2012.[60]

Thirty-eight years earlier, when there was less accountability in government and political misconduct was often more brazen, a patronage scandal broke out involving the governor's appointment to fill the vacant position of Mercer County prosecutor. It was expected that Democratic governor Brendan Byrne would appoint someone from his party, subject of course to advice and consent of the state senate. According to newspaper reports, Mercer County's Democratic senator Joe Merlino, who could exercise courtesy rights over any nominee, arranged for prosecutor hopefuls to be interviewed by George Pellettieri, the county's foremost criminal defense lawyer and an active Democrat. Because much of his practice was defending clients before the county prosecutor, it was no surprise that Pellettieri's conversation with those seeking the position was about the nature of the staff that would populate the prosecutor's office. Comments about "cleaning house," that is, no Republicans in the prosecutor's office, the desire to have a prosecutor "who would not be anti-labor," and that some of the past attorneys in the office had conducted themselves in "an ungentlemanly fashion," were reported. All one had to do was connect the dots to understand how the political powers intended to fill the Mercer prosecutor position. In a surprise move after the unfavorable press reports about the Pellettieri meetings, Governor Byrne nominated a wild card as prosecutor—highly regarded nonpolitical former Trenton magistrate Anne Thompson. Part of the brilliance of this move was that this would be the highest prosecutorial position for any African American woman in the nation, and for Democratic Senator Merlino to block it by invoking senatorial courtesy would be a political mistake.[61]

After the first two years of his tenure, Governor Byrne submitted a report indicating that eighty-five of his nominations—25 percent—had been "delayed or scrapped" because of senatorial courtesy. Senator Merlino had used it nineteen times.[62]

One of the more intriguing cases of senatorial courtesy took place in 2004, when Governor Corzine renominated Candace Ashmun to the Pinelands Commission without first getting her senator's approval. Ashmun, a very active octogenarian, is the guru of environmentalists in New Jersey, having been a founder of the Pinelands preservation effort and many other green endeavors. When her name was not posted on the Senate Judiciary Committee calendar for confirmation, she was asked to check with her home county (Somerset) senator, Walter Kavanaugh. After Kavanaugh hemmed and hawed, word leaked to the press that Ashmun's nomination was being held up by senatorial courtesy. This made no sense in terms of Ashmun's previous service and experience in environmental and land preservation issues. The press asked Kavanaugh if he was holding the nomination. He said he was. When asked why, he responded with refreshing candor—and political indiscretion—that his county chairman had not approved it. When this became news, the absurdity of an unelected political power holding up a nomination that was in the domain of the state senate was too much, even in New Jersey. An embarrassed Kavanaugh wasted little time in signing off.[63]

Senatorial courtesy poisons the integrity of the appointment process, even for low-profile appointments. Lisa Billmeier of Pennington in Mercer County is a mother and homemaker who is not involved in politics. Her lawyer husband served as magistrate in a neighboring municipality, a part-time position. Yet in early 2008, out of the blue, she made a campaign contribution of $900 to then-senator Bill Baroni, a Republican residing in another district in Mercer County.[64] Was this because she had suddenly become a fan of Senator Baroni, or was it because her husband was interested in being appointed a Mercer County Superior Court judge subject to advice and consent of the state senate? There is no evidence that this contribution was solicited by Senator Baroni. Ms. Billmeier's husband was prohibited as a magistrate from making political contributions. This story ends with Mr. Billmeier's nomination and confirmation shortly thereafter as a judge of the Mercer County Superior Court.

There is currently no groundswell among New Jersey lawmakers to end senatorial courtesy. The government reform group Citizens for the Public Good conducted a survey of legislative candidates in the 2007 election asking all 267 senate and assembly candidates whether they would support a constitutional amendment banning the practice. Only fifty-two (less than 20 percent) of the candidates responded, including only twelve incumbents. The unusually low response rate to this type of questionnaire was much more significant than the fact that all but two respondents favored reform.[65]

Back in the legislative session of 1966–67, the newly elected Democratic senate attempted to end senatorial courtesy by adopting a rule mandating that all gubernatorial appointments come before the full state senate for a vote within sixty days. This short-lived change had mixed results. In a key confirmation vote in June 1966 for Democrat David Perskie of Atlantic County to become judge of that county's superior court, the Republican dean of the senate, Frank "Hap" Farley, also of Atlantic, rose in public session and declared that he opposed the appointment "for personal reasons." Perskie's confirmation vote failed; it received zero yes votes, nine no votes, and nineteen abstentions. The vestiges of senatorial courtesy prevailed, yet the process could not be criticized, because the vote was on the record, making senators publicly accountable for the first time for their actions in blocking the appointment.[66]

Defenders of senatorial courtesy advance two basic reasons for its use: one, it is a way to balance the power between the very strong New Jersey governor and the weaker legislative branch, and two, senatorial courtesy will ensure that unqualified nominees are not appointed. Former Republican senate president Ray Bateman of Somerset, a highly respected legislator, argued in favor of senatorial courtesy by saying, "'Courtesy' forces governors to do what the Constitution says to do, advise, and get consent from senators. . . . As a senator, I always tried to anticipate the governor's appointments coming from Somerset County and make a point to discuss them ahead of time with the governor." As a result of this open vetting process, Bateman concluded, "an appointment confrontation never developed with any governor."[67]

In effect, Senator Bateman refuted the arguments for senatorial courtesy by demonstrating how reasoned discourse with the governor is able to influence appointment choices and renders the use of senatorial courtesy unnecessary. As proof, he never had to use it. Any governor and staff member realizes, moreover, that it is good politics to have a dialogue and cooperate with a state senator whose support on other matters will be needed in the future.

But without the secretive system of senatorial courtesy in place, what is there to prevent a senator from using his or her collegial power with other senators, as well as the power of public opinion, to defeat an unqualified or objectionable nominee in the Judiciary Committee—or in open session in the full senate? Governors would be most reluctant to submit a nominee whose political record or competence would be an embarrassment if the governor knew that the Judiciary Committee would seriously commit to doing its job and expose the nominee's failings. And senators would think twice before allowing their objection to a nominee for politically unjustifiable reasons to be aired in public.

One rather unusual senatorial courtesy experience demonstrates its absurdity. This experience involved me as I was completing my first tenure in the legislature. I was a lame-duck senator in late November 1973, having lost my reelection bid earlier that month. Arriving in Atlantic City to attend the League of Municipalities convention, I checked into my hotel room and received a call from former governor Richard Hughes.

He explained that as a resident of Princeton in my district, he was seeking my approval to become the chief justice of the New Jersey Supreme Court, a position to which he was being nominated by Governor Cahill. I immediately said yes, of course. And after a few pleasantries, we hung up. Clearly, Richard Hughes understood the political facts of life. Yet, the system was totally unreasonable: a former two-term governor of New Jersey who was one of the most highly regarded chief executives ever to serve had asked for the consent of a lame-duck one-term senator to be allowed to receive the most prestigious position in the state. Something was out of whack.

If senatorial courtesy is abolished, the culture of the secret and offensive blackball system would end. Instead, a new culture would emerge, a culture where senators and Judiciary Committee members would assume their rightful role of performing due diligence in providing the governor with advice and consent.

## SICK PAY, VACATION DAYS, PENSION DOUBLE-DIPPING

The soft corruption of dual office holding intensifies when elected officials take advantage of generous perks they have legislated or negotiated into the system for all public employees. One such benefit is a liberal government subsidy for sick pay entitling public employees to be paid for a minimum number of days each year for time off when they are sick. If the employee does not use all of his or her allotted days, the benefit is not lost. Unused sick days are banked for future use or for an outright lump sum payment upon the employee's retirement.

The same system applies to vacation days that are allowed under many public employee contracts. Like sick days, lapsed vacation days can be used in future years or banked for payment on retirement.

A series of reports by the *Star-Ledger* in 2012 revealed that fifteen legislators—fourteen Democrats and one Republican—accrued more than $850,000 in unused sick and vacation time from their second government jobs, which they could turn into cash. Assemblymen Charles Mainor and Sean Connors, who were also Jersey City police detectives, had accrued a total of $224,000 in unused time by early 2012.[68] The most blatant sick day jackpot came to multiple officeholder Democratic state senator Nicholas Sacco of North Bergen in Hudson County. Having rarely taken a day off for being sick from his $233,000 salaried position as assistant school superintendent over a forty-three-year period, Sacco had accumulated 445 days of sick leave worth a $143,560 payout upon his retirement. He would have even more credits had he not traded in ninety-one unused vacation days for $101,000 during the five years before 2010. When commenting on his exorbitant unused sick leave retirement benefit, Senator Sacco said: "Is that fair to the people? Maybe not, but that is the contract that existed."

For dual-office-holding legislators, days spent in Trenton or on legislative business are, by law, not deducted from their vacation or sick day allotment.

The sick and vacation day bonanza applies also to officials who have only one public job working for counties, municipalities, school districts, or authorities. Large lump-sum retirement packages representing pay for accumulated unused days is common in many of these jurisdictions, particularly with police and firefighters. These retirement payouts are a heavy burden on local government resources (such as property taxes). This economic stress became especially intense in 2010, when newly elected governor Chris Christie announced his intention to reform these perks, saying, "It's a broken system. People should not be paid for not being sick. The reward should be not being sick." His announcement caused early retirements to skyrocket before any changes could be legislated.[69] Jersey City had to take out $27 million in short-term loans by 2012 to pay retirees. Atlantic City was forced to come up with $7.1 million in 2010 to meet the lump sum payments to its retiring police officers and firefighters.

Reform efforts initiated in 2007 lowered sick and vacation day allowances for which newly hired public officials will be eligible. The reforms also capped the unused days currently credited to public employees, but it was not possible to reduce the amounts they had banked through legally binding contracts.

Another abuse in the form of a special benefit for public employees is double-dipping of the pension system. This occurs when pensions are awarded for past government services to an individual who is a current public employee earning a government salary. Clearly, this extravagance adds to the cost of government. New Jersey Watchdog, an investigative website, conducted a report on pension double-dipping that included the following findings:

- Eighteen state legislators receive public pensions averaging more than $43,000 per year to supplement their $49,000 salaries.
- Forty-five retired school superintendents collect more than $4 million in yearly pensions while also earning executive-level salaries at interim school district positions.
- Seventeen county sheriffs (there are twenty-one in the state), together with twenty-nine undersheriffs, receive $3.4 million in retirement pay from prior jobs as well as $4.9 million in salaries.
- One hundred twenty-five retired law enforcement officers are on the staffs of state and county prosecutors, receiving $8.6 million in pensions and $9.9 million in salaries.[70]

New Jersey has nine separate pension programs covering different employee groups. The Public Employees Retirement System (PERS) is the largest pension system; the vast majority of all public workers in the state are members. Other pension programs cover teachers, law enforcement officials, judges, and members of the state police. If a retiree receives a pension from one system, PERS for example, the employee does not have to forfeit current payments from that system if he or she gets a paying position in a government agency that is under a different pension. And the employee can gain credits in the pension system of his or her new position. But if this person who was in PERS is hired by another government entity in that same system, pension payments from the former job are suspended until he or she retires from the second position.[71]

The amount of a pension is based on the average of the highest three years of salary paid to the employee. For veterans, it is based on the highest single year. In the election of 2001, there was a tidal shift of legislators from Republican to Democrat. Two GOP legislators who were defeated in the election, Senator Lou Kosco and Assemblyman Nicholas Felice, were immediately rewarded by the lame-duck Republican administration with good-paying state patronage jobs.[72] The two men's new positions paid more than double their legislative salaries, which then had been $35,000, Kosco at the State Parole Board and Felice at the

Board of Public Utilities. Both were veterans, and they retired from these appointed jobs as soon as the one year required for pension eligibility had expired. This move qualified Felice for a pension of $46,312 per year, 117 percent higher than due him under the terms of his legislative pension. Kosco received a yearly pension of $54,405, which was 78 percent more than the pension for senate service would have been. Kosco's public statement about his sudden pension bump was blunt: "If anybody don't [sic] like it, that's too bad. Let them go spend thirty-three years in office."

For many years, attorney legislators have been able to maximize their pensions by a process known as tacking, whereby they are retained under personal employment contracts to provide legal services as an employee of a local government entity. Time spent in this arrangement as a member of each local government's pension program adds to the attorney's pension credits. Former GOP senator John Bennett accumulated enough tacking time from municipalities and school boards to build his yearly pension to a total of $82,000 upon retirement.[73] Public outrage over this probably contributed to Bennett's defeat in the 2003 election.

The following are some of the more egregious examples of pension abuse by individual public employees. They demonstrate the seriousness and breadth of soft corruption in conferring special pension benefits to legislators and public officials:

- Lest anyone believe that a political boss who has a very powerful government position at a high salary would be overcome by altruism and renounce all supplemental compensation benefits, consider the case of Joe DiVincenzo. As Essex County executive, DiVincenzo receives a salary of $153,207 per year to which is added a yearly pension from previous government service of $68,856. In his position, DiVincenzo has accumulated 101.5 vacation days with a payout value of $60,000, but he has agreed to abide by county policy and accept payment for only forty days, or about $23,500. Finally, he has an accumulation of 130 sick days, worth more than $16,000, which are not subject to forfeiture.[74]

- Democratic senator Jim Beach of Camden developed his own system of creative pension exploitation. After serving twenty-six years in education, Beach was granted $33,192 per year from the teachers' pension fund with lifetime health benefits for him and his family. He left the field of education and worked in other government jobs, building up service time in a second pension (PERS) while collecting the teacher's pension. He then hit the jackpot when the party tapped him for county clerk at an annual salary of $153,000. This new job would, after ten years, increase the separate second pension to double the amount of his teacher pension. But Beach's grand plan was disrupted when he was drafted by his party for a vacant state senate seat, an offer that no Camden Democrat could refuse. The senate position removed him from his second pension opportunity—the county clerk's job—until the ever-resourceful Beach was able to land a part-time job (ten hours per week at $10,400 per year) with another Camden government agency, which will allow him to eventually compile the necessary years for the second pension.[75]

- As a candidate running for the office of governor in 2009, Chris Christie was openly critical of dual office holding as well as of those who were exploiting the pension system while holding another government job. A former state trooper who had thirty years of service and was collecting a $90,000 pension joined the Christie campaign for governor in 2009, and became the candidate's personal driver. After Christie was elected, he apparently disregarded his criticism of pension padding and nominated his campaign driver to a job on the State Parole Board, a notorious haven for patronage appointments coveted for "inflated salaries and light workloads," adding a salary of $116,305 to his pension.[76]

Recent legislative action has reformed some of the excesses going forward, such as attempting to make professional service contracts ineligible for pension tacking (although a 2012 state comptroller report showed widespread flouting of the statute),[77] reducing benefits for new hires to more reasonable levels, requiring larger employee payroll contributions, and limiting—to the extent possible—bloated retirement payments for sick and vacation days. As with so many government programs that have become unreasonably excessive, or even scandalous, these represent minor efforts at reform because they cannot reform benefits in which current retirees are already vested. And lawmakers, who often have a personal interest in the status quo, resist fundamental systemic reform. This combination has contributed to an even more serious problem involving public pensions: the actuarial viability of the system. As of mid-2014, New Jersey had an unfunded state pension liability of approximately $40 billion. If this deficit is not made up, the state will fall short of paying its contractual pension obligations to the entire universe of retirees in future years. Governors and the legislature have shown little discipline in efforts to make up this shortfall. Clearly, much more needs to be done.[78]

## TITHING

Party organizations and candidates keep lists of potential and past contributors to election campaigns. It is no coincidence that the correlation between the names on these lists and people who have patronage jobs is high. While it is illegal to extract a binding commitment for a campaign donation from someone as a condition of government employment, both parties understand that the beneficiary of patronage has an obligation to reward the benefactor with a regular stipend. This is not much different from the expectation of a church that its members will tithe a portion of their income.

Years ago, strong political organizations made it clear to people who hold public jobs that they should return a certain percentage of their salaries to the party. The Democrats who dominated Mercer County more than forty years ago operated under a tithing system: employees earning less than $5,000 a year would contribute 3 percent of their salaries; those earning more than $5,000 would contribute 5 percent. Party functionaries would receive lists of seventy-five to one hundred public employees to solicit for contributions or for purchasing tickets to fundraising events.[79]

Two Democratic stalwarts in Mercer County who made the rounds collecting party tribute in the mid-1970s were Sam Naples, longtime superintendent of elections, and James McGroarty, county road supervisor. In the process, however, McGroarty stepped over the line with some heavy-handed solicitation of contractors, was convicted of extortion, and was sentenced to prison. Believing his pal had gotten a bum rap for what was common practice, Naples showed his displeasure by going public with the party's tithing system. Thereafter, solicitation of people who held patronage jobs became more discreet.[80]

Enactment of the state campaign finance disclosure law in 1973, combined with more aggressive investigative reporting by journalists, squelched some of the more blatant efforts to extract money from those who held public jobs. But this part of the pay-to-play system still exists, particularly in areas where politics is blood sport. A 2010–11 *Star-Ledger* investigation of the Passaic Valley Sewerage Commission (PVSC) found, among other things, that during work hours supervisors would regularly ask their employees to buy tickets to political fund-raisers, both Democratic and Republican.[81] Records showed that the long-serving state senator from Passaic County, John Girgenti, received 10 percent of his campaign contributions from PVSC employees and vendors. Girgenti claimed he never solicited money from these sources, but he didn't have to—other political players stepped in to do the job to make sure that he would continue to represent them in Trenton. The ongoing investigation revealed that one PVSC computer contained a list of all the authority's employees who bought tickets for a Girgenti fundraising dinner in October 2010. Girgenti's service in the senate ended as a result of the redistricting of Passaic County in 2011.

The amount of political contributions raised from patronage appointees is difficult to determine. If anything, it is understated for the simple reason that contributions of $300 or less do not have to be recorded on campaign finance reports. Most lower-paid public employees are solicited for amounts smaller than $300. This became quite clear in the 2009 election, when reports to ELEC showed $68,360 had been collected from 301 named employees of the office of incumbent Essex County Sheriff Armando Fontoura. It is likely that the computer used for Fontoura's fund-raising was not programmed to block out names of contributors who gave less than the reportable threshold of $300. Most were $200 donations, the normal cost to attend a fundraising dinner. After protesting that he does not solicit his employees, the sheriff observed: "I'm not an aggressive fund-raiser. I hate raising money. But people show up at the door and we don't turn them away. I don't know if they love me that much, but we get a lot of people from the department showing up."[82]

## PATRONAGE ON THE ELIZABETH SCHOOL BOARD

Elizabeth, a city just south of Newark with a population of 125,000, is dominated by a uniquely positioned political machine. The machine exercises its muscle through the city's school board, whose members are elected on a nonpartisan basis but who in fact are Democrats, as are virtually all holders of public office in that section of Union County.[83] The purpose of the Elizabeth school board machine is to gain power for its school board leaders, who have received scarce recognition from normal Democratic Party channels. Tithing is the foundation of this enterprise. It provides the political underpinnings to elect the machine's board members and keep them in power. It is instructive to describe the broad range of political activities in which the Elizabeth school board engages—and important to emphasize that no other school board anywhere in New Jersey has seen the need or desire to exert such political power. And all of it depends on the link between patronage and contributions from school board employees and public contractors.

While nominally nonpartisan, school board elections in Elizabeth are as intense as partisan elections for municipal, county, and state offices in terms of fund-raising, publicity, and get-out-the-vote drives. At odds with the Democrats who control elections for these offices, the school board has sponsored candidates at all levels to run against the regular Democrats in primaries and nonpartisan municipal elections. Former board chair Rafael Fajardo had previously run unsuccessfully for mayor of Elizabeth. And while he stepped down as chair of the board of education in 2010, he did not relinquish his control over the political machine that carries out the goals of the Elizabeth education establishment. In 2011, the school board contributed heavily in money and manpower to the primary slate of three legislative hopefuls who sought, unsuccessfully, to topple longtime incumbents.

The lifeblood of this political juggernaut is the four thousand employees of the school district, including teachers, whose loyalty is controlled through strong-arm patronage methods. They are, for example, counted on to take time off on Election Day to serve as challengers at the polls or to get the vote out. More troubling, board members and other supervisory personnel solicit funds, generally in the form of tickets to events, from teachers and other employees. The proceeds are deposited in accounts used to finance political campaigns. Solicitations have been made on school property using the board of education's personnel lists—and even after a state law was passed in 2012 to ban political campaign solicitation on public property, allegations of its practice in Elizabeth have been made in subsequent elections. One fund-raising e-mail solicited $240 memberships in For the People of Union County, an organization that financed a weekly political publication. In 2010, one board-sponsored election committee raised $105,000, including $85,000 in amounts under the reporting threshold of $300. The incentive for employees to contribute is clear: "If you don't buy tickets, you are not promoted to jobs you may want. You are basically shut out of the system no matter how competent you are," said a former school principal who had become an Elizabeth city council member.

Nepotism flourishes in this political environment. The nine-member board of education has appointed twenty relatives of board members to jobs on the district payroll. Former board chair Fajardo accounts for six of these, including his sister, whose position as truant officer for pre-school children with a salary of $50,000 was under review by the state because there is no requirement for preschoolers to attend school—so what is the justification for a preschool truant officer?

In a political maneuver aimed against local Democrats who were campaigning to reelect their party's candidate for governor in 2009, eight of the nine board members endorsed the Republican gubernatorial candidate, Chris Christie. One school employee, according to a complaint he later filed, was told to put up Christie campaign signs and take down the signs of incumbent Democrat Jon Corzine during regular work hours.[84]

The politicization of the Elizabeth school district, whether through coerced campaign contributions or participation in election events, takes its toll on the professional integrity of its mission and personnel. One aspiring educator who earned a master's degree while teaching social studies realized that advancement "depended on more than hard work and determination." After purchasing tickets and attending political events, he progressed to the position of tenured administrator, and then he had an epiphany. He stopped buying tickets. Thereafter he was removed from a choice assignment and eventually suspended. These actions led him to sue the Elizabeth school board, citing fund-raising pressures and other political irregularities. Other employees in similar circumstances also initiated whistle-blower suits against the board.[85]

The Elizabeth school board officials were proactive in their response to these complaints. First, they hired a firm staffed with former FBI agents to aggressively investigate the complainants. Their second strategy was to negotiate and offer cash settlements with a stipulation that the settlements remain confidential. This strategy failed when reporters used the open public records law to extract information regarding the suits. Attorneys for the school board redacted the names and settlement terms on many of the court papers, but enough information became public to indicate the board had made ninety settlements, a sample of which showed awards averaging $100,000. During the five years leading up to 2011, the Elizabeth Board of Education spent $5.6 million on legal services, more than twice as much as was spent in Newark, the largest school district in the state.[86]

The stakes at issue in order to gain control of the Elizabeth Board of Education have not been lost on the board's political enemies, the traditional Democratic Party of the city and surrounding Union County. In recent years, both factions have mounted heated campaigns against each other in school board elections and in the primaries.[87]

As a sign of the seriousness of the rivalry, a super PAC spawned by the Supreme Court's 2010 *Citizens United* decision has entered the fray at this, the lowest of all government levels. The Committee for Economic Growth and Social Justice, a super PAC with the backing of Union County state senator Raymond Lesniak, provided more than $180,000 to defeat two of the three incumbent Elizabeth school board members running in 2013, but this was not enough to control the nine-member board.

Again in the November 2014 school board election the Lesniak group fielded a team of three challengers opposing Fajardo's three incumbents. A total of $196,000 of super PAC money was spent for the Lesniak candidates, enough to win two seats and control of the board. However, before the new members were settled in, Lesniak incumbent and board president Ana Maria Amin defected to the Fajardo camp, thereby denying control to the Lesniak group.

Of special note are the contributions to this super PAC from Lesniak and his law firm—$30,000—and from special interests that are allied with him on the state scene. Among these are bail bondsmen, alcoholic beverage groups, the longshoremen's union, and online betting interests. As absurd as it may seem for online betting firms to be investing in the defeat of candidates for a board that decides on textbooks and school lunch contracts in one city in New Jersey, it is no coincidence that these firms are heavily involved in supporting the political objectives of Senator Lesniak, since he has championed their role in the New Jersey gambling industry.

The transgressions involving the Elizabeth school board in areas where political corruption is likely to exist—patronage, campaign financing, electoral procedure—are demonstrably clear and run counter to the educational mission expected of the body that governs a school system. As a result of the complaints filed by aggrieved school employees, condemnation by traditional Democratic Party organizations, and the constant drumbeat of critical newspaper stories, law enforcement authorities have been pressured to undertake a full investigation of the political activities of the Elizabeth school board. While the investigation has led to no major criminal violations, fines have been assessed on several school board members for minor infractions. Former board president Fajardo and school superintendent Pablo Munoz were assessed $63,622 for improper legal fees that they charged the board, and there have been several minor infractions for which Elizabeth school board members have been fined.[88]

Patronage per se is not bad. Patronage in the form of public jobs and the awarding of government benefits is an essential component of governing. Patronage is bad only if it is abused, if incompetent people are hired to perform government services, if the distribution of government benefits is rigged to the advantage of a favored few—in short, if this nation's founding principles of honest representative government are compromised by the tactics of those who use government to gain power and personal rewards.

Patronage abuses in New Jersey are sufficiently serious to conclude that citizens of the state are not receiving the quality government to which they are entitled—and for which they pay.

# 7 ▸ THE ELECTORAL PROCESS

"I don't care who does the electing, just so I can do the nominating."

—WILLIAM MAGEAR "BOSS" TWEED (1823–1878),
Tammany Hall, New York City

THESE FOREBODING WORDS about the power over elected officials held by a behind-the-scenes political boss are almost as true today in many parts of New Jersey as they were more than a century ago. The electoral process can be legally bent in a variety of ways to favor the interests of powerful party leaders, shutting out many who might aspire to elective office to serve the public good. The American ideal that highly qualified candidates who champion enlightened public policy are destined to win at the polls is fantasy much of the time in the Garden State.

To be sure, most New Jerseyans in elective office are honorable, competent, and serve to the best of their abilities. Maybe this is because most are products of the state's political farm system, having been elected to municipal office where they put in long hours at little or no pay.

But New Jersey citizens still tolerate shortcomings in the state's electoral system that adversely affect government's ability to perform at the highest degree of proficiency and integrity. This brings up two related issues of major concern: (1) rigging of the process to select candidates in jurisdictions dominated by one party, often blocking the best and brightest from entering or advancing in elective office; and (2) lack of competition in many election contests, much of which is related to the advantages of incumbency, a phenomenon of single-party domination.

In order to get a feel for the critically important candidate selection process commonly used in New Jersey, it is instructive to understand the partisan landscape. Political power resides in the county political organizations, specifically in their leaders. By law, candidate slates as they appear on the ballot are constructed at the county level by county party organizations. Over the years, partisan strongholds have taken hold. Of the twenty-one counties, sixteen are solidly under the control of one of the major parties. Seven are Republican counties, representing 27 percent of the state's population, and nine are Democratic counties, accounting for 52 percent.[1] Although the remaining five counties are reasonably competitive, their candidate selection process is similar to that of the other counties.

## THE PRIMARY ELECTION

In the sixteen counties that are dominated by one party or the other, the real contest as to who will represent the people at the county level, in the congressional district, in the legislative district, and in many of the municipalities is determined in the primary election, not at the general election when voter approval of the dominant party's nominee is a virtual certainty. Party leaders settle on their chosen candidate and bestow on him or her all the advantages necessary for winning the primary, including campaign funds, endorsements, and, most important, ballot position. It is critical to the success of a candidate to be part of the official party slate that appears on the primary election ballot, known in political parlance as the party line.

The candidate slate always includes those running in the county for congressional, legislative, and county positions. In many cases it will include the favored candidates for municipal office and even those for district committee. When a statewide office such as governor or

U.S. senator is contested, the candidates for that office will vie for the endorsement of the county political establishment so as to be part of its ballot slate. Party leaders relish the power this process gives them, particularly with a future governor.

The path toward patching together the party line has many twists and turns. Each of the two major parties has its own primary county ballot on which all qualified candidates are listed. But the most favorable line on the ballot is the first line, which is customarily awarded to the party's official slate of candidate names—that is, to those the party has blessed. Candidates who have not received party approval are relegated to less prominent—even obscure—places on the primary ballot by the county clerk, who generally respects the wishes of the two major parties regarding ballot placement.

Technically, under the law, an insurgent slate of party candidates has as much right as the slate of the party establishment to be placed on line one of the primary ballot, but this seldom happens. The county clerk, who has broad discretion over whose names go where on the ballot, will often come up with a technicality to deny the insurgents the first line. Or if it comes down to a drawing by lot, county clerks have an uncanny ability to always pick the establishment party slate for the first line.

When they go to the polls, most party regulars will pull the lever for the better-known names on line one, generally incumbents, and, if undecided, will most likely choose all the other candidates on the same line. Clearly, being "on the line" means everything in winning the party nomination in the primary. And in the case of incumbency in a dominant party, this is tantamount to being reelected in November.

In some counties, the line is drawn up and submitted at the sole discretion of the party boss. By law, only one person, usually the party chair or the chair's designee, has total power over the line by being officially appointed manager of the candidates who have filed for county office as a joint slate. This enables the manager to certify other chosen candidates to have their names on the same line, thereby excluding from this favored ballot placement all other candidates unacceptable to the manager.[2]

In order to avoid the appearance that one person has such autocratic power over the fate of candidates, many counties have adopted a more open system wherein selection of candidates for the party line is made at a candidate-endorsement convention. The procedures used by endorsement conventions vary from county to county with regard to eligibility of delegates, voting rules, and admissibility of candidates to the party line.

Even here, party chairs have found ways to impose their will over the selection of candidates. One stratagem is to form a nominating committee to recruit and screen potential candidates who are then presented to the party leaders or to an endorsement convention. Chairs are not reluctant to stack nominating committees with their allies to ensure that the outcome reflects their wishes. And in the case of an endorsement convention, the power of the chair, through patronage and fund-raising, often convinces party members to do the chair's bidding.

As suggested by the words of Boss Tweed, primary elections in counties and districts dominated by one party are the elections that really matter, because the winners are virtually assured of being voted into office in the general election in November. Local party leaders recognize this fact and jealously guard the power they have over the procedures that regulate the primary.

Since New Jersey does not have an open primary, voters can vote only in the primary of the party with which they are registered. This system gives each party a known pool of voters to work with in delivering for the party. But a consequence is that participation in New Jersey primaries is very low, generally under 20 percent of all registered voters. Many voters are reluctant to declare their party affiliation, something they have to do when voting in a primary, earning them the letter D for Democrat and R for Republican on the voter registry sheet. Fewer than 50 percent of the state's voters choose to be so identified, which means that more than half of the electorate eliminate themselves from even considering participation in party primaries.

The importance of the primary for New Jersey's Democratic Party was clearly demonstrated by two significant incidents. In 2003, the Democratic legislature, in an attempt to reform wheeling between counties, settled on a half-baked law that prohibited wheeling, but only during primaries, when legislators wanted no outside interference with the campaigns run by their local political leaders (see the section on wheeling in chapter 2). When primaries are over, wheeling is still legal and is effectively used to target competitive races in other areas.

I saw the reluctance to give up control of primaries firsthand in 2006, when I chaired the Citizens Clean Elections Commission. We recommended a pilot program of publicly funded campaigns in selected assembly districts. The program would, of course, benefit non-party-backed candidates by making available to them the financial resources necessary to compete against entrenched, well-financed incumbents. We designed the initiative to apply to the primary as well as to the general election, since the primary was where aspiring new candidates needed help to enter the process. The executive director of the assembly Democratic majority made an urgent plea for us to remove primaries from the scope of the proposal, but we stuck to our recommendation. Nevertheless, the Democrats got what they wanted anyway. By the time the pilot program legislation was approved, it was too late to authorize primary-campaign funds for selected assembly districts. The pilot applied to only one year's general election.

## REDISTRICTING

Legislative districts, which are reapportioned as a result of population changes after each decennial U.S. census, are also vestiges of single-party domination. New Jersey is divided into forty legislative districts, each consisting of approximately 220,000 residents. One state senator and two assembly members are elected to the legislature from each district. Unlike many states, where reapportioning happens through the highly contentious legislative process, with both houses and the governor eventually reaching consensus on the redrawn district maps, New Jersey appoints a bipartisan commission to do the work. The Apportionment Commission charged with drawing district boundaries is nonetheless political; its ten members include five Republicans and five Democrats picked by their respective state party chairs. If they cannot agree on a map, the chief justice of the state supreme court appoints an eleventh member to break the deadlock. Among the standards a new district plan must meet are: the population in the districts must be nearly equal (within several percentage points), the area must be contiguous, municipalities may not be divided between districts to the extent possible, and consideration must be given to the ability of minorities to be elected. While forming compact districts would be an ideal goal, this outcome is seldom achieved. Instead, the configurations of most districts are gerrymandered to enhance political objectives.

It is no secret that in redrawing districts, the members of the commission want to protect incumbents and maximize the opportunity for their party to capture a majority of legislative seats. By generating and analyzing thousands of alternative map designs, using sophisticated computer programs and data on the voting history of the state's 565 municipalities, each party tries to carve out as many safe districts as possible.

Because of the deliberately designed lack of competition between the parties in most districts, voters end up with representatives they have had little power over choosing. This system fosters public apathy and reduced turnout, depriving citizens of the virtues of a meaningful participatory democracy, one of the founding principles of this country.

Studies of recent elections show only two or three of New Jersey's forty legislative districts as highly competitive.[3] Another five to seven districts can be classified as marginally competitive. This means that in the remaining 75 percent of the state's districts, because of a strong majority of Republican or Democratic voters, there is really no contest.

How safe have these districts become? A study by ELEC in 2011 for elections between 1999 and 2009 showed that the reelection rate of incumbents among assembly members in these six elections was 97 percent, and the rate among state senators in their three elections was 91 percent.[4] Even in 2013, when Governor Christie won reelection by a commanding 22 points over his Democratic challenger, no state senate incumbent in either party gave up his or her seat, and only two in the assembly lost—one from each party.

Consider an example from Legislative District 15 in the years immediately following 2000. This district encompasses a heavily Democratic area including the city of Trenton, and is served by longtime incumbent Senator Shirley Turner, whose campaign war chest has always amounted to several hundred thousand dollars. In 2001, Turner won against a token Republican with more than 69 percent of the vote. She won again in 2003, garnering 67 percent of the vote over an opponent who spent $1,175 on his campaign compared to Turner's $12,000. Flush with funds and facing a weak challenger, Turner was able to wheel more than $106,000 to other Democratic campaigns and committees in competitive contests that year.

Suddenly, in 2007, Turner was faced with a serious and well-financed challenge to her safe 15th District senate seat. Republican Bob Martin, an attractive, successful business executive who had considerable personal wealth, mounted an aggressive effort to replace Turner. Martin's campaign was highly visible and presented popular positions on important state policies. He even spent $255,000 compared to Turner's $68,000. But with all his spending and good media coverage, Martin's candidacy barely moved the numbers against the district Democratic machine. Turner won with 63 percent of the vote.

## PARTY ORGANIZATION

Political parties have indirect power over government through patronage, fund-raising, and the electoral process. Misuse of this power can lead to soft corruption.

New Jersey law provides that voting districts consisting of five hundred to one thousand registered voters elect a county committeeman and committeewoman (aka precinct leader) at the primary to represent each major party. The law also stipulates that committee persons elect a municipal chair as well as a county chair one week after the primary. Other than these few functions, party committees are held to few other statutory or regulatory requirements.

In an effort to improve transparency and accountability, the legislature passed the 2009 Party Democracy Act, requiring all county committee organizations to adopt a constitution and bylaws. This document is intended to ensure "fundamental fairness and the rights of members of the county committee in the governance of the county party," but sets no standards or procedures for carrying out this mandate. Neither are there any uniform requirements for the county committee of a party to hold an endorsement convention, nor are there uniform guidelines for placing candidates' names in the party line on the ballot.

Much of the vagueness of the laws that regulate county committees can be attributed to the United States Supreme Court's *Eu* decision of 1989, which invalidated on First Amendment grounds the power of

California state statutes over the internal affairs of political parties.[5] In other words, the organizational and associational freedoms of parties are the same as those of private entities. They cannot be proscribed.

## THE LUCK OF THE BALLOT DRAW FOR NOVEMBER

Much has been made of the party line on the ballot, and for good reason. Again, the primary election has a separate ballot for each of the two parties. In the November general election, however, the candidates of all the parties are combined onto one ballot. Studies have shown that the name that appears first on any list gets an automatic benefit of at least 3 percent over names that follow, based on the presumption that many voters who are unfamiliar with the candidates will choose the first name on the ballot.[6] Line one on the general election ballot, therefore, is fiercely coveted. On the eighty-fifth day before the general election, county clerks are required to draw "by lot" the name of one of the two major parties to be printed on the first line of the ballot. County clerks who are elected to their office as political party members will naturally favor their party in the draw for the line—and they always succeed. It seems that as part of their initiation into the society of county clerks, they are given the secret of how to always pull their party's card or capsule for the favored first line from the closed container that holds the names of the other party—and independent slates, if any.

Hunterdon is a solid Republican county. A review of the general election ballots from 1999 to 2009 showed the GOP had a 100 percent success rate for getting line one, a probability amounting to 1 in 2,048.[7] Results in other counties are the same. Essex, a Democratic bastion, has had a similar record, especially several decades ago, when the party's Nicholas Caputo was county clerk.[8] In a fourteen-year stretch, the Democrats received the first ballot position, line A, for thirteen years. In the one year when they missed, the line was awarded to the Republicans as a result of a feud between the Essex Democrats and then-governor Richard Hughes, also a Democrat. The inside story told in Essex was that the party had such faith in Caputo's ability to draw line A—the first line—that the party's election material saying "Vote line A, all the way" was printed even before he drew for the ballot position.

Caputo's true skill came to the fore in 1973, when the voters of Essex County were charged with electing a nine-member nonpartisan charter study commission to examine the county's structure and make recommendations for change. Democrats who ran Essex did not want a charter study aimed at reforming their county government; they wanted the status quo. The outcome was left in the capable hands of clerk Caputo. Ten Democratic stalwarts, including Caputo, filed petitions to run as commissioners for the charter study. Nineteen others—Republicans, independents, and maverick Democrats—also filed. The order of the names that would appear on the nonpartisan line of the general election ballot over an eighteen-inch span would be determined by the order in which Caputo drew the names of candidates out of a closed drum. Obviously, the first names appearing on the ballot had a distinct advantage, since there was little public awareness of the charter study and since it was very easy for the dominant Democratic Party to instruct its followers to vote for the first names they saw on the line. As luck would have it, Nicholas Caputo's name was the first one drawn, followed immediately by the other nine party faithful. This result was achieved at odds estimated at seven out of ten billion.

The elected charter commission subsequently met and summarily rejected any effort to reform Essex County government. Caputo coyly admitted that he was embarrassed to draw his name first. In any event, this and other feats of ballot legerdemain earned Caputo the title of "the man with the golden hand."

Other states have different ways to award line one on the ballot. Florida gives this line to candidates of the governor's party, which is probably one of the reasons George W. Bush, whose brother Jeb was Florida governor at the time, eked out a narrow victory for president over Al Gore in 2000.[9]

## THIRD PARTIES

Third parties are anathema to Republicans and Democrats in New Jersey. They have virtually no chance to qualify as a party because of a law that is more discriminatory against forming third parties than laws in any other state. It seems that Republicans know, tolerate, and accept the existence of Democrats and vice versa. They are in the arena together; they are familiar with each other's moves. But third parties are different, unpredictable, and, therefore, hard to deal with as friend or foe.

It stands to reason that establishment of third, fourth, or more parties will make elections more competitive, thereby increasing public interest and voter turnout. This will help overcome the condition of voter apathy, one of the consequences of soft corruption.

A third party, in order to become official in New Jersey, would have to recruit eighty candidates for the assembly from all districts throughout the state to file, run, and garner an aggregate of 10 percent of the votes cast for assembly candidates in the election.[10] If the third party recruited only forty candidates, these would have to get double the votes per district than the number required if there were eighty candidates. This is a monumental undertaking, more difficult than other states that have seemingly rigorous thresholds for party qualification.[11] Several states require a vote of at least 20 percent of the votes cast for a statewide office such as governor. But by focusing on one popular candidate for a position such as governor, it is easier to attain the 20 percent than 10 percent of eighty disparate candidates for the "invisible" office of assembly. New York State requires only 50,000 votes for governor for a political organization to qualify as an official party. The 50,000 was slightly more than 1 percent of the total vote for governor in 2010. Other than Republican and Democratic, there are four officially certified parties in the Empire State: Conservative, Independence, Working Families, and Green.[12]

In New Jersey, only an official political party is entitled to have a primary election to nominate its candidates for the general election. Non-party candidates get on the November ballot by filing a petition, but their names do not receive the privileged position of a recognized party line.

The lawmakers who produced this electoral system almost one hundred years ago added another feature that made sense in the early twentieth century when participation in parties and voter turnout were more robust. This feature, as spelled out in the law, states:

[N]o political party which fails to poll at any primary election . . . at least ten percentum (10%) of the votes cast in the state for members of the General Assembly at the next preceding general election held for the election of all the members of the general assembly . . . shall be entitled to have a party column on the official ballot at the general election for which the primary election has been held.[13]

In other words, the same 10 percent standard must be met in the party primary turnout for the party to continue as an official party entitled to a party line on the general election ballot.

With the continuing falloff of primary voters in New Jersey in 1999, less than 5 percent of Republican voters turned out in the primary, and among the Democrats, only 6 percent. Clearly, neither party had attained the legal threshold for primary voters. The New Jersey Conservative political organization, which had never been treated kindly by either the Democrats or the GOP, immediately took legal action against the two parties.[14] A superior court judge in Monmouth County ruled in favor of the Conservatives, advising all county clerks to withhold preferential treatment on the general election ballot for candidates of the two parties. If this verdict held, the entire political establishment in New Jersey would be turned upside-down. Both political parties, the state attorney general, the county clerks, and their contingent of twenty-three lawyers immediately filed an appeal against the Conservatives with their one attorney.

Opponents of the ruling invented some fuzzy math in their appeal. They reasoned that the 10 percent required to vote in a primary did not refer to the number of voters who went to the polls, as interpreted by the Superior Court judge, but to the number of candidates for whom these voters cast their ballots. In other words, if John Smith went into the voting booth and marked his ballot for three candidates—an assemblywoman, a freeholder, and a mayor—this would count as three, not one.[15]

The appeal came before the appellate court and was heard less than a week after the original decision. After one day of review, including oral arguments heard by telephone, the two appellate judges (not the normal three-judge appellate panel) reversed the ruling and instructed the clerks to proceed with making up the ballots in the customary fashion.

With political power concentrated in strong party organizations in New Jersey, it is easy to understand that the rich get richer and the poor stay poor. Third-party candidates face an insurmountable hurdle. No matter how qualified a candidate of a third or independent party is when compared to candidates of the major parties, voters are not inclined to waste their vote on someone who has no chance of winning. These candidates often get tabbed as spoilers. So the downward spiral of third parties continues.

There is a remedy that would make the vote for a third-party candidate count for something. This process, called instant runoff voting (IRV),[16] would require that a candidate receive more than 50 percent of all votes cast to win an election, and it would apply specific procedures to ensure that the winning candidate would receive an absolute majority of the vote in election contests where more than two candidates vie for the same office.

IRV works in the following manner: assume three people are candidates for state senator—a Democrat we'll call Smith, a Republican we'll call Jones, and Wilson, a Libertarian. Voters would cast ballots for their first choice and have the option of indicating their second choice. If any one of the three receives more than 50 percent of the votes cast, he or she would be the automatic winner. However, if no candidate receives at least 50 percent, with Smith getting 46 percent, Jones 44 percent, and Wilson 10 percent, for example, Wilson would be eliminated and the second choice on all Wilson ballots would be added to the totals for Smith or Jones. Absent the unlikely event of a tie, either Smith or Jones would pass the 50 percent mark and would be the winner. And all the voters for Wilson would have their votes counted by virtue of their second choice. This system would work equally well for four, five, six or more candidates running for the one office.

IRV has been used in foreign countries and in some jurisdictions in the United States, such as San Francisco, Minneapolis, and Burlington, Vermont. The implications of this process are profound. Consider the effect IRV might have had in the Florida presidential election in 2000, if those who cast their votes for Ralph Nader could have made a second choice and had this second choice count in order to get a winner with more than 50 percent of the state's votes.

Instant runoff voting has several secondary benefits in addition to ensuring a clear majority of votes for the winner of an election. Clearly, voters will have a greater incentive to participate in the process if they realize they will not be encumbered with the stigma of being a spoiler or casting a wasted vote by supporting a third-party candidate. Further, candidates will be less inclined to use negative campaign tactics against opponents because they will not want to jeopardize their chance of getting the second-choice designation of an adversary.

Although no studies are known as to whether IRV increases voter turnout, simple logic tells us it will increase interest in elections and reduce the apathy that has become so prevalent. IRV eliminates the expense of conducting follow-up elections in those cities and jurisdictions that, failing to get an absolute majority in the regular election, require a runoff one month later. The turnouts in such runoffs are known to be low.

## CAMPAIGNING

Political campaigns have changed over the years. In the early twentieth century, voting was driven by retail politics where party district leaders worked hard going door-to-door to become personally known by the voters and to gain their loyalty in supporting the party ticket. In more recent years, face-to-face contact has been replaced by computers, telephones, polling, television, social media, and direct mail, all made possible by the infusion of vast amounts of campaign money. The current function of county committee persons appears to be limited to voting each year for leaders and recruiting local candidates rather than conducting districtwide registration drives and communicating personally with residents.

Since 1950, virtually all voting districts in New Jersey have been equipped with voting machines. In prior years, people voted by paper ballot, giving rise to many cases of fraud. Jersey City in Hudson County has had a history of voting irregularities under the legendary rule of Democratic mayor Frank Hague in the early 1900s and continuing with his successors. There were years when Hudson County would report more votes cast than there were registered voters, causing former governor Brendan Byrne to quip that when he dies, he wants to be buried in Hudson County so he can remain active in politics.[17]

The problems associated with paper ballots are still present with absentee ballots, but to a lesser degree. A voter no longer has to be sick, out of state, or in military service to apply for and receive an absentee ballot. These are made readily available to any registered voter as a convenient method to maximize voting through the mail. The system allows for "messenger ballots" to be distributed, collected, and turned in by other individuals. But the controls are problematic. Those who handle absentee ballots can focus their efforts on nursing homes, where some occupants with reduced mental acuity are susceptible to scamming. Or the messenger ballot effort can concentrate on known party supporters who simply don't want to take the time to come to the polls. Use of absentee ballots helps political machines gather the vote of their core supporters in advance of Election Day, which is perfectly acceptable. But in a more sinister vein, it can be the source of fraud when the ballot couriers do the voting for the absentee voter.

Investigations, followed by indictments, revealed there was substantial absentee ballot fraud in the Essex County general election in behalf of Senator Teresa Ruiz in 2007. Senator Ruiz's husband, Essex freeholder Samuel Gonzalez, as well as aides to county power broker Steve Adubato and Mayor Cory Booker, were indicted for improper handling and voting of several hundred messenger ballots.[18] In Atlantic City, there was similar ballot manipulation in the 2009 primary, when supporters of mayoral candidates applied for 835 absentee ballots. Of these, the New Jersey attorney general was able to find 130 that were fraudulently filled out, resulting in the arrest of thirteen persons charged with ballot fraud.[19] (In neither Essex nor Atlantic City were absentee ballots decisive in the outcome.)

## NEGATIVE CAMPAIGNS AND DIRTY TRICKS

Negative campaign tactics have become a staple. The objective, obviously, is to cast the opponent in the most unfavorable light possible so that the voter responds by supporting the candidate and the party that is on the attack. It is legitimate for a candidate to vigorously contest an election with honest, hard-hitting criticism of the record and programs advocated by his or her opponent. When these pronouncements contain misrepresentations, half-truths, innuendo, and distortions, they cross the line into negative campaigning. (Representations made in a campaign that are patently false are subject to the laws of libel and slander, and are not part of this analysis. The same applies to campaign materials and media produced without attribution, which is also against the law.)

There are two ways that negativity adversely affects a campaign and erodes the electoral process. First, if not refuted, it clearly detracts from the confidence and electoral support the public will have for the person under attack both in the election and afterward. Second, it can become so troubling to constituents that they decide not to vote. Campaign managers often attempt to reduce voter turnout of certain population segments as a strategy to benefit their candidates.

In recent years, a new campaign trick called push polling has been devised. This process involves a contrived telephone polling survey organized by the campaign of one of the candidates. By way of explanation, assume Mr. Brown is the candidate using the push polling tactic, and his opponent is Mr. Johnson. People hired by the Brown campaign make telephone calls to voters in the contested district purporting to represent a political poll. The caller will ask: "In the coming election, do you plan to vote for Mr. Brown or Mr. Johnson?" If the respondent says, "Brown," the caller expresses thanks, terminates the call, and notes for the get-out-the-vote drive that this is a favorable voter. If, however, the respondent is for Johnson, the caller will enter into a conversation, asking such questions as: "Would you still vote for Johnson if you knew that he voted ten times to raise your taxes?" or "that he voted against additional funding for our children's education?" or "that he has missed votes on fifteen key issues?" The questions, whether they contain half-truths, distortions, or even irrelevancies, are effective in sowing the seeds of distrust. Although push polling has been widely condemned, it is still used by unethical candidates.

The political mind is very clever and resourceful. Perhaps this is the reason why election campaigns are replete with dirty tricks that generally involve staged political happenings that are clandestinely hatched and executed. While dirty tricks do not always violate legal strictures, they usually break standards of ethical conduct and human decency. A few examples, steeped in the lore of New Jersey politics, are instructive in understanding this phenomenon.

Back in 1948, Senator Sam Bodine of Hunterdon County was in what many thought would be a close reelection race against Democratic assemblywoman Mildred Preen.[20] Several of Bodine's supporters came into the possession of an interesting hotel receipt, a copy of which they had published as a display ad in the weekly Hunterdon County newspaper of record on the Thursday before the election. The receipt was from the Hildebrecht Hotel in Trenton, showing that Mildred Preen, a single woman, had occupied a room in the hotel for one night several years prior with an "M. Doremus." No explanation was given, but none was necessary to arouse the suspicions of curious Hunterdon County voters. Why was Preen, a Hunterdon resident living so close to Trenton, spending the night in this hotel with an unknown M. Doremus? The timing of the publication five days before the election made it too late in the campaign for any kind of rebuttal. Bodine handily won reelection on the following Tuesday.

The story that ultimately unfolded exonerated Preen of any impropriety or wrongdoing. Early on the night in question, she had left Trenton only to be faced with a fog that was so dense that she turned around and went back to stay at the Hildebrecht. At the hotel, she ran into one of her friends, Miss Mattie Doremus, a lawmaker from Passaic County who was in Trenton for a hearing and who had booked a room that they both shared for the night.

A classic dirty trick was perpetrated in the late 1960s in the run-up to a referendum on the county ballot to approve a harness race track and its sponsoring organization in the Hudson County town of Secaucus.[21] A decaying community at the northern terminus of the New Jersey Turnpike and the site of stockyards for pigs, Secaucus was home to a white lower-middle-class population. In order for the track to win approval, the referendum had to get a majority vote in Secaucus as well as all of Hudson County. There would be no trouble meeting the latter requirement, because Hudson Democratic leaders were connected with the principals of the new track enterprise. Another group, reported to have ties to organized crime, had been turned down in its application to sponsor the new track. This group quietly implemented a plan to defeat the referendum in the hope it could get a second chance to apply for ownership of the proposed race track.

Shortly before the balloting took place, many of the homes in Secaucus were visited by black men who would ask the owners if they had a room to rent. The black visitor would explain that the proposed harness track would mean new jobs he and his friends would be taking, and they planned on moving into town. Secaucus voted down the referendum by a small margin, while Hudson as a county voted in favor by better than four to one. It was reported afterward to a state senate committee that the group opposing the referendum had hired eleven black and Puerto Rican canvassers to "generate a white backlash" among the town's voters to defeat the proposal.[22]

Voter suppression in urban areas is a strategy Republicans sometimes use, surreptitiously of course. Simple math tells us that elections are won not only by those who vote, but also by those who don't—or can't—vote. By reducing turnout of groups of voters with a history of favoring one party, the percentage of the other party's voters will increase, giving them a better chance at the polls. The 1981 contest for governor in New Jersey between Democrat Jim Florio and Republican Tom Kean was hard fought and, according to preelection poll projections, very competitive. The Republican National Committee funded creation of the National Ballot Security Task Force as part of a plan put into effect in New Jersey to reduce voter turnout as much as possible in cities, thereby impairing Florio's chances. It is doubtful that this initiative was carried out with the knowledge and blessing of candidate Kean, whose standards of integrity have always been above reproach.[23]

In Trenton, signs were posted outside polling stations warning of criminal penalties for anyone violating the election laws and declaring: "This Area Is Being Patrolled by the National Ballot Security Task Force." The signs offered a "$1,000 reward for information leading to arrest and conviction of persons violating New Jersey election law" (see figure 7.1). Off-duty police officers still in uniform and task force members with armbands reading "National Ballot Security Task Force" were recruited to be present at city polling places, and word was spread that automobile repossession agents would be on the lookout for cars whose payments were overdue. The atmosphere was definitely intimidating to those urban voters who weren't that enthusiastic about coming to the polls in the first place. Tom Kean won the election by a margin of only 1,797 votes out of 2,317,000 votes cast, an exasperating experience for Democrats.

Data on voting patterns began to show that reforms enacted over the past several decades to make it easier for citizens to vote, particularly

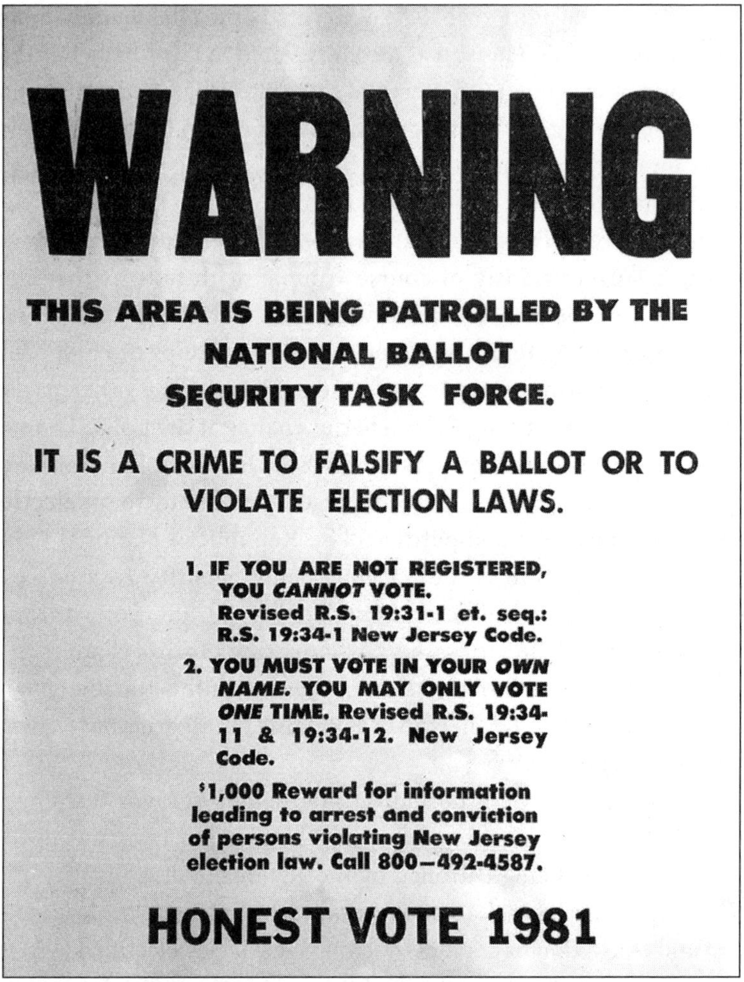

FIGURE 7.1. Poster displayed in New Jersey urban polling stations by the National Ballot Security Task Force in the November 1981 election.

minorities in urban areas, were producing greater success at the polls for Democratic candidates. As reported by the Brennan Center for Justice, less than 4 percent of the public in 2000 participated in early voting before Election Day, and only 10 percent voted by absentee ballot. Eight years later, the number of early voters increased to 18 percent and voting by mail almost doubled to 19 percent of votes cast. Much of this total—more than one-third of the voting public cast their ballots before Election Day, with heavy concentrations in the South and among black voters—was a major contributor to Barack Obama's success in 2008.[24]

The Obama results, along with the 2010 mid-term election success of Republicans at the national level and in state legislatures, combined to spark a new strategy by Republicans across the country who wanted to reverse the trend of "easy" voting by pursuing serious voter suppression efforts. It should come as no surprise that one national group that is actively engaged in promoting restrictions on voting is ALEC, the conservative American Legislative Exchange Council.

Under the Constitution, it is up to the states to regulate elections. Since 2011, many states have introduced—and even passed—legislation making it more difficult to vote based on the rationale that they needed to attack fraud that exists in the electoral process. Among the laws already enacted in a handful of states or currently in legislative hoppers are measures that:

- require voters to show a photo ID before they are allowed in the voting booth. Texas law allows voters to use a concealed weapons ID card but disallows ID cards for students attending state universities;
- require proof of citizenship, such as a birth certificate, in order to register to vote;
- repeal Election Day registration where it exists;
- impose rigorous standards on those who assist in registering voters;
- reduce time periods for early voting. Ohio law eliminated all in-person early voting on Sundays, while Florida canceled voting on the Sunday before an election, a day on which black churches had traditionally rallied members to the polls; and
- impede the process for restoring the voting rights of people who have changed their address and of those who have past felony convictions.

Most observers of the political scene believe that the incidence of voter fraud is grossly overstated by those who are using this strategy. A two-year study begun in 2012 by the Iowa Division of Criminal Investigation of 117 allegedly fraudulent votes cast in the state (where turnout often exceeds one million voters) produced charges against only twenty-seven of the suspects and six criminal convictions.[25]

Although New Jersey is not in the vanguard of the movement to make it more difficult to vote, the concerns that have been raised about it are serious enough for the state to be on guard against imposing any of these voter suppression tactics on the body politic.

The electoral process is critical in determining who has power and who controls government. The many examples outlined in this chapter are clear evidence of the threats posed by political manipulators to undermine the integrity of elections, thereby disrupting the bedrock of our democracy.

# 8 ▸ AGENDA FOR REFORM

$\mathsf{A}$s THE PRECEDING chapters have demonstrated, New Jersey government at every level has been compromised by soft corruption— the use of political subterfuge, nonetheless legal, to achieve government results that work against the public interest. Now that we have a wide-ranging picture of the ethical misconduct, unfair policies, and shady practices that prevent New Jersey government from serving the state more effectively, how can we fix the problem? Upon analyzing the laws, regulations, and traditions that allow this conduct to exist, the specific remedies become fairly obvious. In fact, many reforms have already been advanced in public debate and proposed legislation.

Political reform is not for the faint of heart. Perhaps it would be wise to propose only modest or "safe" recommendations, thereby avoiding con-troversial options that entrenched opponents—the status quo politicians or their backers—would love to seize upon as implausible or draconian in order to discredit an entire reform package. But to be faithful to the true mission of political reform, it is essential to air all options, no mat-ter how unconventional they are or farfetched they might be labeled. This chapter outlines more than forty reforms focused on the areas examined in the previous six chapters: campaign finance, lobbying, conflict of interest, patronage, and the electoral process. Some reforms are fairly easy to implement—such as changing the date for campaign finance reporting or increasing the cooling-off period before state officials can become lobbyists—while others will require a major shift in the way political business is conducted, such as abolishing senatorial courtesy, establishing a full-time senate and assembly, and reducing the power of legislative leadership committees. But all of them deserve consideration as part of a concerted effort to restore the public's faith in New Jersey government.

## CAMPAIGN FINANCE

The largest and most profound issue crying out for reform is the harmful effect of the inordinate amount of political money that pours into the system. More than a decade ago, Robert Byrd of West Virginia, the dean of the U.S. Senate, shouted on the Senate floor: "It is money, money, money! Not ideas, not principles, but money that reigns supreme in American politics."[1] Conditions have only grown worse in the intervening years. In fact, they have grown worse, not only at the national level but also within states such as New Jersey.

The number-one villain causing outrageous sums of money to be spent on influencing election outcomes—initially at the federal level but increasingly in state elections as well—is *Citizens United*, the 2010 U.S. Supreme Court decision that allows corporations, unions, and nonprofit organizations to make unlimited expenditures and disseminate electioneering communications as long as they are not coordinated with a specific political campaign. It is noteworthy that the decision also reaffirmed the authority of government to limit direct contributions to candidates and political committees.

The United States Court of Appeals for the District of Columbia Circuit subsequently ruled, in *SpeechNow.org v. Federal Election Commission*, that it would also be unconstitutional to limit contributions by individuals to groups that make independent expenditures in campaigns.[2] Contributions in unlimited amounts, largely from unidentified donors, are collected by an array of newly spawned super PACs to fund these political expenditures.[3] As noted in chapter 2, the volume of independent expenditures has become concentrated in the hands of a very small minority of wealthy individuals.

While the initial impact of *Citizens United* consisted of an explosion of independent political spending in federal election campaigns, recent trends show a similar growth in state elections. In New Jersey's 2013 election, independent groups spent more than $41 million on independent expenditures, a 275 percent increase over 2009.

The U.S. Supreme Court handed down another ruling on April 2, 2014, that exacerbates the surfeit of campaign money entering the American electoral scene. This ruling, *McCutcheon v. Federal Election Commission*, struck down aggregate limits of direct contributions for federal elections.[4] This means that total direct campaign contributions made in a two-year election cycle by a single source to all candidates for federal office are no longer subject to an aggregate limit of $46,200; similarly, direct contributions to all PACs and party committees involved in federal elections do not have to be limited to $70,800 in the aggregate. This ruling does not change the existing caps on individual contributions made directly: $2,600 per election to a single candidate; $5,000 per year to a PAC; and $32,400 to a national party committee. The *McCutcheon* decision simply ruled that the contributor can now give up to these maximum amounts directly to as many candidates and party committees as desired. The Center for Public Integrity conjectured that similar types of limits on aggregate contributions in eight states and the District of Columbia will probably be overturned as a result of *McCutcheon*.[5] While New Jersey does not have similar laws limiting aggregate contributions to candidates and parties, any thought of enacting such laws as a reform for excessive campaign spending will have to be abandoned.

The recommendations that follow address measures New Jersey can take to mitigate the corruptive effects that campaign money can have on government and the political system.

1. There must be full and timely disclosure of the source of funds and expenses of super PACs and other entities that make independent expenditures in the state's election campaigns.

While it is not now possible under *Citizens United* to limit donations for such expenditures or to make them subject to pay-to-play regulations, the state can take measures to require disclosing their sources, thereby providing the general public with the background information it needs in order to make voting decisions. New Jersey should enact laws immediately requiring super PACs to register with ELEC and make full disclosure of both sources and expenditures.

A 2014 California law supported by a coalition of good-government groups may provide a model; the law requires nonprofit super PACs to disclose the names of donors who give more than $1,000 for political activity in the state if the PAC spends more than $50,000 in any one year or $100,000 in four years.[6]

More important, in an effort to mitigate the damage done by the decision, the problems created by *Citizens United* should be addressed at the federal level. One proposal would require the Securities and Exchange Commission to impose a system for listed corporations to obtain stockholder approval and identify their CEOs by name when they make contributions to super PACs. Another proposal would require full public disclosure to the Federal Election Commission of all contributions and expenditures made to and by super PACs, the same as recommended above for disclosure at the New Jersey state level.

Some have advanced a strategy that borders on heresy: to amend the U.S. Constitution's First Amendment provision of free speech by establishing that campaign money, in its totality, is not just speech. A proposed amendment by U.S. senator Tom Udall of New Mexico that would establish the authority of Congress and the states to regulate and limit how money for elections is raised and spent has gained traction in the nation's capital. As improbable as such a constitutional upheaval may seem, by mid-2014, forty-one U.S. senators, 123 U.S. representatives, and more than 1,700 state legislators favored such an amendment. So did sixteen states, which called for this constitutional amendment by ballot referenda, legislative resolution, or letters signed by a majority of their legislators. After the House of Representatives passed a resolution approving the constitutional amendment, the Senate came up short on its vote in September 2014. But as described by Meredith McGehee, policy director of the Campaign Legal Center, "the Senate's consideration and debate provided an avenue to keep people who are appalled by the current campaign finance system energized and engaged."[7]

Senator Udall's amendment would reject the Supreme Court's position that campaign finance regulation can only be justified to prevent quid pro quo corruption. Rather, other campaign finance regulatory objectives are vital to the public interest, such as advancing "the fundamental principle of political equality for all" and assuring the integrity of the electoral process. The changes recommended by Udall, moreover, could in no way be used to restrict freedom of the press.

2.  Public financing programs for legislators, county executives, and even big-city mayors should be developed and put into effect.[8]

Government dollars can either fully fund these contests or can be used as a match against private donations. Admission into publicly funded campaigns would be voluntary and would require a minimum number of small contributions to the campaign as a threshold to qualify. Public financing should apply to primary elections as well as to the general election, because meaningful access to the primary offers the most strategic avenue for aspiring candidates to advance up the political ladder. Public financing should also be instituted for elections to fill vacancies in offices for which this reform is adopted.

In recent years, Maine, Arizona, and Connecticut have adopted public financing for candidates running for the legislature or for statewide office such as governor and, where applicable, secretary of state, attorney general, and so forth. New Jersey implemented public financing for gubernatorial candidates in 1977, a program that has been largely successful in removing special interest direct contributions from dominating these contests. For almost twenty-five years the Campaign Finance Board of New York City has administered a comprehensive and highly regarded public financing program covering all city elected officials.

The benefits of publicly financed elections are many. Most important, they mitigate the corrupting influence, perceived and real, associated with contributions of special interest money. Other advantages include enforced spending limits on candidates who accept public funds, and a requirement that participating candidates engage in debates.

Of special significance is that candidates are freed from the inordinately time-consuming demands of raising funds and therefore can spend more time working on issues and programs vital to their constituents. This obligation to raise funds is assumed not only by candidates but also by incumbent lawmakers. A stark example was provided in a speech by former Federal Election Commission chairman Trevor Potter, who said that in 2012, incoming Democratic members of Congress were directed that 40 percent of their work time should be allocated to making fund-raising telephone calls.[9]

Some public finance programs that use the matching fund system limit, or even prohibit, contributions from certain classes of donors such as corporations, PACs, and professional service providers. Connecticut has an outright ban on contributions from lobbyists and their spouses. New Jersey reformers might take note that New York City has recently adopted many creative features in its laws that level the playing field for all candidates:[10]

- The threshold contributions that city council candidates receive to qualify for public financing must come from at least seventy-five residents of their district.
- While the contribution limit from a single donor source to a council candidate is $2,750, only the first $175 of the contribution is eligible for the match, which is $6 of public funds for each dollar contributed (for example, a contribution of $175 will fetch $1,050 in public money). Since there is no match for a contribution's excess over $175, there is not as great an incentive to seek funds from "fat-cat" contributors.
- If candidate A chooses not to accept public funds and spends more than the limit of $168,000 allowed to be spent by candidate B, a publicly financed city council candidate, the Campaign Finance

Board can provide "rescue" money by permitting candidate B to raise and spend over the $168,000 limit.

- Contribution and spending limits for the New York City offices of mayor and borough president are substantially higher, but the maximum match of six-to-one in public funds for the first $175 of a contribution applies to all offices.
- Credit card contributions made over the Internet are allowed, thereby encouraging more and easier participation by donors.

Many of these features were applied in the New York City 2009 election and yielded an increase in the percentage of small donors, a reduction of special interest money from businesses and developers, and greater competition among candidates in many districts. Insurgent candidates defeated five incumbent city council members, the greatest turnover in a generation.[11]

Former California congressman, Clinton chief of staff, and CIA director Leon Panetta offered strong words about the evils of campaign fund raising by elected officials when he said in 2007: "If you're not independently wealthy, you're a person who has to sell your soul to a lot of interests so you can raise the money you need to run a campaign. . . . We're not going to get back to getting the kind of people we want in politics unless we break this addiction to money. It's all about winning, it's not about governing anymore. If all you care about is winning, you're not going to care about solving problems."[12]

3.  Contribution limits from all sources to all candidates and political organizations should be reduced.

Table 2.1 illustrates how high these limits are, and they are constantly inching higher due to indexing with cost-of-living increases. Reducing contribution limits will lower the political arms race. Present maximum contribution limits in the major categories are:

a)  $2,600 to individual candidates,
b)  $7,200 to continuing political committees (PACs) and to municipal party committees,
c)  $8,200 to candidate committees,

d) $25,000 to legislative leadership and state party committees, and

e) $37,000 to county party committees.

These limits are more than adequate to finance campaigns, even ones that are hotly contested.

More egregious is the concentration of power in the partisan political committees (d and e), which, after building up huge treasuries, can make unlimited contributions among themselves and to all entities. It would be reasonable to cut contribution limits to legislative leadership and party committees in half. Just as important, low limits must be established on currently unlimited contributions from these committees (d and e) to candidates and other party committees, particularly to ones that are out-of-district.

As a corollary, the contribution limits to candidates for lower-level offices (municipal and school board) should be steeply reduced. Clearly, candidates running for town council or school board in a constituency of several thousand residents do not need the same financial resources from the $2,600 denomination contribution as legislative or freeholder candidates running in districts of more than two hundred thousand. The U.S. Supreme Court validated this concept when it upheld a Missouri law that set limits for local candidates at 25 percent of the amount permitted for those running for state office.[13]

Implementation of any initiative to reduce campaign contribution limits for all categories must be balanced so that the legitimate interests of all the political players are harmonized.

There are some who advocate major increases in contribution limits to political parties as a way of offsetting the tremendous inflow of campaign money from *Citizens United*. Because these contributions are direct, moreover, they are fully reportable under New Jersey law. This position asserts that political parties have an established legal responsibility for financing election campaigns and therefore will provide more transparency and accountability than the super PACs created by *Citizens United*. A more convincing argument against this proposal reasons that no amount of private direct contributions will come close to competing financially with money pouring in from super PACs. Such a move would only give greater power to the present small group of institutionalized campaign financiers who are accustomed to giving—and receiving credit for—direct contributions.

4. The power of legislative leadership committees should be reduced.

As explained in chapter 3, these are not really committees, but rather single-member PACs that give the individual leader of each major party in each house tremendous power to control the legislative agenda. This power is magnified by the ease with which leaders can raise funds from special interests and lobbies who wish to influence legislative outcomes. Able to collect up to $25,000 from any source and to give unlimited amounts to political committees and candidates—a cash stream not permitted to minor parties— these leaders can provide generous financial help to the campaigns of colleagues, thereby gaining their loyalty and automatic support on future legislative matters.

It has been advanced in other campaign finance reform recommendations that contributions from leadership PACs to candidates and political committees be significantly lowered, which would have the collateral benefit of reducing the wheeling of money from leadership PACs to campaigns around the state. In order to further diffuse the exercise of so much unilateral power by the legislators who operate leadership PACs, these entities should be converted into genuine committees under the control of at least four members of each caucus. This change would be in concert with the recommendations of the Rosenthal Commission of 1993 and would give individual senators and assembly members, working through their caucus, greater influence in shaping policy and developing legislative initiatives.

5. Wheeling large sums of money from the treasuries of affluent candidates and party committees to benefit candidates in other districts should be curtailed.

New Jersey has recognized that wheeling distorts the electoral process and gives inordinate power to a few political entrepreneurs. The legislature was pushed into action against this practice in 2004, but in halfhearted fashion when it restricted wheeling only between county political parties and only in primaries. As part of the process of reducing campaign contributions across the board, substantially lower limits should apply to the allowable amounts transferred (wheeled) from individuals, candidate committees, and PACs to political committees and candidates in other jurisdictions. Low limits should also be imposed on transfers from legislative leadership and political party committees where there presently are no limits whatsoever on wheeling campaign funds (see also number 3 above).

6. Loopholes in the pay-to-play laws must be closed.

Under New Jersey pay-to-play restrictions, vendors who contract to sell products, provide services, or engage in construction or redevelopment projects with the state are prohibited from contributing more than $300 per year to various political entities if their government contract exceeds $17,500 in value.[14] The most important pay-to-play reform would be to establish a state-administered system that applies rules uniformly to county and municipal vendor contracts in the same manner as for state contracts.

Under present conditions, pay-to-play rules for vendors of local government contracts do not apply if the contracts are made under a "fair and open" bidding process. But the standards for "fair and open" are so lax that local governments using this bidding process can effectively avoid pay-to-play restrictions. Under a statewide system, this process should be abolished and replaced with true competitive bidding that meets the requirements of state pay-to-play regulations.

All service contracts for attorneys, engineers, planning consultants, and other professionals should be subject to pay-to-play and competitively bid under prescribed standards in an open process.

Vendors subject to pay-to-play strictures are not prohibited from contributing to candidates (except governor) or to PACs. Those vendors with government contracts exceeding $50,000 are required to file their campaign finance data with ELEC. This requirement gives regulators and the public an opportunity to see if vendor contributions to candidates and PACs have any correlation to contracts that are awarded subsequently. Laws and procedures protecting against donations to PACs used to circumvent pay-to-play should be developed and implemented to the maximum extent possible. To further this end, the state should reduce the $50,000 contract value threshold for reporting under anti-pay-to-play rules to the present $17,500 threshold reporting figure for pay-to-play.

7. Direct corporate and union contributions to campaigns should be prohibited.

This prohibition already exists for federal candidates, and a majority of states do not allow corporations to make campaign donations.

This stipulation, first recommended by the Election Law Enforcement Commission in 1988,[15] will help facilitate pay-to-play enforcement while permitting corporations and unions to use more strictly regulated PACs for collecting and dispensing contributions. New Jersey now bans direct contributions from regulated industries, such as banks, insurance companies, and utilities. It would make just as much sense to extend the prohibition to other corporations that are subject to state regulation on matters involving environment, public health and safety, workplace standards, and more.

8. Bundling contributions should be limited to donors who give of their own volition and their own resources.

When partners of a professional firm amass a large bundle of funds to give to a campaign, the donation, in reality, is from the firm. But it is split into partnership attribution shares in order to take advantage of individual contribution limits. This practice should be disallowed when it is used as a dodge to increase the contribution limit of a firm. A donation attributable to partner B from a firm which is under the control of partner A is really a donation from A, and should be treated as such. New York City law prohibits bundled contributions if the firm is under the control of single partner, and has been able to determine when such a condition exists. New Jersey should do likewise.

9. Funds in a candidate's election campaign account should be used only for campaign and political purposes, not for extraneous or personal expenses.

The *Star-Ledger* has reported a steady stream of inappropriate use of campaign funds by New Jersey lawmakers. Among the major abuses are:

- $250,000 in miscellaneous expenses racked up on credit cards belonging to Essex County executive Joe DiVincenzo, including two dozen rounds of golf and travel expenses to Puerto Rico with political friends over Super Bowl weekend, all reimbursed from the DiVincenzo campaign account;
- gifts of watches valued at more than $14,000 given to political colleagues and staffers by Senate President Stephen Sweeney;
- $21,000 in unspecified credit card expenses picked up by the campaign account of Senator Diane Allen; and
- payment of $9,000 for a trip to Scotland for Congressman Rob Andrews and his family to attend the wedding of the daughter of one of his donors—an amount Andrews repaid from personal funds after a congressional ethics investigation was launched.[16]

The explanation DiVincenzo gave for using campaign funds, much of which were raised from county vendors, for junkets and personal expenses contained the logic that there are no taxpayer consequences: "I have used these funds to carry out the duties as an elected official so that taxpayers are not burdened with these expenses," DiVincenzo said.[17] This logic was reinforced when his political ally, Governor Christie, chimed in: "From my perspective, I think you'd much rather have donors paying for these kinds of things than having vendors pay"—as if donors and vendors don't give from the same pocket!

New Jersey law is not totally clear regarding limits on campaign money spent by a candidate. Expenses paid by campaign funds for dinners during which government-related business is conducted are legitimate. The same applies to car and travel expenses. Lawmakers incur many other expenses that are necessary and ordinary to their function of holding public office, such as tickets to political and civic events, flowers for funerals, program ads supporting local charities, sponsorship of community activities, and similar miscellany. Some of the political sages used to call this "walking-around money." But expenditures cross the line when they are wholly unrelated to holding public office. The DiVincenzo record showed that his campaign money paid for gym membership, bicycle repair, tickets to sporting events, and more. Because the present system of personal expenses is subject to abuse, precise legal limits should be established on the amounts and purposes of such public office-related expenditures. The Election Law Enforcement Commission should ensure that record keeping by candidates and political committees conforms with these high standards. Credit card use should conform to the same detailed restrictions and disclosure requirements.

It is further recommended that campaign accounts be terminated once an elected official leaves office and has not declared an intention to seek office in the future. The purpose of this recommendation is to avoid clearly unreasonable situations such as that of former sheriff, Essex County executive, and Democratic Party chair Thomas D'Alessio. D'Alessio vacated his office in 1994 to serve a term in federal prison for money laundering and bribery—making him ineligible for elected office.[18] After being released on parole in 1998 and with his campaign account still intact, D'Alessio used $1.3 million of the unspent funds to set up the Evergreen Fund Foundation for the stated purpose of making charitable gifts to youth organizations. The fund paid D'Alessio more than $65,000 in annual salary, plus expenses for leasing a luxury automobile.

Another example of inappropriate use of leftover campaign funds involved Donald DiFrancesco a full year after he had left the joint offices of senator and acting governor. When bowing out of the race for governor in April 2001, he stated: "I will never run for another office. Never."[19] But DiFrancesco kept his campaign account open, even after leaving office. He then quietly accepted two campaign contributions from members of the CME Associates PAC totaling $14,000, and three days later, contributed the same amount to the accounts of two Republicans running for the Sayreville municipal government. CME Associates is retained as the municipal engineer for Sayreville, and was paid $1.3 million in fees in 2002 by the municipality.[20]

Present law allows a former public official the same use of leftover campaign funds as an officeholder who continues to serve. This should be changed so that the former officeholder, after paying off campaign debts, can return leftover funds only to contributors, political entities in limited amounts, or charitable organizations where no benefits can accrue to the former candidate or his or her relatives. After leaving office, there should be a time limit of ninety days for closing out the campaign account.

10. PACs should be subject to regulations designed to achieve greater accountability and transparency.

At present, PACs are little more than paper organizations involving as few as two individuals. These entities, generally associated with a special interest, solicit funds and make campaign contributions to candidates and political committees. They operate outside the jurisdiction of pay-to-play regulations.

A major scandal broke in 2012 in Middlesex County linking contributions from government contractors, primarily engineering firms, to a select group of PACs with feel-good names such as Democracy in Motion, Coalition for Government Efficiency, Women for Good Government, and New Expectations. These PACs would then make sizable contributions to municipal candidates and party organizations and *voilà*, the original contributing organization—the engineering firm—would be hired under professional service contracts by the local officials who had received the PAC money. No pay-to-play laws were broken.

The Middlesex County Improvement Authority (MCIA) also participated in this system of rewarding vendors who channeled campaign contributions through PACs to local candidates and party organizations. The MCIA effort was facilitated by its executive director, Richard Pucci, who also was serving as mayor of Monroe Township in Middlesex and chaired the local Democratic Committee. MCIA contractors, through this select group of PACs, made indirect contributions to Pucci's campaigns for mayor of $48,000 in 2007 and $67,000 in 2011. Vendors that took part in this political financing process received more than $8.3 million in contracts for services from MCIA in the five years following 2007.[21]

This circumvention of pay-to-play was perfectly legal as long as there was no collusion between the contributing vendor and the government contracting entity. But there didn't have to be collusion, because all the players understood how the system works and where the money was supposed to end up. In order to prevent PACs from being mere conduits for special interest money, the following recommendations (introduced in a prior legislative session by Assemblyman Joe Cryan) are made to reform PACs and to discourage their proliferation:

- There should be a minimum number of principals in order to form a PAC. Nine principals are required for a federal PAC.
- PAC principals must make full disclosure of any other PAC or political affiliation with which they are associated.
- Principals must certify their understanding of and compliance with the basic requirements of New Jersey's campaign finance laws, including the stipulation that to conspire to circumvent these laws is a violation.
- PACs should file a statement of purpose in accordance with specific guidelines that would be subject to approval by ELEC.

Federal law regulating the formation of a multicandidate PAC, where the purpose of the committee is to assist in funding multiple candidates, offers a good guide for reforming the structure of New Jersey PACs. Under the federal system, a multicandidate committee must have at least fifty contributors, be registered with the Federal Election Commission for at least six months, and contribute to five or more candidates for federal office.[22]

11. Campaign finance reporting should start earlier than the present twenty-nine days preceding an election.

An earlier candidate report should be required, due sixty days before the election, to give the public more time to analyze and pass judgment on a candidate's financial sources.

12. Rules regulating campaign contributions from casinos should be tightened.

New Jersey law prohibits candidates running for any office in the state from receiving contributions from casinos, a reflection of the notion that undesirable elements often associated with gambling might try to corrupt lawmakers by contributing to their campaigns. This prohibition does not apply to candidates for Congress, who are subject to federal law. However, there have been instances when incumbent New Jersey elected officials have been candidates for Congress and have accepted casino money for such contests. In 1994, when State Senator William Gormley and Assembly Speaker Chuck Haytaian each waged unsuccessful bids for congressional office, they received nearly $100,000 in casino campaign contributions. Both sponsored legislation, which passed in the ensuing session, to lighten regulations on casinos.[23] The prohibition of casino campaign contributions to any person who holds a New Jersey public office must apply to everyone, regardless whether the person might also be running as a candidate for federal office.

13. Candidates running for certain political party office should be subject to the same campaign finance regulations as candidates for public office.

Although usually of short duration and seldom involving the expenditure of significant sums of money, the campaigns of individuals for party office are often hotly contested. There is the most competition for chairs of county party committees, and securing the support of county committee members to get elected in these contests is generally done through personal contact.

Nevertheless, should the situation arise where a candidate for party office spends substantial funds, either from personal resources or from donations, party members and the public have a right to know the financial underpinnings of this candidate who aspires to a political leadership position. In California, a candidate for election to a county central committee of a qualified political party must file a disclosure statement if the candidate receives or spends more than $1,000.[24]

Some would argue that applying campaign finance restrictions to persons seeking party office might not pass constitutional muster because associational rights of a private organization (for example, a political party entity) are protected as a First Amendment right and cannot be proscribed, as articulated in the Supreme Court's *Eu* decision in 1989. Yet since these elections are mandated by statute, it is reasonable to apply financial strictures to the election of party leaders. Besides, county committees as legal entities are not political clubs. In the interest of removing the corrupting influence of excessive money in the political process, therefore, it would be prudent for the legislature to approve this recommendation and let the courts make further rulings as to the constitutionality of such a change.

As with procedures for regular candidates, no reporting would be required in the election of county chairs unless expenditures exceed $2,000 or if any single contribution to such a campaign is more than $300. It is conceivable that an aspiring candidate for chair of a county party could reach these thresholds by engaging consultants, developing sophisticated electronic communication programs, and holding lavish receptions.[25]

A similar situation exists in the case of conventions held by law to fill vacancies in legislative and county offices. If money is spent over the minimal thresholds for the benefit of candidates to fill such a vacancy, this should also be made subject to reporting in accordance with campaign finance laws.

14. The terms of the four Election Law Enforcement Commission (ELEC) members should be lengthened from three to five years, and the ELEC chair should not be subject to removal by the governor once he or she is appointed unless the chair is guilty of malfeasance as determined by a judicial finding.

In addition, holdover status for any commissioner whose term has expired without being reappointed or without filling the seat with a replacement should be limited to ninety days, after which the commissioner is automatically reinstated to a full term. It is important to have dedicated and knowledgeable public servants who have a sense of security in their positions. A greater degree of longevity will add to the stability and integrity of the commission, thereby encouraging the independence of thought and action so necessary to carrying out the mission of ELEC. Every effort should be expended to maintain an adequate level of funding for ELEC so it can operate and enforce New Jersey's campaign finance regulatory system effectively.

## LOBBYING

It has been shown that special interests, often under the guidance or through the instrument of lobbyists, exploit the campaign contribution system as a way of gaining influence over governmental decisions. To the extent that campaign financing is reformed as proposed by the recommendations in the previous section, the behavior and conduct of lobbyists will also be reformed. Lobbyists have a legitimate role to play in the process of governing; it is in the public interest, therefore, that the state ensure maximum transparency, accountability, and integrity in their operations.

1. There should be comprehensive disclosure of lobbyists' involvement in raising campaign funds for candidates and political organizations.

   Contributions collected by a lobbyist from the lobbyist's clients that go to candidates and parties (such as legalized bundling) should be fully disclosed and recorded. Expenditures, including the in-kind variety incurred in organizing and sponsoring fund-raising events, should also be reported and the lobbyist's name should appear clearly on promotional materials.

2. Activities of registered lobbying firms hired by clients for public relations and general consulting services not related to legislation or administrative decision making should be subject to full disclosure in lobbyist reports.

   These relationships create spheres of indirect influence over government functions.

3. The same regulatory framework that applies to lobbying state agencies and officials should be imposed when lobbyists are hired to influence local government decisions.

   Local programs, over which there are now no lobbying strictures, can be just as vital to a special interest as state programs.

4. By the same token, lobbying engaged in by any government entity— municipal, county, state, or independent authority—should be subject to full financial disclosure and reporting.

Local governments and independent agencies are not now required to disclose what they spend for lobbying (although these expenditures when made for lobbying the state are included in the financial reports filed by the lobbyists involved).[26] Clearly, when the Passaic Valley Sewerage Commission or the City of Newark hires lobbyists to use their power and influence to get results in Trenton, Washington, or with any public agency, this practice applies the same influences on public officials as similar lobbying on state matters. All such activity should be fully disclosed, along with justification for hiring a lobbyist. Normally, such agencies would use their legislative representatives to intercede with other levels of government, so hiring a lobbyist can be perceived as excessive.

5. The cooling-off period for former state officials and legislators after leaving office and before becoming lobbyists should be extended from one to two years.

Many other states and the U.S. Congress have a two-year cooling-off period. This discourages the revolving-door syndrome where present lawmakers get too cozy with potential clients if they have only one year to wait before joining a lobbying firm.

6. Financial reporting by lobbyists, now done annually, should be combined with lobby representation reports, which are compiled quarterly.

This joint data will give the public and regulators a more timely picture of all aspects of lobbying.

7. The maximum fine of $1,000 for violating the lobby laws should be increased to a more meaningful $10,000.

The current maximum is at best a slap on the wrist; a $10,000 fine would be much more likely to change behavior.

## CONFLICT OF INTEREST

Nothing is more important to the citizens of a representative democracy than to have lawmakers governing them who are guided by the highest standards of honesty and integrity. New Jersey has adopted three general categories of conflict-of-interest regulatory schemes to implement this goal: full disclosure by public officials of financial and business interests; a comprehensive list of do's and don'ts covering the activities of these officials; and strong enforcement mechanisms to ensure compliance with the law.

But the record clearly shows that New Jersey's conflict of interest laws need to be improved. They are not uniformly administered and enforced throughout all government levels, and lawmakers are still not disposed to regulate some practices.

1.  The task of administering ethics laws and regulations should be consolidated for full-time and part-time public employees at all levels of government—state, county, municipal, school board, independent authorities—under one governing body, the State Ethics Commission (SEC).

    This would allow the state to apply uniform standards to ethics training, nepotism, financial disclosure (including for family members), gift bans, and ethics enforcement for officials in every governmental agency of the state.

2.  The SEC should be reconstituted and reformed.

    Members appointed to the SEC must have records of impeccable integrity and independence. To accomplish this, several changes are recommended in the appointment of SEC commissioners by the governor. The present provision that three members are selected from the executive branch of state government should be removed; all members should be from the general public. It is further recommended that a special task force of retired judges be empowered to recruit, interview, and submit a pool of highly qualified citizens with proven records of independence as nominees for the SEC. How the SEC is to be reconstituted should be contained in enabling legislation and should include specific provisions regarding such matters as the composition and tenure of the judicial panel, the terms of commission members, their political affiliations, and the filling of vacancies.

    The governor will then select from the pool of those nominated by the judicial panel to go before the state senate for confirmation.

This process should allay any concerns about interference by the executive branch in attempting to influence decisions by the SEC and dictating whom it should pick as executive director.[27]

3. The Joint Legislative Committee on Ethical Standards should change its method of selecting members in order to become a more effective enforcement unit.

Although the change in 2008 to remove sitting legislators from serving on this committee was beneficial, the power to appoint the eight public members still resides in the hands of legislative leaders of both houses. Experience has shown that this system leads to the appointment of political allies who are reluctant to rule harshly against legislators charged with ethics violations. Instead, the power of appointment should be given to a nonpartisan, independent panel. One suggestion is to have a committee of retired judges (as proposed in SEC recommendation 2 above) who would follow guidelines regarding the experience and qualifications for the appointments they are required to make.

It must be noted, of course, that the New Jersey constitution provides that each house of the legislature shall be the judge of the qualifications of its members. Absent a constitutional change, therefore, it is likely that the separate Joint Legislative Committee will continue to administer ethics standards for legislators.

4. Holding more than one elected or appointed government office should be prohibited, with minor exceptions.

The grandfather provision in the present law allowing officials in two elected positions to continue in their positions should be rescinded so that, hereafter, no elected official is able to hold another elective office. Present holders of two elected offices would have to give up one of their positions the next time they are up for election to either.

After study and analysis, legislative standards should be adopted that define specific categories of appointive office that pose a conflict of interest and cannot be filled as a second job by an elected official. An exception, for example, might be for teachers, who present no conflict if they also serve in most other government positions. It is recommended that a panel—or the SEC—be empowered to pass judgment on situations when established legal standards for dual office holding are in dispute.

Appointed professional service positions in governments and their agencies (lawyers, engineers, consultants) should be classified as offices that fall under dual office holding rules and should not be filled by anyone who holds elected office unless specifically exempted by standards in the law.

5. Attorneys who serve in elective office should be barred from representing clients before local government agencies in their district.

The same restriction should apply to other professions such as engineering and planning consultants. Rules should be promulgated for permissible representation of clients before boards outside of the lawmaker's district.

6. Personal financial disclosure requirements for lawmakers who, in private life, are professional service providers should be expanded to identify clients who pay them or their firm more than $10,000 in yearly fees.

This would apply only to clients whose interests are in the public domain and can be affected by government actions. It would not apply, for example, to legal services in divorce cases and similar nongovernmental matters.

When questions arise regarding this requirement, it would be reasonable to submit them to a review agency such as the SEC to determine, in accordance with specific standards, whether the client's identity should be publicly disclosed.

A case in point is Washington State, which has a law requiring legislators to disclose any business or government client who pays $7,500 or more per year to a lawyer/legislator or to the firm where the legislator serves as a principal.[28]

7. The ultimate reform for addressing legislative conflicts of interest is to have a full-time senate and assembly, and to pay members a full-time salary.

As with members of Congress and the New Jersey judiciary, legislators would be barred from holding other jobs. Reforms such as eliminating dual office holding and prohibiting representation of private clients before government agencies would be moot.

Opponents of a full-time legislature claim that the state benefits from the diversity of the present system, which they call a "citizens' legislature." But does New Jersey really have a citizens' legislature? A 2015 demographic profile conducted by Stockton University concluded, "The New Jersey State Legislature does not resemble the statewide constituency it represents" with respect to age, education, ethnicity, gender, occupation, and other attributes.[29]

It seems, moreover, that the principal qualification for gaining membership to the legislature is political acumen and loyalty. No, the legislature is populated by fully committed politicians, not by citizens whose nonlegislative pursuits are significant factors in their livelihoods.

Another objection to full-time legislative service is that it would cost more to pay its members higher salaries. The logical answer to this objection is to take the draconian step of reducing the number of legislative districts. A 25 percent reduction would mean thirty senators and sixty assembly members. A 50 percent reduction would mean twenty and forty. After all, if full-time legislators would be spending 100 percent of their working hours on government matters, it is reasonable to expect them to cover more territory and serve more constituents than they do now. The state of California is like New Jersey in that it has forty state senators with eighty assembly members.[30] California has a population of more than 38 million people, about four and one-half times that of New Jersey. Also, legislators in California serve full-time; they cannot have secondary employment, thereby reducing the potential for conflicts of interest. And with salaries of $95,000 per year plus $142 per diem for legislative days, the California legislator is well paid.

Clearly, individual California legislators have more constituents and greater governmental management responsibilities than their counterparts in the Garden State. These conditions serve to refute naysayers' argument that the proposition of a full-time New Jersey legislature with half its present members, paid appropriate salaries, is an unreasonable fantasy.

8. Procedures governing open public meetings and open public records must be reformed to provide timely and relevant information to the citizens of the state.

   The promise of the Open Public Meetings Act, which declares "the right of the public to be present at all meetings of public bodies, and to witness in full detail all phases of the deliberation, policy formulation, and decision making of public bodies,"[31] is not being fulfilled. Subcommittee and task force meetings should be open to the public; the records of executive sessions of government bodies need to be accessible under reasonable conditions so that the public can inspect all pertinent data on a timely basis. The Government Records Council, which administers open meetings and open records, should be placed under control of the State Ethics Commission.

   Enforcement of open government laws should be strengthened by increasing the $100–$500 penalties for violations by as much as tenfold and by adding negligence to the present "knowing and willful" reasons for prosecution.

## PATRONAGE

Patronage is more than doling out jobs. In its broader sense, patronage involves awarding government benefits ranging from vendor contracts to program approvals to individual perks and everything in between. Too often in New Jersey, these awards are made to secure political power or to reap financial gain, and they are not in the public interest.

Patronage abuse thrives when government decisions are cloaked in secrecy. As with problems of conflicts of interest, recommendations for greater transparency and accountability through full and timely disclosure will do much to reform the patronage excesses that now exist.

1. The practice of senatorial courtesy should be outlawed by a constitutional amendment requiring that all nominations by the governor subject to advice and consent of the senate be submitted to the full

senate for a vote within ninety days unless rejected in the interim at a duly held—and public—senate committee meeting.

Senatorial courtesy is the most egregious of patronage and appointment abuses. It is a blackball system for which there is no justification or redeeming value.

Once the constitution is changed by this amendment, senators who wish to object to a nominee can argue and vote against the nominee's appointment based on his or her qualifications. If a proposed appointment has serious shortcomings, it is not unreasonable to expect a senator or senators to make the case for rejection to the Judiciary Committee or on the senate floor.

Under this proposal, senators can still join together to vote against a nominee for purely political reasons. But they must do so in open session as intended under the advice and consent clause of the state constitution. This change will do much to elevate the caliber of gubernatorial nominees while reducing the obscene bartering that some senators use through the mechanism of senatorial courtesy.[32]

2.  Rigorous disclosure of all activities of independent authorities should be required by law and enforced by the department in the executive branch that has jurisdiction.

    Specifically, budgets and vendor contracts need the scrutiny of independent audits. Personnel records showing employee work history, salaries, and hiring referrals require full public exposure. If these reforms had been enacted and enforced, incidents such as the $100,000 in hidden incentive bonuses and allowances paid yearly to the top executives of the Middlesex County Utilities Authority might have been avoided.[33]

3.  Commission sharing of government payments for vendor contracts by brokers should be disallowed, or at least regulated by the state's bidding laws.

    This issue came to light when the state comptroller investigated the finances of the Delaware River Port Authority (DRPA), which admitted it paid $410,000 to the Norcross insurance brokerage firm for the simple chore of steering a DRPA insurance contract to a favored underwriter.[34] In the state of New York, for example, a law requires full disclosure of commission sharing and the work that is performed to justify such payment.

4.  All possible steps should be taken to prohibit pension abuse where public employees collecting a pension for past government service also receive a paycheck for another full-time government job.

    Although contractual provisions governing public employees and pension rights under present law allow for this arrangement, it is recommended that the practice be sharply curtailed for new hires entering the state's pension system. A reasonable proposal offered by Senator Jennifer Beck stipulates that a retired person earning a pension would have to forgo the pension if he or she accepts a new public service job that pays more than $15,000 per year; the pension benefits would resume once he or she leaves the higher-paying job.[35]

    Pension reform that prevents public employees from gaming the system would create substantial savings for taxpayers. The process is legally complex and has many stakeholders. In order to achieve the most balanced and equitable reform program that has the support of the public as well as lawmakers, it would be prudent to establish a high-level task force to review all aspects of pensions and make recommendations, ensuring that the pension system properly serves in providing income for retirees and does not become an all-you-can-eat buffet for political manipulators.

5.  Legal measures should be taken to abolish pay for unused vacation and sick days.

    While there is justification for compensating a public employee who misses work due to sickness, it's hard to justify banking unused sick days for a payout when the official retires. The obvious reward for not being sick is being healthy. The same recommendation applies to unused vacation days in excess of a nominal yearly amount of perhaps fifteen. Reform clearly calls for abolishing pay for unused vacation and sick days for new hires and reducing past accumulations of these perks. But as with pensions, reforms will not be easy because of the contractual arrangements that apply to these benefits. Again, commissioning a blue-ribbon panel would be helpful in studying and developing a reasonable program to abolish these insults to responsible government.

6.  The Citizens Service Act, which encourages the appointment of citizen volunteers to local boards and agencies by requiring municipalities to publish vacancy lists of appointive positions and how to apply for them, should be expanded and actively promoted.

   Government in New Jersey and across the nation will be more effective and responsive to the public interest if citizens become more active as stakeholders. The Center for Civic Responsibility, founded by reform activist Harry Pozycki, has involved thousands of New Jerseyans through the Citizens Service Act and other programs as participants at the local level in a bottom-up effort to reform and reinvigorate government.

## THE ELECTORAL PROCESS

At the very heart of democracy is the election process, which is intended to provide an open, fair, accessible, and representative system to realize the American dream: government of the people. Unfortunately, New Jersey falls short of this ideal. The process by which candidates emerge and rise to the top in New Jersey is often shrouded in secrecy and manipulated by political bosses. The following recommendations address these problems head-on:

1.  A new paradigm must be developed for creating legislative districts that results in more competitive elections.

   Currently, only a handful of New Jersey's forty legislative districts are truly in play to be contested by candidates of the major parties. Because of the way districts are carved up to heavily favor one major party or the other, the remainder are safely in the hands of incumbents. The manner for selecting members of the apportionment commission needs to be changed—a reform that would require a change in the state constitution.

   At present, the state chair of each of the two political parties picks five members, ensuring politicization of the process. In the future, commissioners should not be elected officials, past and present, or those involved in political activities. Most important, selecting apportionment commissioners should be done in a nonpartisan manner by a panel of public citizens or retired judges chosen by the state supreme court. Three states—Arizona, California, and Iowa—allow their citizens to submit their names into a pool from which redistricting commissioners are chosen.[36] In the case of a deadlock by commissioners as they try to agree on a district plan, most states assign the task of making a final judgment to a judicial body.

Additionally, in an attempt to immunize the process from politics, some states prohibit information about incumbent candidate residency from being entered into the computer analysis. Others have established standards of competitiveness to apply to a minimum number of districts in the state. One such standard might be that a competitive statistical spread between the number of Republican and Democratic voters, perhaps 10 percent or less, must be met in at least 20 percent of the districts that make up a new map. Further, the law should mandate a series of public hearings on a proposed districting plan before final approval.

It follows that if one party can emerge from this process as the clear winner (as was the case in New Jersey with Democrats in 2001 and 2011), an independent, nonpartisan approach using the same research techniques is capable of producing a redistricted map with a greater degree of competitiveness.

This has happened in California, which established a "citizens commission" to conduct redistricting after the 2010 census. In the words of Nicholas Stephanopoulos, a University of Chicago law professor who has studied redistricting in the various states: "Structurally, it [the California system] shields [commission] members from political pressure. Aesthetically, its districts are compact and respect community boundaries, and electorally, they are competitive and politically balanced compared to the ones they replaced."[37]

2. When change in the legislative redistricting process is undertaken, consideration should be given to having assembly members represent a single district rather than the present two members per district.

This recommendation would also require a change in the constitution. Multimember legislative districts have been on the decline across the country, going from two-thirds of all states fifty years ago to just eleven in 2011.[38] California has single-member assembly districts.

Much of the impetus for this trend has been the federal Voting Rights Act, which has been used to "create constituencies where minority groups are concentrated enough to elect candidates of their choice."[39] By the same token, other states have used the multidistrict stratagem for arranging population groups in the redistricting process to maximize a party's political advantage.

In Vermont, which is 95 percent white, the debate about reforming the state's system of multimember districts has been about whether citizens are better served by a legislator who must appeal to a broader spectrum of citizens in a multimember district or one who represents a smaller, closer-knit, and more demographically similar community.

Under a single-member system, current assembly districts would be split into two, with each of these new districts likely to have different demographic composition (ethnicity, income levels, cultural attributes) from each other and from that of the original district. Such a change would produce greater diversity in legislative representation, and there would likely be more competition in electing an assembly majority. At present, thirty-eight of the forty assembly districts in New Jersey are represented by members of the same party, and only one of those thirty-eight districts has a senator whose party affiliation differs from the assembly members.

Under such an arrangement, assembly representatives would have greater independence—they would not have to be constantly looking over their shoulder to see that their actions comport with their district colleague. Further, it can be expected that they would build a more positive personal connection with constituents.

3. The high barrier imposed on forming additional political parties should be lowered.

The present requirement for a new party to qualify—capture at least 10 percent of all the votes for assembly candidates in the state at a general election—is a virtual impossibility. In order to encourage diversity and greater political participation, the requirement should be reduced to 3 percent, and only individuals casting ballots should be counted in computing this percentage. In order for a party to continue having a ballot in the primary election, it would have to have a turnout of a specified minimum percent of the same base of voters in succeeding primary elections.

4. Election administration and regulation should be transferred from county to state control.

The present system allows for procedural inconsistencies, inefficiencies, and in many cases, partisanship. The Election Law Revision Commission proposed in 1975 that such a transfer in responsibility take place, with county election offices staffed by state personnel appointed by merit rather than through political patronage.[40] Further, the federal Help America Vote Act (HAVA) of 2002 established standards that states must follow to ensure the integrity of elections, standards that can most effectively be administered through a state system. Uniform procedures—from voter registration, to record keeping, to staffing polls, to vote tallying—would apply to all areas of the state. To further aid in ensuring the integrity of elections, voting machines equipped with paper trail mechanisms to authenticate every vote should be in use in all New Jersey polling places.

5. Voter-friendly registration initiatives should be maximized.

The state should maintain a data bank of all registered voters. If a voter moves within the state, he or she would not have to reregister. Standards to prevent voter fraud from absentee, mail-in, messenger, and provisional ballots should be closely administered by trained, nonpartisan election personnel.

Further, the closed primary system that now exists in New Jersey should be opened in order to encourage greater public participation in the critically important process of selecting candidates. At present, people who vote in the primary of one party cannot vote in the other party's primary in following years unless they affirmatively change their voter registration at least fifty-five days before the primary. The law should be changed to its pre-1975 status, which allowed a voter to be free to vote in either party's primary after a one-year hiatus of not voting in a primary election.

Efforts to restrict or suppress voting by methods such as requiring voters to present photo ID cards at the polls should be vigorously opposed. Voter registration should be as user-friendly as possible. To that effect, the Nebraska legislature passed a bill in early 2014, becoming the twentieth state to provide online voter registration.[41] Impediments to voter registration, such as requiring the submission of a birth certificate, should be disallowed.

The signature of the applicant affirming location of residence and other eligibility information should be adequate for verification by registration officials—as is now the case.

6. Procedures should be established to make candidate selection by political parties as fair and open as possible.

The following recommendations respond to the previous chapter's saga regarding the manipulative efforts of party insiders to determine who is chosen or endorsed to run for office on the party's primary ballot line. There are three distinctly different tracks for bestowing the politically crucial endorsements on candidates who seek elective office. The first track is statutory, and extremely limited in scope. It regulates the procedures for filling vacancies of candidates nominated in a primary to run for legislative and county offices. This law states that a convention of county committee members of the same party as the individual who vacated the nomination must be held within a specific time frame to vote on a replacement. At such a meeting, there must be a quorum consisting of at least a majority of the county committee members, all of whom must have held their offices at least seven days before the meeting, and the vote must be by secret ballot.[42] This track is rare because it applies only to filling vacancies of those candidates elected in a party primary; it does not apply to vacancies of legislators or county officials after they have been elected to office.

The second track for selecting candidates is the ad hoc process employed by many county parties by which their members participate in a convention to choose candidates. No laws apply to this process, which is governed by a county party's constitution, by tradition, or by chairman fiat. And not until 2010 was there a requirement in New Jersey that political parties adopt a constitution and bylaws to regulate their operations. While these constitutions are intended to ensure "fundamental fairness and the rights of the members of the county committee," they are nothing more than advisory—they have no force of law. Nor are there statutory provisions that formalize how to call meetings and to define qualifications of those who will vote as in track one.

The third track is the totally closed system where a party boss, with occasional help from political cohorts, will choose candidates secretly, proclaim that they are the party's endorsed candidates, and assign them the party line on the primary ballot. Hudson County is notorious for its use of this closed system. This process violates all the principles of open, representative democracy and should be abandoned wherever it is now in use.

In virtually all cases, receiving the party endorsement and favored ballot position is critical to winning the primary and becoming a viable candidate. A concentrated effort to implement a fair and open regulatory scheme for county party endorsement conventions generally operating as the second track should be, where possible, adopted by state law. And if not by law, these reform procedures should be codified in the constitutions and bylaws of county parties. The Party Democracy Act of 2010 requires that the constitution and bylaws of county political parties contain several reform provisions,[43] but only for conventions to fill vacancies as spelled out in the first track. These same provisions should apply to track two county endorsement conventions. Other provisions applicable to track two conventions should be added, including:

- a candidate who garners more than 50 percent of the convention vote receives the party endorsement and placement on the party ballot line, and shares the party slogan of no more than six words with other endorsed candidates;
- a candidate who gets less than 50 percent but more than 20 percent of the convention vote shall be allowed to be on the party line but without the party slogan and in an inferior spot compared to the

party's endorsed candidates (see figs. 8.1 and 8.2 for a visual depiction of the primary ballot structure discussed in this section);

- a candidate who gets less than 20 percent of the convention vote is placed elsewhere than on the party line of the primary ballot in a drawing by the county clerk;
- candidates for municipal and statewide office use the same procedure to qualify for placement on the official line of the county political party;
- an alternative candidate slate can form a party line and compete with the "official" party slate in the primary election. Challenging slates should have an equal chance with the "official" party for receiving the favored ballot line in the primary election; and
- a county political party that does not observe this process for candidate endorsement will not be entitled to a special line on the primary ballot.

Some will contend that the U.S. Supreme Court's *Eu* decision declares that internal affairs of a political party, which are largely determined in primaries, are private activity and cannot be regulated, and efforts might be used to thus invalidate any laws circumscribing the operations of a political party.[44] Yet, the entire primary election process, including the timing, ballot conditions, and political officers elected thereat, is already governed by New Jersey law. Moreover, the recommendations proposed here are critical in protecting the integrity of one of the most vital elements of the electoral system—the primary—where the state has a compelling interest to ensure an orderly, fair, and inclusive process. Indeed, the recommended procedures and conditions for the candidate endorsement convention do not intrude upon internal party activities any more than the provisions of existing law that controls how a political party fills vacancies of candidates nominated in a primary for elective public office by the track-one process.

It is recommended that the New Jersey legislature pass the necessary laws to regulate endorsement conventions, and then let the courts decide. If such laws are stricken, political ethicists, the media, and good-government groups have recourse to every possible tactic of political pressure to get county and municipal political

| OFFICE TITLE | Column **A** Democratic | Column **B** Democratic | Column **C** Democratic | Column **D** Democratic |
|---|---|---|---|---|
| **U.S. Senate** 6 Year Term - Vote for One | Cory **BOOKER** [1A] | | | |
| **House of Representatives** 2 Year Term - Vote for One | Bonnie **WATSON COLEMAN** [2A] | Upendra **CHIVUKULA** [2B] | Linda R. **GREENSTEIN** [2C] | Andrew **ZWICKER** [2D] |
| **Sheriff** 3 Year Term - Vote for One | John A. "Jack" **KEMLER** [3A] | | | |
| **Board of Chosen Freeholders** 3 Year Term - Vote for Two | Lucylle RS **WALTER** [4A] | | | |
| | John A. **CIMINO** [5A] | | | |
| **Mayor** 4 Year Term - Vote for One | Bert H. **STEINMANN** [6A] | | | |
| **Council** 4 Year Term - Vote for Two | Kathleen Culliton **WOLLERT** [7A] | | | |
| | Sarah **STEWARD** [8A] | | | |
| **Male Member of County Committee** 2 Year Term - Vote for One | NO PETITION FILED | | | |
| **Female Member of County Committee** 2 Year Term - Vote for One | Anne M. **ZAMONSKI** [10A] | | | |

*OFFICIAL PRIMARY ELECTION SAMPLE BALLOT JUNE 3, 2014 DEMOCRATIC*

FIGURE 8.1. A Recent Example of the Primary Ballot in New Jersey

The endorsed candidates of the Mercer County Democratic Party are placed on the "party line," which is column A on the primary ballot. All candidates on this line have the slogan "Regular Democratic Organization" printed by their names. (The slogan is not shown on this ballot sample because the print would be too small to be readable.) Assemblywoman Bonnie Watson Coleman, candidate for the U.S. House of Representatives, was endorsed by the Mercer County Democratic Committee at its meeting in March 2014, receiving more than 60 percent of the vote of county committee representatives (Mike Davis, "Watson Coleman Lands Endorsement of Mercer Democratic Committee," *Times of Trenton,* March 27, 2014). Her name appears as 2A on line A. Three other candidates for Congress, including State Senator Linda Greenstein of Middlesex County, were also seeking endorsement at the meeting. Greenstein received more than 25 percent of the vote, but she was not placed on the party line and instead was relegated to the less favorable location 2C on the ballot. Watson Coleman won the primary that June, garnering 46 percent of the vote; Greenstein came in second with 30 percent.

committees, through their constitutions and bylaws, to strengthen, codify, and enforce the way they endorse candidates.

One benefit that can be expected from an open and fair candidate selection process is that more women will run for and be elected to public office. This was the conclusion drawn from a *Star-Ledger* editorial that stated: "Party leadership is male-dominated and

**OFFICIAL PRIMARY ELECTION SAMPLE BALLOT** JUNE 3, 2014
**DEMOCRATIC**

| OFFICE TITLE | Column **A** Democratic | Column **B** Democratic | Column **C** Democratic | Column **D** Democratic |
|---|---|---|---|---|
| U.S. Senate<br>6 Year Term · Vote for One | Cory **BOOKER** ⒈Ａ | | | |
| House of Representatives<br>2 Year Term · Vote for One | Bonnie **WATSON COLEMAN** ⒉Ａ | Upendra **CHIVUKULA** ⒉Ｂ | | |
| | Linda R. **GREENSTEIN** ⒉Ｃ | Andrew **ZWICKER** ⒉Ｄ | | |
| Sheriff<br>3 Year Term · Vote for One | John A. "Jack" **KEMLER** ⒊Ａ | | | |
| Board of Chosen Freeholders<br>3 Year Term · Vote for Two | Lucylle RS **WALTER** ⒋Ａ | | | |
| | John A. **CIMINO** ⒌Ａ | | | |
| Mayor<br>4 Year Term · Vote for One | Bert H. **STEINMANN** ⒍Ａ | | | |
| Council<br>4 Year Term · Vote for Two | Kathleen Culliton **WOLLERT** ⒎Ａ | | | |
| | Sarah **STEWARD** ⒏Ａ | | | |
| Male Member of County Committee<br>2 Year Term · Vote for One | NO PETITION FILED | | | |
| Female Member of County Committee<br>2 Year Term · Vote for One | Anne M. **ZAMONSKI** ⒑Ａ | | | |

FIGURE 8.2. A Ballot Illustrating a Recommended Improvement

If the recommendation to make the selection of candidates fairer to those who receive significant support (more than 20 percent) at the party's endorsement meeting but who do not receive the party line on the ballot were adopted, this is what the ballot would look like. Having earned 25 percent, Senator Greenstein would have been placed on the more favorable line A with other endorsed Democratic party candidates. Her name would appear beneath Watson Coleman but with a different slogan. In that location, she would have had a much better chance of getting the voters' attention—and their support. She would also avoid the stigma of "party renegade."

decision-making on who gets to run for office—and who doesn't—is made behind closed doors by men such as Steve Adubato and George Norcross who aren't elected or accountable."[45]

These fundamental changes in the candidate selection system would reinvigorate the public's faith in its government by recognizing genuine political leadership in its legitimate role of influencing party members in the choice of candidates rather than allowing these choices to be made either out of sight by party bosses or by manipulation of the process.

7. The county clerk, a partisan elected official, should not make the draw to determine which party gets the first line on the November general election ballot.

   Studies have shown that the first line, by virtue of its position, is generally worth more votes than subsequent lines. Superior Court judges can perform this task, and they can alternate from year to year between Republican-appointed judges and Democratic ones. As an alternative, consideration should be given to changing a party's line on the general election ballot from voting district to voting district so that each party would appear first on approximately the same number of ballots—a reform adopted in a dozen or more states.[46]

8. New Jersey should require at least a 50 percent majority of the votes for a winner in contests where a single candidate is elected to office.

   This can be done by establishing instant runoff voting (IRV) in situations where three (or more) candidates run for the same office. Under IRV, which was described in detail in chapter 7, each voter designates a first choice and is permitted but not required to designate a second choice. If neither of the top two vote-getters receives more than 50 percent of the votes cast, the second choice of those voting for the third candidate is added to the totals of the first two, thereby assuring that one candidate gets more than 50 percent. IRV has several clear advantages over the present system:

   • The winner will always receive a majority of votes cast, a desirable result in representative government. In multi-candidate races, it is often expressed that a winner who receives less than 50 percent of the vote does not have a legitimate mandate for the position.
   • Some jurisdictions (cities such as Newark and Trenton) now require a runoff election for the two highest vote-getters if no candidate has more than 50 percent. When this happens, there is extra cost—paid by taxpayers—for the second election, and, generally, a lower turnout due to voter fatigue. But under IRV, there is no need for a second election; IRV is the runoff.
   • A third- or independent-party candidate who gets only a small percentage of the vote is no longer considered a spoiler, because the

second-choice votes of this candidate's supporters will ensure that there is a winner with more than 50 percent.

- People who vote for a long-shot candidate based on issues and principle are not wasting their vote, because they have made a second choice who might very well be the winner.
- IRV will foster the development of more parties and more independent candidacies and, therefore, more electoral competition.

Since elections are conducted under state law, the legislature of New Jersey or any other state can enact IRV for elections for a seat in the U.S. Senate and the U.S. House of Representatives, as well as for state senator, county executive, and mayor. IRV can even work for multiple at-large candidates, although the math to adjudicate outcomes in such cases is more complex.

9.  Fair and clean campaign practices should be implemented to the maximum extent—by statute where possible, or by public pressure.

Negativity and personal invective have become epidemic in New Jersey campaigns as well as in other states. There should be incentives for candidates to run under a "fair campaign practices" system monitored by a strong good-government group such as the League of Women Voters or Common Cause. The monitoring organization would require participating candidates to abide by a set of standards of fair play, including in its provisions: no voter suppression, for example, push polling; no personal vilification or character defamation of one's opponent or family; no use of unfounded accusations; and public repudiation of any support they may derive from sources that employ these prohibited tactics. Additionally, fair campaign candidates would be required to participate in a minimum number of public debates.

Candidates who so qualify would be entitled to use the "fair campaign practices" slogan on their radio, TV, and print advertisements in the same context as household products use the *Good Housekeeping* seal of approval. Publicly recognizing a candidate whose campaign tactics meet fair and honorable standards has precedence in New Jersey. In 2007, the state adopted a Clean Elections pilot program for public financing for assembly races in three districts.[47]

Candidates had to collect more than eight hundred contributions of $10 or more and agree not to use private funds in their campaigns in order to qualify for a state subsidy of $92,000. The candidates who met these requirements on time were allowed to use the label "Clean Elections Candidate" next to their name on the general election ballot. Although the pilot program was not successful enough to expand to other districts, it did prove that the use of a favorable slogan, "Clean Elections Candidate," was eagerly sought by the participants as a badge of honor.

Other states have passed truth-in-campaigning laws that establish a nonpartisan panel to review and evaluate material candidates submit for fairness and accuracy.[48] These states have incentivized candidates to run clean campaigns in accordance with prescribed standards by permitting them to use the "fair campaign" label in their electoral literature and next to their name on the ballot.

An underlying theme runs throughout these recommendations as an effective instrument in fighting political corruption and restoring integrity to government: disclosure. Whether it be campaign contributions, lobbying by and for special interests, public officials with hidden conflicts, patronage and privilege abuses by insiders, or manipulation of the electoral process, the best protection against these ills is transparency and disclosure. To repeat the words of former Justice Louis Brandeis: "Sunlight is said to be the best of disinfectants; electric light the most effective policeman." Full disclosure will give citizens—and the press that serves them—the opportunity to see where government is failing, and will guide the public toward actions necessary to renew the fundamental promise of America.

# 9 ▸ HOW TO ACHIEVE REFORM

THE PRECEDING CHAPTERS have demonstrated the prevalence of soft corruption in New Jersey. The problems are real, and there is no sign that things are getting better. The task of remedying ethical challenges in New Jersey government will be long and daunting. What makes comprehensive reform especially difficult is that those who are best positioned to address these ethical failings—legislators and their political godfathers—are not enthralled with the prospect. Their political success depends on the status quo. And there is no inclination to remedy existing practices if calls for reform can simply be ignored without any electoral punishment or other political consequences.

Well-intentioned people have offered several panaceas for perceived shortcomings in governmental integrity and competence. Upon close examination, however, implementing these cures would not necessarily be consistent with the premises and values of our representative democracy, and, indeed, would not be valid reform. They can be called faux reform—and should be dispensed with in short order.

## FAUX REFORM

### Initiative & Referendum (I & R)

The first faux reform involves initiative and referendum, commonly referred to as I & R, by which the public uses the petition and referendum process to make new laws regarding matters on which the legislature fails to act. Growing out of the populist and progressive reform movements of a century ago, I & R was intended to counteract the power of lobbies and special interests that had strangleholds on state legislatures. A total of twenty-four states, including every state on the West Coast, as well as most of those in the Great Plains and Rocky Mountain regions, adopted this "direct democracy" process.[1]

In its early years, I & R worked well as the only way to get results on intractable issues ignored by state lawmakers. Initiatives for women's suffrage, direct election of U.S. senators, wage and hour labor laws, and regulation of the inordinate economic powers of banks, railroads, and corporations improved existing conditions for the public.

Eventually, however, the dark side of I & R emerged. Special interests realized that the strategic use of I & R was an easier way to get government results than the conventional procedure of electing candidates and then lobbying them on legislation. Sophisticated polling, public relations, and advertising developed as powerful forces for molding public opinion, which could then convert policy issues into government outcomes through I & R.

The I & R process, in states that allowed it, became a dominant force by which to bypass the legislature. But it is no longer used solely as an instrument for reform. Instead, according to *Washington Post* columnist David Broder: "It has given the United States something that seems unthinkable—not a government of laws but laws without government."[2]

Of all the states that use I & R, California is the most notorious, probably because of the passage of Proposition 13 in 1978, which lowered and essentially froze homeowner property taxes by constitutional amendment. Proposition 13, which voters approved 65 percent to 35 percent, was very popular with Californians, whose property taxes had been soaring. Immediately thereafter, annual revenue for local government declined by $6 billion, two-thirds of which benefited corporations that Proposition 13 relieved from paying. Further initiatives were implemented requiring approval of two-thirds of the voters to increase local taxes and a two-thirds vote of the legislature to raise state taxes and approve the annual state budget. Because the resulting fiscal turmoil shifted the focus of spending from the local level to the state level, public school funding, which had been capped by Proposition 13, was severely affected. In the twenty years following passage of Proposition 13, California schools, which had been ranked near the top, fell to forty-second in public funds spent on education.[3]

Despite the damage to California's economy and governmental institutions in the aftermath of Proposition 13, I & R flourished there and in other states where its use is permitted. A cottage industry of consultants, special attorneys, and professional petition gatherers was spawned to carry out the objectives of special interests in gaining government advantages. Believing that paying people to solicit and gather petitions was inconsistent with the true spirit of the reform movement, some states tried to enact laws prohibiting it, but the U.S. Supreme Court struck down these efforts.[4]

The sums of money directed into I & R campaigns soon reached major proportions. California Indian tribes spent more than $66 million in 1998 on a winning initiative to support their casino interests, overcoming opposition from the Las Vegas gambling industry, which spent $25 million in an effort to defeat it. In the twenty-two years following 1976, yearly spending on California initiative campaigns went from $9 million to $224 million. Spending on I & R had become a big-bucks enterprise in the Golden State, where the median cost to finance an initiative campaign rose from $45,000 in 1976 to more than $1 million by the end of the 1990s.

Other states experienced the same profligacy in I & R spending. Multibillionaire Paul Allen, a founder of Microsoft who owns the Seattle Seahawks football team, spent $10 million, $6.3 million of which went toward securing petition signatures, on a successful initiative to get government to pay for a share of a new $425 million stadium.[5]

The variety of issues that have been the subject of initiative campaigns is extensive, ranging from medical marijuana, to animal protection, to taxes, to affirmative action, to immigration, to gambling, to many, many more. One ballot question will often inspire opponents to create a cleverly worded countermeasure to confuse the voters. If there are two ballot questions on the same issue, each offering a different result, courts have ruled that the one getting the most votes prevails.

As I & R has matured, the process has become big business, and the legitimate efforts of one hundred years ago by populists and progressives to keep it pure have largely been thwarted by opportunistic special interests. Only a small portion of current I & R proposals are focused on issues that benefit the common good. The words of President Theodore Roosevelt, even during the heyday of progressivism, were prescient. He issued a strong warning against the misuse of I & R when he said: "I believe in Initiative and Referendum, which should not be used to destroy representative government but to correct it whenever it becomes misrepresentative."[6]

It is also clear that in their deliberations at the constitutional convention and in the *Federalist Papers*, the nation's founders chose representative government over direct democracy. They structured the legislative system and the separation of powers accordingly.

### Term Limits

A second faux reform, term limits, is closely allied with I & R. Driven by the notion that after several years in the same office lawmakers lose their edge, are consumed by the politics of reelection, have failed to make a difference, and are protected by incumbency, citizens conclude that someone else can do better and deserves the opportunity to represent them. In the name of reform, laws are proposed—and passed—to limit the terms of state legislators, usually to a maximum of ten or twelve years. In the 1990s, eighteen states adopted legislative term limits, mostly through the I & R process.[7] Logic tells us from the private sector that experience in a job should be nurtured and recognized; certainly, experience in business, in the professions, and with skilled artisans is not an ipso facto negative. Political columnist David Broder provided additional illumination when he observed: "We are supposed to believe that term-limited legislators will take better care of the public purse than those who know they will have to face the electorate in the future."[8]

Legislators who have been in office for a shorter time lack governmental expertise. This shortcoming is often filled by another resource, namely advice and assistance from unelected players in the lawmaking process: lobbyists and government administrators. It is not likely that the public wants its representatives to delegate their responsibilities in this manner.

Alan Rosenthal of the Eagleton Institute of Politics at Rutgers University once described by Broder as "probably the leading academic scholar of state legislatures," argued in the August 1999 issue of *State Legislatures* for the importance of continuity in the successful functioning of state legislatures:

> Some continuity of membership and staff not only provides for greater knowledge and skill on the parts of lawmakers, but it promotes institutional values. Continuity does not require extremely low turnover of membership, but only that some members serve for a decent period of time. By requiring that everyone turn over with relative brief regularity and by discouraging legislators from identifying with an institution they are passing through, term limits run counter to institutional continuity. The eighteen states that currently limit terms are at a disadvantage when it comes to having a good legislature.[9]

"Change the players and the system will change," as proffered by proponents of term limits, is an illusion. Only by vigorous and comprehensive reform promoted by lawmakers who have developed leadership skills will we be able to cure these ills and return to the American ideal of honest, representative government subject to the will of public citizens who will be sufficiently involved to impose term limits on any malefactor in the next election.

## Supermajority Votes

Ordinarily, legislatures and other governmental bodies operate under rules by which a simple majority of 50 percent plus one of the membership is necessary to approve a law or resolution. Yet some states take the position that there are certain issues of such importance that a supermajority of two-thirds or three-quarters of the membership of the governing body should be required for approval. Most of the matters calling for a supermajority vote in these states are financial, such as imposing new taxes and approving budgets. While intended to ensure that the legislature takes a more serious and deliberative view on certain critical state issues, supermajority requirements often elevate the importance of such issues to artificially high levels and deny lawmakers their traditional role of participating in legislative dynamics where the primacy of majority rule should prevail.

After 2010, there were sixteen states in which tax increases could only be passed with a supermajority vote of the legislature.[10] The supermajority restrictions in many of these states have been implemented by I & R, while some have even been imbedded in state constitutions. This was the case with California's infamous Proposition 13, which not only constitutionally capped property taxes at their 1975 levels but also required that any vote to raise taxes by the legislature or by local government would have to pass with a two-thirds majority.[11]

State finances have to be addressed each year through the budgetary process. No matter how difficult, these are decisions officials are elected to make so that government continues to function. In cases of routine government responsibilities, the supermajority concept rejects the principle of majority rule. Yet majority rule is, in fact, fundamental to the political divisions in governing bodies. The dynamics of a political majority involving accountability and the obligation to deliver enough votes to enact its program is a key factor in representative democracy. Supermajority rules encourage highly charged political partisanship in the decision-making process whereby minorities of a legislative body can thwart the will of the majority by extorting significant legislative concessions before providing the votes to pass a budget or impose necessary revenue measures. The public deserves representatives who can make decisions rather than being procedurally blocked from doing so.

Nevertheless, there are special circumstances in government where the bar for change should be set high—when a supermajority of votes by an official body to enact a proposal is in order. For example, New Jersey requires a 60 percent supermajority vote of the legislature followed by public referendum to effect a change in the state constitution. If the vote by the legislature on a constitutional amendment gets a majority but less than 60 percent, the measure can get legislative approval if it receives a simple majority in the succeeding year (the governor plays no role in the approval process for a constitutional change). Passing a local bond ordinance that encumbers the financial obligations of a municipality needs two-thirds approval by the governing body. The common thread is that these are matters of major consequence that only crop up occasionally, usually after experiencing genuine need accompanied by great public concern. They are anything but routine.

In 1996, Republican governor Christie Whitman urged the legislature to approve a constitutional amendment requiring that any future increase in state taxes be approved by a two-thirds vote by the state senate and assembly. After the measure failed, the *Times of Trenton* editorialized: "To demand a super-majority for the Legislature to do something as fundamental to governing as raising revenue betrays a deep distrust of representative government."[12]

## A ROAD MAP FOR ACHIEVING REFORM

Public interest groups have said the only way government will reform itself is if there is a major scandal or if there is "fire in the belly" of a popular governor crusading for reform. As for scandals being precursors to reform, Connecticut is a good example. A combination of the governor's imprisonment on bribery charges, ethical misdeeds in the legislature, and a well-financed effort by several good government organizations resulted in sweeping campaign finance reforms enacted in 2005 by the state's legislature.[13]

But scandals cannot always be relied on to produce a similar outcome. In New Jersey, the Karen Kotvas shakedown scandal of 1989 (described in chapter 3) led to the blue ribbon Rosenthal Commission, whose recommendations produced the controversial leadership PACs in the name of reform. So what caused the Rosenthal proposals to go awry? With very little media or organized public outrage, legislative leaders watered down the commission's suggestions on contribution limits and leadership PAC structure to suit their own political ends.

New Jersey legislators have thus far responded to calls for reform with a minimalist approach, consistently shying away from comprehensive measures and instead adopting palliatives such as the inadequate efforts to fully ban pay-to-play, the primaries-only prohibition of wheeling political funds to other counties, and the partial elimination of dual office holding. Regarding some of the more serious reform issues such as senatorial courtesy, creating competitive legislative districts, and the negative influence of excess money in the political system, there is little interest in change.

But has the tipping point arrived where these corrupting influences just have to be faced and dealt with?

Having exposed the significant flaws of several faux reforms, I believe there is an ultimate reform solution that can raise New Jersey out of this soft corruption quagmire. It is limited I & R, which reassembles the basic components of standard I & R into a hybrid structure. While this might sound like a repudiation of my arguments against standard I & R, there is a distinct difference between the two.

### Limited I & R

Voter initiative in states that have general, unrestricted I & R cover all manner of proposals. Many of the subjects considered in such states, particularly those issues affecting taxes, business regulation, and personal conduct, have been contentious and have generated politically charged and expensive campaigns, both pro and con. Worse, their passage has often had disastrous governmental consequences, most dramatically in California. This type of activity earned I & R the faux label.

There is, however, a limited spectrum of government reforms that states have adopted through I & R that do not involve the negatives associated with the faux measures. These are reforms relating to political money, government integrity, and the electoral process. Seldom opposed by moneyed interests, they are almost always approved by the voters. In recent years, I & R has been used in Arizona, Maine, and Massachusetts to pass clean-election laws allowing public financing to subsidize campaigns.[14] In New York City, which operates under a charter allowing voter initiative, the public was asked at the November 1988 election to approve a campaign finance board to manage public financing of city elections, a measure that passed with 79 percent of the vote.[15]

Across the country, it is more common for such reform programs to be adopted through Initiative and Referendum in states where this process is allowed than through the legislative process. Commenting about this phenomenon, the Pew Center on the States observed on its stateline .org website: "The more progressive of the public financing measures have become law only because of voter initiatives, an indication that incumbent lawmakers are extremely reluctant to do anything to upset a system awash in special interest money that helps them get re-elected."[16] The use of I & R as a mechanism for reform in the twenty-four states where it is now permitted has shown significant success, particularly on the issue of campaign financing. In a sample survey between 1996 and 2000, there were sixteen initiatives to reform campaign financing in ten of these states. Of this total, thirteen were approved by the voters, demonstrating that the people can—and do—use I & R to reform government.[17]

In New Jersey, evidence points to the conclusion that reform of the magnitude necessary to change the culture in Trenton will not come incrementally through normal legislative channels or from scandal. And there is no governor on the horizon who has the political will to lead the charge. So what can be done? How can the I & R process, condemned as faux earlier in this chapter, be recast as a favorable strategy to achieve reform?

It is possible to restructure Initiative and Referendum into a tactically balanced process for delivering the reforms we seek without the overreach of conventional I & R. This is the approach I took in the New Jersey Senate in the mid-1990s. After extensive research of experiences in other states and consultation with state constitutional experts, I proposed a legislative framework to establish a system of limited I & R in New Jersey applying only to four specific areas: campaign finance, lobbying, government ethics, and the electoral process. The legislation would give the people of New Jersey the power to draft and enact laws to reform aspects of the four issue areas through a tightly administered I & R process. For example, exorbitant campaign contribution levels could be reduced by amending the statute through a voter-approved initiative; or instant runoff voting could be adopted to ensure that election winners get more than 50 percent of the vote; or the law could be changed to eliminate all forms of dual office holding—and so on. Impetus for the use of limited I & R would result when the citizenry senses a growing need to reform these basic areas, and they perceive clear evidence that the legislature refuses to act.

The limited I & R legislation contained checks and balances to avoid "tyranny of the majority" and other defects so prevalent with faux I & R. The checks and balances include:

- restricting the process to a very limited number of issue areas related to the behavior of political players, not to the substance of governance;
- subjecting each petition proposing a reform initiative to an impartial judicial review before it goes on the ballot to ensure that it conforms to legal and constitutional strictures;
- requiring a significant number of petition signers for the initiative to be valid (8 percent of those voting in the last gubernatorial election is a well-recognized standard), and limiting the time period for collecting signatures to one year;
- permitting the legislature, after the initiative petition is filed, to enact a law that is "substantially similar" to the petition proposal, thereby avoiding the need for a referendum. Petition proponents would have the right to determine if the legislation is substantially similar;
- offering "proponent amendability" whereby proponents—and only proponents—can amend the initiative consistent with its original intent before placing the final revised measure on the ballot. Proponent amendability may occur if unforeseen defects crop up following hearings by the legislature and during public forums;
- voting on the referendum at the general election, ensuring the greatest public participation;[18]
- requiring expedited state supreme court review for legal challenges to the initiative;
- mandating distribution of informational material to all voters; and
- prohibiting changes in the statute created by the initiative for the ensuing five years.

The legislation would later draw praise from Craig Holman, a nationally recognized authority on campaign finance and reform issues, as "an effective marriage between the legislative process and direct democracy." In a study he conducted as senior policy analyst at the Brennan Center for Justice at New York University School of Law, Holman concluded:

The New Jersey model . . . is a unique hybrid of institutional structures designed in light of the experiences of other states. For those concerned with excessive initiative activity, the "limited initiative" will reduce the frequency and costs of the initiative process seen in other states. "Proponent amendability" . . . a dynamic feature that no other state offers . . . All too often, initiatives are drafted without appropriate review and a full understanding of the initiative's consequences. . . .

The New Jersey model provides citizens with the major benefits of the initiative—a means for seeking redress for pressing government problems when the legislature declines to act—while avoiding some of the major pit-falls associated with . . . I & R.[19]

I introduced the proposed legislation, Senate Concurrent Resolution 24, in the state senate on January 18, 1996, with the bipartisan support of twelve senate cosponsors. The resolution was assigned to the Judiciary Committee, where it languished for over a year. Growing impatient and seeing no sign of interest on the part of senate leadership, I employed an obscure legislative maneuver known as "Relieve a Senate Committee of a Bill" to seek action on the measure.[20] On March 10, 1997, I made the motion to remove the bill from committee and bring it directly to the senate floor for a vote. My admittedly quixotic effort was killed by a nondebatable tabling motion (19–14) by opponents who argued that this was an unorthodox, radical move that short-circuited established senate procedures.[21]

Deliberation over this legislative proposal over the years has shown a need for several refinements. The scope of limited I & R, which addresses statutory changes, should be extended to address constitutional changes. And the four issue areas I proposed for reform in past legislation should be expanded to five to include appointive powers of those in government—patronage. Petition proposals need to have statewide legitimacy, so a provision should be inserted stipulating that no more than 25 percent of the qualifying petition signers reside in a single county. In order to avoid confusion caused by a plethora of reform initiatives submitted by referendum at a single election, there should also be a limit on the number of initiatives (perhaps the first four that qualify) to be placed on the ballot at a single election. And finally, the process should ensure funding of an anticipated proposal by combining it with an appropriation so that the legislature cannot kill a reform by starving it of money, as happened in Massachusetts, where the legislature was able to derail the citizen-passed clean-election effort by withholding the necessary funds.

## Passing the Enabling Legislation

As logical and beneficial as limited I & R may sound, its adoption in New Jersey will be difficult. An amendment to the state's constitution is necessary, requiring a 60 percent favorable vote by each house of the legislature followed by a vote of the people ratifying the amendment at the next general election. Naysayers will contend that if legislators are not willing to enact reforms under present conditions, what makes one think they will authorize a constitutional amendment to go on the ballot, thereby giving up this power and handing it over to the people?

It will take a huge but not insurmountable effort by citizens and the media to convince legislators to take the next step on this proposal. Legislators can be assured that they will not be totally giving up power, because the recommended I & R process still gives them the opportunity to shape and act on any reform before a public vote. And this is not standard, unlimited I & R, which gives away the right to pass laws on any subject.

A strong and convincing argument advocating adoption of limited I & R to reform conditions in New Jersey was advanced by John Kolesar, former editor of the *Times of Trenton*, when he wrote in an op-ed:

> In New Jersey we have an opportunity to gain control of the election process by total, vehement support of the proposed [limited I & R] amendment to the state constitution. It would give the people the right to initiate state-wide referendums controlling election finance. This . . . is the most important piece of legislation to come before the Legislature in more than 50 years. Any legislator who does not support this amendment should be opposed for re-election by every voter, regardless of the candidate's position on any other issue.[22]

It is useful, although not totally analogous to conditions in present-day New Jersey, to examine how the twenty-four states adopted I & R in the first place. This was one of the key reforms promoted by the populist and Progressive movements of more than a century ago. Five states approved I & R by means of a constitutional convention,[23] but legislatures in most of the remaining nineteen states submitted the question to their voters for their acceptance. Certainly, letting the people decide this crucial question was not then anathema to the legislators. In fact, in many cases, the proportion of legislators who voted in favor of submitting the matter to a referendum was greater than that of voters who approved the question in that referendum.

It is unlikely that legislators will vote against this proposal if it is posted in the assembly and senate for a vote. The key is to get the political powers in the state, including the legislative leaders, to agree that it should be posted. Considerable pressure will be required to move these leaders to that step. There will have to be citizen uprisings of major proportions at the grassroots level, using social media and other modern political tools, to demand this change. Organizations such as the Citizens Campaign, League of Women Voters, AARP, Common Cause, New Jersey Public Interest Group, Citizen Action, and environmental groups could mobilize their memberships into a formidable "power of the people" political force to generate this uprising and make it successful. More venturesome individuals could use adoption of limited I & R as a single-issue political strategy to gain party and elective office. Party bosses would be hard-pressed to silence an overwhelming chorus for reform coming from party members and candidates for office. And, of course, the media, recognizing the significance of the movement for improving integrity as well as responsiveness in government, would have to put on a full-court press in its editorials and candidate endorsements.

Candidates for governor and the legislature could be put on the spot by asking them in questionnaires and at public forums to endorse the proposal. Former governor Jim Florio wrote an op-ed supporting limited I & R, stating, "Legislators will be judged not by their pronouncements for reform in the abstract but by their vote for or against allowing citizens to control special-interest political contributions."[24]

The use of limited I & R to reform soft corruption in government has the potential to become a defining political issue in New Jersey. With favorable advocates lining up behind the effort—reform groups, individual candidates, lawmakers, the media, and particularly legions of ordinary citizens—the chances of passing limited I & R legislation are good. And based on the history of I & R referenda in other states, when this proposal is presented to the voters, their approval would be virtually automatic.

### After Limited I & R Is Approved

Should a state constitutional amendment permit I & R on a limited range of reform issues, it is likely that good-government groups will quickly coalesce to hammer out proposed improvements in the processes of government that will engender broad public and media support.

Prospects for enacting ballot initiatives should be excellent in reform-starved New Jersey. Experience in other states demonstrates the ease by which petition signatures can be obtained. In Maine, for example, more than one thousand volunteers collected sixty-five thousand signatures in one day to qualify the clean election referendum for their ballot.[25] Once reform initiatives make the ballot, there has never been a need for large sums of money to finance the campaign for public approval. As history has shown, special interests that might not like the results of a reform are reluctant to spend money to oppose it for fear of alienating citizens who are engaged in a populist cause.

A program of limited I & R can provide an opportunity for New Jersey to finally overcome the soft corruption that has caused so much dysfunction in government. Will there be a tidal wave of change? Not necessarily. It is more likely that these reforms will be achieved incrementally. But the potential outcomes are significant:

- curtailing the excesses of political money that buys government favors and results;
- improving lobbyists' disclosure and professionalism so they focus more on communicating information than on peddling influence;
- establishing a high level of integrity, transparency, and accountability in the conduct of public officials;
- reducing cronyism, nepotism, and political payoffs when government jobs and benefits are awarded; and
- opening up the electoral process to greater fairness, transparency, and competition.

Government reform in New Jersey, and in states like it, will require a focused—even outraged—citizenry to use every political means possible to force their representatives to give them greater control over the integrity of their government. Our mission is to reinvigorate representative democracy by fighting soft corruption—so that every taxpayer dollar is spent well, so that government makes good decisions on behalf of the people it serves, and so that citizens are motivated to participate. This is not only a political objective, but a moral imperative. To quote an adage used by American presidents and sometimes erroneously attributed to French philosopher/historian Alexis de Tocqueville, who visited America in the mid-1800s:

> I sought for the greatness and genius of America in her countless harbors and ample rivers—and it was not there; in her fertile lands and boundless forests—and it was not there. . . . Not until I went to the churches of America and heard her pulpits aflame with righteousness did I understand the secret of her genius and power. America is great because she is good—and if America ever ceases to be good, America will cease to be great.

Is the prevalence of soft corruption in New Jersey a sign that governance of the state is ceasing to be good? Can New Jerseyans become so inflamed with righteousness that they will rise up and reverse this ominous trajectory?

Let this be a call to arms! The stakes are high, the obstacles are many, and the challenge must be met so that government service in New Jersey can indeed be a noble calling.

# NOTES

## CHAPTER 1    SOFT CORRUPTION—THE PROBLEM

1. While serving as U.S. attorney for the District of New Jersey for eight years, Chris Christie, who became governor in 2010, successfully prosecuted more than 130 cases of government corruption.

2. For a widely cited definition of corruption, see J. S. Nye, "Corruption and Political Development: A Cost-Benefit Analysis," *American Political Science Review* 61 (June 1967): 419.

3. Editorial, "Retired, Rehired, Remunerated," *Newark Star-Ledger,* July 6, 2011.

4. William L. Riordan, *Plunkitt of Tammany Hall* (New York: E. P. Dutton, 1963), 3–6.

5. Barbara G. Salmore and Stephen A. Salmore, *New Jersey Politics and Government,* 3rd ed. (New Brunswick, NJ: Rutgers University Press, 2008), 260.

6. Richard L. McCormick, "The Discovery That Business Corrupts Politics; A Reappraisal of the Origins of Progressivism," *American Historical Review* 86, no. 2 (April 1981): 266–267.

7. Nathaniel Persily and Melissa Cully Anderson, "Regulating Democracy through Democracy: The Use of Direct Legislation in Election Law Reform," *Southern California Law Review* 78, no. 997 (May 2005): 1024.

8. Beth A. Rosenson, *The Shadowlands of Conduct* (Washington, DC: Georgetown University Press, 2005), 6, 101, 102, 111, 141, 144, 145.

9. Tom Moran, "An Eye on the White House—10 Ways NJ Is Paying the Price for Christie's Presidential Ambitions," *Newark Star-Ledger,* July 13, 2014.

10. Monmouth University/Gannett New Jersey Poll, August 9, 2009, Monmouth University Polling Institute, West Long Branch, NJ.

11. Edward Buttimore, "Who Are These Guys Working For? The Voters or the Governor?," op-ed, *Newark Star-Ledger,* October 9, 2015. Under great pressure, the senate did pass a second vote to override by the bare two-thirds majority on October 22, 2015.

12. Susan K. Livio, "What Record Did Last Month's N.J. Elections Set?" NJ Advance Media for *NJ.com,* December 2, 2015, http://www.nj.com/politics/index.ssf/2015/12/november_2015_election_saw_lowest_voter_turnout_in.html. The 22 percent voter participation figure would be much lower if the hundreds of thousands of unregistered citizens were taken into account.

13. David S. Broder, *Democracy Derailed* (New York: Harcourt, 2000), 3.

CHAPTER 2    CAMPAIGN FINANCING: HOW IT WORKS

1. "Soft money," sometimes called "dark money," refers to contributions and expenditures for electoral purposes that are not made directly to a candidate's campaign or political party. A candidate for governor or other high office often will establish an independent nonprofit organization that collects and spends what is known as soft money to publicize the record and positive features of the candidate. Soft money is also associated with independent (that is, indirect) expenditures made by groups that raise substantial amounts for the purpose of influencing election outcomes.

2. Lynda Powell, *The Influence of Campaign Contributions in State Legislatures: The Effects of Institutions and Politics* (Ann Arbor: University of Michigan Press, 2012), 153.

3. Ibid., 152.

4. New York Times News Service, "GOP Returns Contribution from Adult Bookstores," *Times of Trenton*, September 1, 1994.

5. Joe Donohue, "Political Parties Accused of Violations," *Newark Star-Ledger*, November 5, 2004.

6. The four leadership PACs were established by law in 1993. Each is under the total control of a single leader: the Speaker and minority leader of the assembly and the president and minority leader of the senate.

7. Deb Dawson, "Dems Pass Cash to Ocean County," *Hunterdon County Democrat*, October 30, 2003.

8. Darryl R. Isherwood, "Who Has Inside Track for Hamilton Project?" and "Project Carries Pair's Imprint," *Times of Trenton*, August 22, 2004.

9. Joe Donohue, "For County Bosses, the Wheel Deal," *Newark Star-Ledger*, April 4, 2004.

10. Ibid.

11. Ibid.

12. Isherwood, "Who Has Inside Track."

13. Jonathan Schuppe, "Corporate Donors Filling Campaign Coffers," *Bridgewater Courier News*, September 26, 1999.

14. Editorial, "'Pay-to-Play' Bill Belongs Atop Assembly Fall Agenda," *New Brunswick Home News Tribune*, June 20, 2002.

15. Campaign contribution data and comments by officials regarding the Parsons contract are contained in a series of newspaper accounts from August 1998 through March 2002, including Joe Donohue and Tom Johnson, "State Hands Over Car Inspections to Private Company," *Newark Star-Ledger*, August 8, 1998; Kathleen Cannon, "Democrats: Connors a Watchdog for Taxpayers, Motorists," *Burlington County Times*, October 22, 1998; Sherry Sylvester, "Cash & Carry—Parsons Gives $$$ to Burlco GOP," *Trentonian*, October 22, 1998; Associated Press, "Say Goodbye Today to State-Run Inspection Stations," *Times of Trenton*, November 6, 1998; Associated Press, "Auto Checks Switch Gears," *Newark Star-Ledger*, November 6, 1998; Sandy McClure, "Task Farce," *Trentonian*, May 19, 2000; Dunstan McNichol, "Auto-Test Probe Cites Blunders, SCI Chief Says Whitman Aides 'Mismanaged' Contract Bidding," *Newark Star-Ledger*, July 11–12, 2001; Editorial, "The Price of Influence," *Newark Star-Ledger*, July 15, 2001; Editorial,

"End Pay-to-Play," *Newark Star-Ledger*, August 15, 2001; Dunstan McNichol, "Probe Calls Auto-Testing Deal a Waste," *Newark Star-Ledger*, March 14, 2002; John Curran, Associated Press, "A Hotbed of Graft, New Jersey Tries to Clean House," *Asbury Park Press*, August 17, 2003; Joe Donohue, "Pay-to-Play Ban Working . . . Some Say Too Well," *Newark Star-Ledger*, June 11, 2006.

16. Associated Press, "Auto Checks Switch Gears."

17. New Jersey Commission of Investigation, *N.J. Enhanced Motor Vehicle Inspection Contract*, March 2002, Trenton; McNichol, "Probe Calls Auto-Testing Deal a Waste."

18. In addition to the SCI report, I am grateful for the information supplied by reporter Dunstan McNichol (cited in notes 15 and 17), which provides further basis for this account. The Division of Motor Vehicles' name was changed to Motor Vehicle Commission by the New Jersey Motor Vehicle Security and Customer Service Act in 2003.

19. New Jersey Commission of Investigation, *N.J. Enhanced Motor Vehicle Inspection Contract*, March 2002, Trenton.

20. McNichol, "Probe Calls Auto-Testing Deal a Waste."

21. McNichol, "Auto-Test Probe Cites Blunders."

22. Jeff Whelan and Joe Donohue, "While Reform Waits, Cash Flows to Democrats," *Newark Star-Ledger*, May 12, 2003.

23. Robert Schwaneberg, "Order Toughens Law but Leaves Some Loopholes," *Newark Star-Ledger*, September 23, 2004.

24. Donohue, "Pay-to-Play Ban Working . . . Some Say Too Well."

25. James W. Prado Roberts, "Municipal Organizations Give to County Parties, Get around Law," *Asbury Park Press*, October 5, 2007.

26. James W. Prado Roberts and Gregory Volpe, "Money Flows through Pay-to-Play Loopholes," *Asbury Park Press*, October 5, 2007.

27. Heather Taylor, "At Local Level, Pay-to-Play Still Alive and Kicking," op-ed, *Times of Trenton*, November 30, 2011.

28. Ibid. At the time, Taylor was affiliated with the Citizens Campaign.

29. Herb Jackson, "Reforms Won't Close Campaign Cash Spigot," *Hackensack Record*, August 15, 2004.

30. The information that follows regarding EnCap relies heavily on financial data and commentary in a series of newspaper stories and editorials, including John Brennan and David Sheingold, "Politicians, Law Firms Have Reaped $13M from EnCap," *Hackensack Record*, April 9, 2007; editorial, "End Game—EnCap's Over, but the Questions Remain," *Hackensack Record*, February 15, 2009; John Brennan, "EnCap Acknowledges End of Golf Project, Pledges Landfill Help," *Hackensack Record*, April 28, 2009; Jeff Pillets, "State Probe on EnCap Project Found a Trail of Deception," *Hackensack Record*, June 21, 2009; Charles Stile, "EnCap Case Shows Trenton's Ugly Side," *Hackensack Record*, September 29, 2010; John Brennan, "State Takes Over EnCap Property after Suit Tossed," *Hackensack Record*, April 5, 2011; editorial, "EnCap Redux," *Hackensack Record*, June 7, 2011; Jeff Pillets, "Four Years after EnCap Collapse, Former Lawmaker Faces Trial," *Hackensack Record*, January 31, 2012; Jeff Pillets, "Lobbyist Testifies on How EnCap Got Breaks and Money," *Hackensack Record*, February 8, 2012; Jeff Pillets, "Former Lawmaker Cleared over EnCap," *Hackensack Record*, August 11, 2012.

**31.** Brennan and Sheingold, "Politicians, Law Firms Have Reaped $13M."

**32.** Ibid.; Stile, "EnCap Case Shows Trenton's Ugly Side."

**33.** Alan Guenther, "Two Sides of Bryant Long Evident," *Asbury Park Press*, October 2, 2007; George Anastasia, "Questions Swirl around Latest Charges against Former New Jersey Legislator Bryant," *Philadelphia Inquirer*, November 22, 2010. Other transgressions of Senator Bryant are noted in chapter 6.

**34.** Brennan and Sheingold, "Politicians, Law Firms Have Reaped $13M."

**35.** James W. Prado Roberts and Gregory Volpe, "Money Still Finds Its Way to Candidates," *Asbury Park Press*, October 2, 2007.

**36.** Josh Margolin and Joe Donohue, "In Political Circles, He Was a Ringmaster," *Newark Star-Ledger*, July 14, 2004.

**37.** Primary election campaign finance report for James E. McGreevey (2001), filed with the New Jersey Election Law Enforcement Commission, Trenton.

**38.** Raymond Hernandez, "Call Him a Soft Touch for Democratic Candidates," *New York Times*, July 11, 2004.

**39.** Jeff Pillets and Clint Riley, "Paying for Power," *Hackensack Record*, June 16, 2002.

**40.** Ibid.

**41.** Ibid.

**42.** David Kinney, "Governor's Ally Is Challenged on Bank Stock," *Newark Star-Ledger*, February 25, 2003.

**43.** John P. Martin and Russell Ben-Ali, "P.A. Nominee Comes under Fed Scrutiny," *Newark Star-Ledger*, February 12, 2003; Jeff Whelan, "A Defiant Kushner Quits P.A. Board," *Newark Star-Ledger*, February 27, 2003.

**44.** Hernandez, "Call Him a Soft Touch for Democratic Candidates"; Clint Riley, "McGreevey Can't Cut Lawyer Link to Kushner," *Hackensack Record*, August 9, 2004; Clint Riley, "Kushner, State Prosecutors Had Deal Months before Settlement with Feds," *Hackensack Record*, August 9, 2004.

**45.** Ted Sherman, "The Family: Five Years of Bad Blood," *Newark Star-Ledger*, July 14, 2004.

**46.** John P. Martin, "Kushner Undercut Inquiry, U.S. Says," *Newark Star-Ledger*, July 14, 2004, and "Kushner Sentenced to Two Years in Witness Plot," *Newark Star-Ledger*, March 5, 2005.

**47.** Unless otherwise noted, all data about contributions and fees in regard to the DeCotiis firm come from four stories by reporters Shannon Harrington, Clint Riley, and Jeff Pillets of the *Hackensack Record*: "He Pays, You Play; Generous Law Firm Gets Lots of Work," "Seems Like Clock Is Always Ticking on Legal Bills," and "Following Paper Trail of Legal Giant Meant Doing Our 'Homework,'" December 28, 2003; "Calls to Reform 'Pay-to-Play' Go Unheeded," December 29, 2003.

**48.** Harrington, Riley, and Pillets, "He Pays, You Play."

**49.** Shannon Harrington and Clint Riley, "Dead Man Giving: Political Donations from Late Lawyer," *Hackensack Record*, January 18, 2004.

**50.** Harrington, Riley, and Pillets, "He Pays, You Play."

**51.** Ted Sherman, "Special-Interest Cash Greases Political Wheels; Firms Bankroll Candidates Who Repay the Favor," *Newark Star-Ledger*, October 21, 2001.

52. Joe Donohue and Jeff Whelan, "Watered-Down Law Will Let Cash Flow," *Newark Star-Ledger*, June 13, 2004; Jim Edwards, "Pay to Play Isn't Always Quid Pro Quo," *New Jersey Law Journal*, December 22, 2003.

53. Joe Donohue, "Democrats Receive $1.2M from Corzine's Deep Pockets," *Newark Star-Ledger*, March 27, 2007.

54. Joe Donohue and Deborah Howlett, "Corzine Cash Shadows His Climb to Top," *Newark Star-Ledger*, February 6, 2005.

55. Election Law Enforcement Commission (ELEC) Reports, 1999–2009; Joseph Donohue, deputy director of ELEC, e-mail to author, March 4, 2012.

56. Elise Young, "He Fights System but Funds It Too," *Hackensack Record*, October 6, 2009.

57. Josh Margolin, "The $50,000 Loan That Became a Gift," *Newark Star-Ledger*, August 31, 2006.

58. Ibid.

59. Tom Moran, "Friends of Jon, Yet Enemies of Reform," op-ed, *Newark Star-Ledger*, March 28, 2007.

60. Adam Nagourney and Jeff Zelleny, "Obama Forgoes Public Money in First for Major Candidate," *New York Times*, June 20, 2008.

61. Meredith McGehee, policy director, Campaign Legal Center, Washington, DC, "What's Next for Campaign Finance Reform," *HuffPost Politics*, September 19, 2014, http://www.huffingtonpost.com/meredith-mcgehee/campaign-finance-reform_b_5847164.html.

62. Trevor Potter, president and general counsel, Campaign Legal Center, speech before the California Fair Political Practices Commission, September 19, 2014.

63. Anthony Corrado, *Campaign Finance Reform* (New York: Century Foundation Press, 2000), 39; Corrado, letter to author, March 11, 2001. See also Herbert E. Alexander and Anthony Corrado, *Financing the 1992 Election* (Armonk, NY: M. E. Sharpe, 1995), 8–9.

64. Michael J. Malbin, Peter W. Brusoe, and Brendan Glavin, "Small Donors, Big Democracy: New York City's Matching Funds as a Model for the Nation and States," *Election Law Journal* 11 (November 1, 2012); Campaign Finance Institute, based on data from the National Institute on Money in State Politics and the New York City Campaign Finance Board.

65. Ted Sherman, "Special-Interest Cash Greases Political Wheels," *Newark Star-Ledger*, October 21, 2001.

66. Independent expenditure data at the various levels of government contained in the following two paragraphs are from White Paper No. 24 published in March 2014 by the New Jersey Election Law Enforcement Commission, Trenton, NJ.

67. Mary Ann Spoto, "Elizabeth Ed Board, Lesniak Clash over Election Campaigning," *Newark Star-Ledger*, March 27, 2014.

68. Greg Hitt, "527 Groups Use Tax Loopholes to Promote Politicians," *Wall Street Journal*, May 25, 2000.

69. Herb Jackson, "Governor's Race Takes the Stage; DiFrancesco Airing TV Ads," *Hackensack Record*, November 9, 2000.

**70.** Joe Donohue, "Disclosure Law Nips at Heels of 2 at GOP's Top," *Newark Star-Ledger*, July 11, 2000; Herb Jackson, "Governor Hopefuls Exploiting Issue Ads," *Hackensack Record*, May 1, 2000.

**71.** John Reitmeyer, "Advocacy Groups Sidestep N.J. Disclosure Rules as Non-profits," op-ed, *New Jersey Real-TimeNews*, June 11, 2010; Tom Moran, "Secret Donors, Big Checks, and a Broken Promise," op-ed, *Newark Star Ledger*, July 25, 2010; Josh Margolin, "Gov. Works with Group That Skirts Pay-to-Pay," *Newark Star-Ledger*, July 13, 2010.

**72.** Matt Friedman and Ginger Gibson, "'Reform Jersey' Releases Donor List," *Newark Star-Ledger*, December 30, 2010.

## CHAPTER 3    CAMPAIGN FINANCING: THE NEW JERSEY VERSION

**1.** Details of the September 21 meeting were first reported in the following: Jim Goodman, "Assembly Fund-raisers Seek Lobbyists' Support," *Times of Trenton*, October 6, 1989; Jim Goodman, "Hoping for Florio Coattails," *Times of Trenton*, October 9, 1989; Chris Mondics and Patrick McGeehan, "Lobbyist Says She Was Shaken Down," *Hackensack Record*, January 7, 1990.

**2.** Many of the details of the Kotvas visit to the lobbyists were contained in news stories, and she confirmed and expanded on them when interviewed by the author on October 12, 2010, at the Somerset Hotel, Franklin Township, New Jersey.

**3.** Chris Conway, "Lobbyist Accuses Legislators," *Philadelphia Inquirer*, January 9, 1990.

**4.** Chris Conway, "Money Talks—and So Did One Angry Lobbyist," *Philadelphia Inquirer*, January 15, 1990.

**5.** Comments by the four legislators at the press conference appeared in the following news stories: Chris Mondics and Patrick McGeehan, "Democrats to Lobbyist: You're a Liar," *Hackensack Record*; Chris Conway, "Lobbyist Accuses Legislators," *Philadelphia Inquirer*; Robert Schwaneberg, "Lobbyist Sticks with 'Shakedown' Charge Despite Denial by Assemblymen," *Newark Star-Ledger*; Jim Hooker, "Dems Refute Shakedown Charge," *Times of Trenton*; Rich Linsk, "Democrats Accused of 'Shakedown' Try," *Asbury Park Press*, all January 9, 1990.

**6.** Mondics and McGeehan, "Democrats to Lobbyist: You're a Liar."

**7.** Nancy Becker, conversation with author, January 8, 1990. It is not likely that Becker would have been invited to the "shakedown" meeting because her clients were not business or special interest groups, which customarily made heavy political contributions.

**8.** Hazel Gluck, conversation with author, January 12, 1990. Gluck's clientele was similar to Becker's (see note 7).

**9.** Schwaneberg, "Lobbyist Sticks with 'Shakedown' Charge."

**10.** Joe Katz, interview by Michael Aron, *On the Record*, New Jersey Network Television, January 14, 1990.

**11.** Conway, "Money Talks."

**12.** Kotvas, interview by author.

13. Audrey Kelly, "FBI Joins Probe of Five Dems," *New Brunswick Home News Tribune*, February 15, 1990; Peter Kerr, "Ethics Questions in Trenton Bring Call for Reform," *New York Times*, March 2, 1990.

14. Patrick McGeehan and Chris Mondics, "Democrats Escape Lobbyist's Charges," *Hackensack Record*, April 5, 1990.

15. Ibid.

16. Democrat Carmen Orechio, state senate president, 1982–1985; Republican Donald DiFrancesco, state senate minority leader, 1982–1984; Democrat Thomas Deverin, then assembly majority leader pro tem; Republican Garabed Haytaian, then assembly minority leader.

17. *Findings and Recommendations of the Ad Hoc Commission on Legislative Ethics and Campaign Finance: A Report to the President of the Senate, the Speaker of the General Assembly, and Members of the New Jersey Legislature*, October 22, 1990; Chris Mondics, "N.J. Ethics Panel Calls for Reforms," *Hackensack Record*, October 23, 1990.

18. Public hearing, Ad Hoc Commission on Legislative Ethics and Campaign Finance, Trenton, July 11, 1990; Daniel Hays, "State Campaign Fund Law Called a National Model," *Newark Star-Ledger*, August 8, 1973.

19. Four senate bills, S-3530, S-3531, S-3532, and S-3533, introduced in the New Jersey State Senate on June 10, 1991, New Jersey legislative session 204. The four bills remained in committee and received no further action for the remainder of the 204th session, which ended in January 1992.

20. Daniel LeDuc, "Reform Stalls with Campaign Underway," *Philadelphia Inquirer*, November 22, 1992.

21. Owen McNany, Stanley Bedford, and David Linett to Governor Jim Florio, February 25, 1993. McNany, Bedford, and Linett were the ELEC commissioners. ELEC records are retained in the agency's office at 28 West State Street, Trenton.

22. Leonard J. Lawson to state senator William Schluter, April 26, 1993. Lawson was first assistant legislative counsel in the Office of Legislative Services when he wrote this opinion.

23. Center for Analysis of Public Issues, "1993 Campaign Finance Reform Was a Flop," press release, March 8, 1994.

24. Joe Donohue, "Campaign Finance Law Fails to Curb Big Money," *Newark Star-Ledger*, March 14, 1996; Robert Schwaneberg, "Democrat Blames 'Big Money' for Tainting Politics," *Newark Star-Ledger*, February 23, 1997.

25. Joe Donohue, "Agency Proposes Cap on Donations to Legislative Leadership Committees," *Newark Star-Ledger*, July 18, 1996.

26. Herb Jackson, "Suit Says Leadership Committees Give Parties Unfair Advantage," *Hackensack Record*, October 14, 1998.

27. Chip Stapleton, memorandum to Republican senators, March 8, 1994. Stapleton was executive director of the New Jersey Senate.

28. Kelly Richmond, "A \$100,000 Loophole for Senate Leader," *Hackensack Record*, August 7, 1995.

29. Aron Pilhofer, Greg Trevor, and Bonnie Freestone, "Legislators Use Loopholes to Cozy Up to Each Other," *Bridgewater Courier News*, July 19, 1998.

**30.** Dan Zegart and Peter Page, "Bills Aimed to Curb Tobacco Industry Influence," *Times of Trenton*, September 19, 1994.

**31.** Stapleton probably would have been more accurate had he said: "Tobacco money helped elect Jack Sinagra." This exchange was recorded in written notes by the author, who was present at the forum.

**32.** Sandy McClure, "Griping GOP, Republicans Irked by Donnie D's Use of $$$," *Trentonian*, September 5, 2000. Also in 2000, DiFrancesco donated $23,000 from the fund for his own state senate campaign to the Warren County Republican Committee and was subsequently endorsed for governor by the committee's chairman, Walter Orcutt. Jeff Pillets, "Governor Pressured by Ethics Concerns; DiFrancesco Aides Deny He Will Quit Race," *Hackensack Record*, April 18, 2001; ELEC website.

**33.** McClure, "Griping GOP, Republicans Irked by Donnie D's Use of $$$."

**34.** Joe Donohue, "Report Spotlights Legislative Chiefs' Cash Committees," *Newark Star-Ledger*, September 14, 1999; Pilhofer, Trevor, and Freestone, "Legislators Use Loopholes."

**35.** Ibid.

**36.** Information about the pension bond issue appeared in the following series of stories in the *Newark Star-Ledger*: Ron Marsico and Cynthia Burton, "10 Men on a Fence Test Whitman," April 27, 1997; Ron Marsico and Cynthia Burton, "Whitman Pressures Bond Plan Holdouts," April 30, 1997; Joe Donohue and Ron Marsico, "Bond Sale Vote Faces Further Delay," May 6, 1997; Ron Marsico and Joe Donohue, "S & P Warning Deepens Split on Bond Sale," May 21, 1997; Joe Donohue and Ron Marsico, "Bond Plan Muscles Past Last Obstacles," June 6, 1997; Joe Donohue, Ron Marsico, and Tom Johnson, "Whitman's Deals Sealed Bond Vote," June 8, 1997.

**37.** Donohue and Marsico, "Bond Plan Muscles Past Last Obstacles."

**38.** Donohue, Marsico, and Johnson, "Whitman's Deals Sealed Bond Vote."

**39.** Election Law Enforcement Commission filings, July 1, 1996, through 1997.

**40.** Jim Goodman, "LaRossa Tapped for $89G State Job," *Times of Trenton*, January 14, 1998; John McLaughlin, "About That Reform Bill: Never Mind," *Newark Star-Ledger*, February 1, 1998; David Voreacos, "Whitman Recommends Bubba for Seat on State Parole Board," *Hackensack Record*, May 29, 1998. According to these reports, Scott received $84,500, LaRossa received $89,500, and Bubba received $83,435.

**41.** Mark Magyar, "'One Sheriff, One Paycheck' Campaign Targets Pension/Pay Double-Dipping," *NJSpotlight*, September 5, 2014. Of this amount, the state's portion of the unfunded liability is estimated at 73 percent based on the $40 billion state unfunded liability as reported by Sal Rizzo, "Christie Challenges Pension Lawsuits," *Newark Star-Ledger*, September 3, 2014.

**42.** Center for Analysis of Public Issues, "1993 Campaign Finance Reform Was a Flop."

**43.** Donohue, "Report Spotlights Legislative Chiefs' Cash Committees."

**44.** David Kinney and Joe Donohue, "State Democrats Hike Fund-raising Bar, Again," *Newark Star-Ledger*, January 21, 2004.

**45.** Joe Donohue, "Party Bigs Gain Clout through PACs," *Newark Star-Ledger*, September 30, 2007. The year 2003 is comparable to 1993, since both the senate and assembly were up for election in those years.

**46.** Joe Donohue, "Legislative Races Set a New High for War Chests," *Newark Star-Ledger*, December 3, 2003.

**47.** Ibid.

**48.** Herb Jackson and Benjamin Lesser, "Highs and Lows of Political Fund Raising," *Hackensack Record*, August 16, 2004; Benjamin Lesser, "Party Leaders' Fund Transfers Aid Senator's Rise," *Hackensack Record*, August 12, 2004. One example of wheeling funds into the Sarlo campaign is seen in contributions from the local plumbers unions, which contributed $9,800 directly to the candidate. The same plumbers unions donated $92,250 to the senate president's leadership PAC, which gave $644,000 to Sarlo.

**49.** From ELEC website: www.elec.state.nj.us.

**50.** ELEC, "Legislative Election 2003: The Rise of Party-Oriented Campaigns," White Paper no. 17, July 2004, 33–34.

**51.** ELEC, "Legislative General Elections: An Analysis of Trends in State Senate and Assembly Elections," White Paper no. 20, January 2009, 15–16.

**52.** ELEC-Tronic NEWSLETTER, Issue 31, January 2012, Published by the Election Law Enforcement Commission, Executive Director Thoughts, Jeff Brindle.

**53.** Matt Friedman, "How PACs Are Skirting the Law on Pay-to-Play—Ledger Traces Millions Funneled to Politicians," *Newark Star-Ledger*, April 8, 2012.

**54.** Benjamin Lesser, "Lawyers Won War of Dueling Donations," *Hackensack Record*, August 11, 2004.

**55.** Ibid.

**56.** Joe Donohue, "Pensions and Transit Are Key as Labor PACs Aid Candidates," *Newark Star-Ledger*, October 25, 2005; Joe Donohue, "PAC Money Gushing into Campaigns," *Newark Star-Ledger*, October 23, 2007; Matt Friedman, "Unions Spent $24M on Election," *Times of Trenton*, August 10, 2010. Also, see ELEC White Papers: no. 19, "The 2005 Election: New Trends on the Horizon," September 2006; no. 20, "Legislative General Election 2007: An Analysis of Trends in State Senate and Assembly Elections," January 2009; no. 22, "Trends in Legislative Campaign Financing in the Era of Pay-to-Play Reform: Self Funders and Recession 1999–2009," September 2011.

**57.** New Jersey Election Law Enforcement Commission, Trenton, news release, September 10, 2014.

**58.** Letter from New Jersey Optometric Association to members of the legislature, October 24, 1991. Bill approved by senate December 19, 1991 (21–11), and by the assembly January 10, 1992 (41–18), signed by Governor Florio January 16, 1992 as C.385, P.L. 1991, and New Jersey legislative website, elec.state.nj.us.

**59.** From contemporaneous notes taken by author at the caucus meeting, October 18, 1990.

**60.** The Auditor, "Crass Pitch," *Newark Star-Ledger*, May 11, 2003. The Auditor is a Sunday editorial column.

**61.** Darryl R. Isherwood, "Mountain Creek Forked Over Campaign Cash Days before Favorable Bill Made Law," PolitickerNJ.com, April 28, 2011.

**62.** Ibid.

63. David Giambusso, "Contractor: Bribes, Donations Are Just Part of Business in N.J.," *Newark Star-Ledger*, September 15, 2011. The Newark official was subsequently convicted of steering contracts for money.

64. Contemporaneous notes taken by author at February 17, 1993, meeting.

65. Craig Horowitz, "Jim McGreevey and His Main Man," *New York Magazine*, September 20, 2004. Earlier in the year, Marcus was quoted as saying, "I've found that fund raising has become legalized extortion." Herb Jackson and Benjamin Lesser, "Under the Influence: Money in Trenton," *Hackensack Record*, August 8, 2004.

66. Chris Conway and Craig R. McCoy, "PACs Rally to the Cause on High-Stakes Issues in Trenton," *Philadelphia Inquirer*, February 28, 1988.

67. Staff and wire reports, "Senators Claim Influence Peddling," *Easton Express-Times*, April 18, 1997; Jeffrey Kanige, "The Best Houses Money Can Buy," *New Jersey Reporter*, May 1988; ELEC reports 1987–2001.

## CHAPTER 4    LOBBYING

1. Brian O'Reilly, "Lobbying, a Survey," *New Jersey Magazine*, published by Center for Analysis of Public Issues, Princeton, New Jersey, February 1978, 9.

2. Frederick Herrmann, "Stress and Structure: Political Change in Antebellum New Jersey" (PhD diss., Rutgers University, 1976), J974.9, H568.

3. This and other anecdotes in this chapter about lobbyists are from the personal experiences of the author while serving in the legislature from 1970 to 1973.

4. John Weber of Citizen Action, "Quotes—Year in Review," *Newark Star-Ledger*, December 30, 2003.

5. All of the information about private meetings with Governor McGreevey arranged by the Democratic State Committee with lobbyists and their clients in exchange for contributions of $25,000, and references to fundraising by previous governors, are contained in: Jeff Pillets, "Governor Woos Substantial Donors," *Hackensack Record*, November 24, 2002. The account of the "shakedown" of the businessperson seeking face time with the governor was told to the author confidentially by the lobbyist who represented the businessperson.

6. Ibid.

7. John Solomon, Associated Press, "GOP Checks to Ensure PACs Don't Split Donations," *Newark Star-Ledger*, August 1, 2000.

8. Pillets, "Governor Woos Substantial Donors."

9. Ibid.

10. David Kinney, "Democrats Tapping Lobbyists for Cash," *Newark Star-Ledger*, February 2, 2004.

11. All of the information about the Johnson family dispute and related legislation is found in: David Kinney, "How J & J Heirs' Pet Bill Backfired," *Newark Star-Ledger*, December 20, 2001; Herb Jackson, "Shaping Paternity Legislation: Bill Advances after Sculptor's Donations," *Hackensack Record*, August 9, 2004.

12. Center for Public Integrity, "Revolving Door Swings Freely in America's Statehouses," www.publicintergrity.org, January 16, 2013; National Conference of State

Legislatures, "'Revolving Door' Prohibitions against Legislators Lobbying State Government after They Leave Office," December 2012 update.

13. The amendment sponsored by then-Assemblyman Richard Codey stated: "Any legislative agent who knowingly causes, influences, or otherwise secures the introduction of any legislation or amendment thereto for the purpose of thereafter being employed to prevent the passage thereof, shall upon conviction be guilty of a misdemeanor." N.J.P.L. 1977, c.91, approved May 16, 1977.

14. *Lobbying Manual* (Trenton: New Jersey Election Law Enforcement Commission, January 2013), 8.

15. National Conference of State Legislatures, 50-State Chart, "Contingency Fees for Lobbyists," March 2013.

16. N.J.P.L. 1977, c. 90.

17. Tom Baldwin, Gannett State Bureau, "2 Parties Agree When It Pays Off," *Asbury Park Press*, October 7, 2007; Barbara G. Salmore and Stephen A. Salmore, *New Jersey Politics and Government*, 3rd ed. (New Brunswick, NJ: Rutgers University Press, 2008), 357–358.

18. Bob Ingle, "Brash Even for New Jersey," blog on *Politics Patrol*, APP.com, March 17, 2010.

19. Martin C. Bricketto, Gannett New Jersey, "Wearing 2 Hats Gives Dale Florio Twice the Clout," *Asbury Park Press*, October 4, 2007; ELEC News Release, March 3, 2016.

20. The 100 percent record was broken in November 2015 when Democrat Andrew Zwicker was elected by less than 100 votes in a district that includes Somerset and three other counties.

21. Bricketto, "Wearing 2 Hats Gives Dale Florio Twice the Clout."

22. Frederick M. Herrmann, *Lobbying in New Jersey 2008* (Trenton: New Jersey Election Law Enforcement Commission, 2008), 1.

23. David Kinney, "An Effort to Sharpen Blurry Lobbying Line," *Newark Star-Ledger*, May 5, 2003.

24. Herrmann, *Lobbying in New Jersey 2008*, 2.

25. *Lobbying Manual* (Trenton: New Jersey Election Law Enforcement Commission, January 2013), 14.

26. Joe Donohue, "Senate Puts Curbs on Gifts to Lawmakers," *Newark Star-Ledger*, December 12, 2003.

27. Associated Press, "Fewer Freebies for Lawmakers," *Times of Trenton*, February 27, 2005; Charles Stile, "This Year, Cardinale's Trips Are Fair Game," *Hackensack Record*, October 18, 2007.

28. Laurie Hollman, "Legislators Accept Free Trip to Fla.," *Philadelphia Inquirer*, April 21, 1988.

29. Deborah Howlett and Jeff Whelan, "Lobbying Limits Spur Reduction in Trenton Gifts," *Newark Star-Ledger*, February 26, 2005.

30. ELEC, Lobbying, Summary reports at: elec.state.nj.us; ELEC News Release, March 3, 2016.

31. Nicholas Kusnetz, "Grading the Nation: How Accountable Is Your State?" *State Integrity Investigation*, a collaborative project of the Center for Public Integrity, Global

Integrity, and Public Radio International, March 19, 2012; State Elections Enforcement Commission (Connecticut), Revised Contribution Limits and Restrictions, Chart 2— Special Donor Restrictions, July 2013, CT general statutes, Chapter 155, Section 9–611.

32. ELEC, "Summary of Activities of Governmental Affairs Agents," first quarter, 2013; New Jersey Election Law Enforcement Commission (ELEC), news releases, March 7, 2013, and March 3, 2016.

33. Joe Donohue, "Making the Most of a Government Job," *Newark Star-Ledger*, March 11, 2007; elec.state.nj.us, Annual Lobbying Reports, 2014.

34. Matt Friedman and Chris Megerian, "Municipalities Cut Funding after Drawing Governor's Ire," *Newark Star-Ledger*, March 10, 2011.

35. John Reitmeyer, "N.J. Is Wild West for Campaign Lobbyists," *Hackensack Record*, September 13, 2009.

36. The following newspaper stories contain information about AshBritt and the Christie fund-raising event held by AshBritt's lobbyist: Jenna Portnoy, "Head of Lobbying Firm Hired by AshBritt Will Host Christie Fundraiser," *Newark Star-Ledger*, February 7, 2013; editorial, "The Empire Strikes Back," *Newark Star-Ledger*, February 7, 2013; Jarrett Renshaw, "FEMA Warned Christie Administration That AshBritt Contract Would Jeopardize Federal Funding," *Newark Star-Ledger*, March 29, 2013; Jarrett Renshaw, "AshBritt CEO Has Financial Stake in Subcontractor," *Newark Star-Ledger*, April 1, 2013; editorial, "Gov. Christie's Baseless Tantrum over AshBritt," *Newark Star-Ledger*, May 1, 2013.

37. Portnoy, "Head of Lobbying Firm Hired by AshBritt Will Host Christie Fundraiser."

38. ELEC, news release, March 3, 2016.

39. The amounts spent on legislative races when both the assembly and senate stood for election in 2007 and 2011 were $72,670,958 and $73,884,330 respectively. These totals included expenditures for both primary and general elections. ELEC website.

## CHAPTER 5　CONFLICT OF INTEREST

1. Common Cause, "Conflict of Interest Legislation in the States," newsletter, January 10, 1975.

2. New Jersey Uniform Ethics Code, N.J.S.A. 52:13D-23.

3. In passing the bill, the legislature carved out several exceptions to this injunction— including the Public Employees Relations Commission, Workers Compensation Court, Division of Tax Appeals, Inheritance Tax Bureau, Division of Civil Rights, and State Board of Mediation—at the behest of attorney legislators who had substantial practices before the agencies in question.

4. Legislators may accept during a year gifts from special interests (lobbyists) that have a value less than $250, total, from each interest and may accept travel expenses with certain limits. Restrictions on gifts do not apply to campaign contributions to a candidate for public office.

5. N.J.A.C. 19:61–7.4.

6. New Jersey Briefs, "Assemblyman Drops Consultant Job," *New York Times*, May 26, 1973.

7. Campaign Monitoring Report for 1973 Legislative /elections, vol., Senate, published by Common Cause New Jersey, 1975; also, Senate bills 461 and 1088 signed into law, c. 91 and c.92, May 8, 1975; Legislative Index, Legislative Index of NJ Inc., Somerville, NJ, vol. 62, no. 11.

8. Information on the appointment of William Watley and his chief of staff, Lesly Devereaux, is from the following newspaper accounts: Jonathan Schuppe, "Minister Prepared to Lead Jersey Commerce," *Newark Star-Ledger*, February 3, 2002; Jeff Whelan and Josh Margolin, "Senate Clears Cleric for Commerce," *Newark Star-Ledger*, March 5, 2002; Jeff Whelan, "Watley's Two Jobs Put City Officials in the Middle," *Newark Star-Ledger*, July 3, 2004; Jeff Whelan, "State Finds Commerce Secretary in Conflict," *Newark Star-Ledger*, July 9, 2004; Jeff Whelan, "Embattled Commerce Chief Quits," July 15, 2004; Jeff Whelan, "Audit Bares Agency's Unchecked Spending," *Newark Star-Ledger*, September 21, 2004; Jeff Whelan and Jonathan Schuppe, "Ex-State Official Indicted in No-Show Job Scam," *Newark Star-Ledger*, December 7, 2004.

9. Whelan, "Watley's Two Jobs Put City Officials in the Middle."

10. Richard Kuh, *Foolish Figleaves? Pornography in—and out of—Court* (New York: Macmillan, 1967), 63.

11. George Amick, "The American Way of Graft," report by the Center for Analysis of Public Issues, Princeton, NJ, 1976, 4.

12. "Mulvihill Buys Mountain Creek," *Sussex County Advertiser News*, June 2, 2010.

13. Jeff Whelan, "Key Senator's Wife Works as Consultant to Resort Developer," *Newark Star-Ledger*, June 1, 2002; Colleen O'Dea, "Senator Brokered Land Deal with Resort His Wife Represented," *Asbury Park Press*, September 27, 2003.

14. Diane C. Walsh, "Senator Raises Stir with List of Clients," *Newark Star-Ledger*, May 20, 2007; editorial, "A Lawyer-Legislator Conflict," *Newark Star-Ledger*, May 24, 2007; Jonathan Tamari, "Senator Sees No Conflict in Land-Use Law," *Asbury Park Press*, September 23, 2003.

15. Walsh, "Senator Raises Stir with List of Clients."

16. B. L. Raynor, *The Life of Jefferson* (Boston: Lilly, Wait, Colman & Holden, 1834), 356.

17. Kathleen Wiechnik, former executive director of State Ethics Commission, discussion with author, July 8, 2015.

18. New Jersey Uniform Ethics Code, N.J.S.A. 52:13D-18(b); N.J.P.L. 1971, c.182, s.7; amended 2004, c.23.

19. Information involving Assemblyman Roberts and George Norcross in the U.S. Vision matter was contained in: Dunstan McNichol, "Trenton's Hollow Conflict-of-Interest Ban," *Newark Star-Ledger*, May 11, 2003; Alan Guenther, "Roberts and the Boss: Perfect Together," *Asbury Park Press*, September 30, 2007.

20. It is questionable whether Roberts was required to report the U.S. Vision financing deal, because it involved a loan repayment provision of $400,000 per month. As a personal liability, Roberts would have been obliged to detail this on his financial disclosure report.

21. O'Dea, "Senator Brokered Land Deal with Resort His Wife Represented."

**22.** Jonathan Tamari, "Lawmakers Hide Conflicts by Keeping Clients Secret," *Asbury Park Press*, October 1, 2007.

**23.** New Jersey Office of Legislative Services, Legislator's Financial Disclosure Statement for Calendar Year 2009, Gerald B. Green, May 5, 2010.

**24.** Alan Guenther, "$71G a Year to Meet and Greet," *Asbury Park Press*, October 1, 2007.

**25.** Background on DiFrancesco's career is provided by: Jeff Whelan, "The Quiet Donnie D Leaves the Shadows," *Newark Star-Ledger*, December 24, 2000.

**26.** Eugene Kiely, "DiFrancesco Spends Big to Win Seat He Bypassed," *Philadelphia Inquirer*, March 27, 2001.

**27.** Ron Marsico, "DiFrancesco Forms Group to Market His Views," *Newark Star-Ledger*, January 21, 2000.

**28.** Joe Donohue, "DiFrancesco's Laws Often Let Clients Thrive," *Newark Star-Ledger*, March 25, 2001.

**29.** Dunstan McNichol and William Swayze, "Contractor Still Unpaid for DiFrancesco Work," *Newark Star-Ledger*, February 15, 2001. Additional commentary regarding the Parsons project can be found in chapter 2 of this book (pay-to-play section).

**30.** Dan Weissman, "Florio Names Senate Chief's Friend to Sports and Exposition Authority," *Newark Star-Ledger*, September 13, 1992; David Kinney, "DiFrancesco Is Leaving but His Friends Won't Be," *Newark Star-Ledger*, December 13, 2001.

**31.** Joe Donohue and Dunstan McNichol, "DiFrancesco: 'There's No Real Conflict,'" *Newark Star-Ledger*, February 13, 2001; Dunstan McNichol, "Acting Governor Cleared in Loan Deal," *Newark Star-Ledger*, May 10, 2001.

**32.** David M. Halbfinger, "New Jersey's Acting Governor Defends Loan from a Home Builder," *New York Times*, March 1, 2001; Jennifer Golson and Jeff Whelan, "Secret Report Rips DiFrancesco Ethics," *Newark Star-Ledger*, April 18, 2001; John Hassell, "DiFrancesco's Blind Spot," *Newark Star-Ledger*, April 22, 2001.

**33.** Ted Sherman and Dunstan McNichol, "DiFrancesco Goes Public with Stack of Financial Details," *Newark Star-Ledger*, March 24, 2001; Ted Sherman, "DiFrancesco Netted Windfalls from IPOs," *Newark Star-Ledger*, April 3, 2001; editorial, "Raising Suspicions," *Newark Star-Ledger*, April 4, 2001.

**34.** David M. Halbfinger, "New Jersey's Acting Governor Was Faulted on Ethics in 1998," *New York Times*, April 17, 2001; Golson and Whelan, "Secret Report Rips DiFrancesco Ethics."

**35.** John Hassell, "DiFrancesco Drops Out; Awash in Scrutiny, Acting Governor Says, 'I've Just Had It,'" *Newark Star-Ledger*, April 26, 2001.

**36.** Data on dual office holding are from the following sources: Tom O'Neill, "One to a Customer: The Democratic Downsides of Dual Office Holding," New Jersey Policy Perspective, Trenton, and Demos: A Network for Ideas and Action, New York, 2006; Tom O'Neill and Bill Schluter, "How Much Is Enough?" New Jersey Policy Perspective, Trenton, July 2007; Jean Mikle and Alan Guenther, "Critics Fault Exceptions to Dual-Office Ban," *Asbury Park Press*, October 5, 2007; Barbara G. Salmore and Stephen A. Salmore, *New Jersey Politics and Government*, 3rd ed. (New Brunswick, NJ: Rutgers University Press, 2008), 175; Monday Minute, "And Then There Were Ten," New

Jersey Policy Perspective, Trenton, August 30, 2010; Matt Friedman, "Piling Up the Public Paychecks," *Newark Star-Ledger*, June 1, 2011.

37. N.J.S.A. 40A:9–7.2. A similar provision applies to legislators employed by public education institutions: N.J.S.A. 18A:6–8.1.

38. O'Neill, "One to a Customer: The Democratic Downsides of Dual Office Holding."

39. Jonathan Tamari and Jean Mikle, "Had Enough? Change Is Up to You," *Asbury Park Press*, October 7, 2007.

40. Jonathan Tamari, "Senator Sees No Conflict in Land-Use Law," *Asbury Park Press*, September 23, 2003.

41. Joseph P. Smith, "Assemblyman Brian E. Rumpf, 43, R-Ocean," *Asbury Park Press*, October 7, 2007.

42. Friedman, "Piling Up the Public Paychecks."

43. Jonathan Tamari, "Delivering a One-Two Punch," *Asbury Park Press*, October 3, 2007.

44. O'Neill and Schluter, "How Much Is Enough?"

45. Ibid.

46. Bill Mooney, "Christie: Sacco 'Poster' Boy for Triple-Dipping Public Workers," http://www.politickernj.com, October 11, 2012.

47. Friedman, "Piling Up the Public Paychecks." The legislators are Senator Teresa Ruiz, who draws $88,073 as deputy chief of staff for DiVincenzo; Assemblywoman (and former Speaker) Sheila Oliver, who is administrator of Essex County at a salary of $83,048; and Senator Nia Gill, earning $52,500 as attorney for the Essex County Improvement Authority, whose commissioners are appointed by DiVincenzo.

48. O'Neill and Schluter, "How Much Is Enough?"

49. Lee Procida, "Van Pelt to Resign Seat in Ocean Twp.," *Press of Atlantic City*, February 9, 2009; Lee Procida, "Van Pelt Resigns His Seat," *Press of Atlantic City*, August 1, 2009; Donna Weaver, "Bribery Gets Van Pelt 41 Months," *Press of Atlantic City*, November 20, 2010.

50. O'Neill and Schluter, "How Much Is Enough?"

51. George Amick, *The American Way of Graft* (Princeton, NJ: Center for Analysis of Public Issues, 1976), 201.

52. Gregory J. Volpe, "Ethics Panel: All Bark, No Bite," *Asbury Park Press*, October 3, 2007.

53. Ibid.

54. Ibid.; Ted Sherman, "Ex-NJ Sen. Joseph Coniglio Faces Resentencing after Appeals Court Dismisses All but One Charge," *Newark Star-Ledger*, March 8, 2011.

55. Dunstan McNichol, "Ethics Panel Spurns Calls to Probe Two Democrats," *Newark Star-Ledger*, May 6, 2005; Ted Sherman and Josh Margolin, "UMDNJ Probe Finds Senator Had Phony Job," *Newark Star-Ledger*, September 17, 2006; Alan Guenther, "Two Sides of Bryant Long Evident," *Asbury Park Press*, October 2, 2007; George Anastasia, "Questions Swirl around Latest Charges against Former New Jersey Legislator Bryant," *Philadelphia Inquirer*, November 22, 2010.

56. Volpe, "Ethics Panel: All Bark, No Bite."

**57.** Gabriel Neville, senior legislative counsel, Office of Legislative Services, e-mail to author, August 27, 2013; Matthew McGrath, "Rumana May Face Rehearing on Ethics Charges," *Hackensack Record,* January 21, 2012.

**58.** Salvador Rizzo, "Christie Accused of Interfering with Ethics Agency," *Newark Star-Ledger,* April 13, 2014.

**59.** Division of Local Government Services, "Report on Local Ethics Boards," June 9, 2009.

**60.** Report of the Governor's Local Government Ethics Task Force, September 2010.

**61.** School Ethics Act, P.L.1991, c.393 (C.18A:12–21 et seq.).

**62.** Mike Davis, "Tenure for Biz Chiefs a Century-Old Tradition," *Times of Trenton,* August 25, 2013.

**63.** Information about the City of Elizabeth Board of Education is contained in the following: Ted Sherman, "Education in Elizabeth: A Study in Politics," *Newark Star-Ledger,* May 22, 2011; Ted Sherman, "At Least $1.5M Paid Out Secretly by Elizabeth Schools, a Fraction of Workers' Settlements," *Newark Star-Ledger,* July 24, 2011; Max Pizarro, "Top Ten Contests of the Last Five Years," PolitickerNJ.com, June 19, 2012; Matt Friedman, "Outside Groups, Money Taking Control of Race for Lesniak Seat," *Newark Star-Ledger,* May 20, 2013. (Additional information about the political activities of the Elizabeth school board is found in chapter 6 of this book.)

## CHAPTER 6    PATRONAGE: JOBS, CONTRACTS, PERKS

**1.** Martin Tolchin and Susan J. Tolchin, *To the Victor: Political Patronage from the Club House to the White House* (New York: Random House, 1971), 311.

**2.** This procedure was explained to the author by Jack Ewing, who held positions as freeholder, assemblyman, and state senator representing Somerset County.

**3.** "The Bad Old Days in Trenton," *New Jersey Magazine,* February 1978, 28.

**4.** So declared Senator William Learned Marcy, a prominent machine Democrat in New York, in his rejoinder to critics of what they regarded as a patronage appointment: Martin Van Buren as ambassador to the Court of St. James. Speech in the United States Senate, January 25, 1832, vol. 8, col. 1325.

**5.** William L. Riordan, *Plunkitt of Tammany Hall* (New York: Penguin Group USA, 1995), 11.

**6.** Neal R. Peirce, "Will Civil Service Lose Its Tenure?" *Times of Trenton,* October 26, 1975.

**7.** Dave Neese, "'Shadow Government' Causing Trouble for Christie," *Trentonian,* December 23, 2013.

**8.** Information about George Norcross from: Alan Guenther, "Norcross Describes Extent of Influence," *New Brunswick Home News Tribune,* September 30, 2007; "They Have No Choice," *Philadelphia Magazine,* September 2005; Jason Method, "South Jersey Power Broker Stepping Out from Shadows," *Asbury Park Press,* February 12, 2012.

**9.** "Display of Arrogance," *Jersey Journal,* November 23, 2001; Peter Aseltine, "Only in New Jersey Politics," *Times of Trenton,* November 19, 2001.

**10.** Information about the secret tape recordings of George Norcross is from the following: Maureen Graham, Angela Couloumbis, and George Anastasia, "Secret Recordings Surface in Corruption Probe," *Philadelphia Inquirer*, October 16, 2001; Jeff Whelan and Deborah Howlett, "Bare-Knuckle Jersey Politics Bared; On Tapes, Democratic Power Broker Norcross Boasts His Influence Affects All Levels," *Newark Star-Ledger*, April 1, 2005.

**11.** Whelan and Howlett, "Bare-Knuckle Jersey Politics Bared"; Method, "South Jersey Power Broker Stepping Out from Shadows."

**12.** Information regarding campaign contributions and political connections involving the Commerce banking organization is contained in the following news stories: David Kinney and Joe Donohue, "State Cash Flows to Commerce Bank Vaults," *Newark Star-Ledger*, January 26, 2003; Sam Ali, "Commerce Continues to Branch Out and Cash In," *Newark Star-Ledger*, January 26, 2003; David Kinney and Joe Donohue, "Commerce Defers PAC Donations," *Newark Star-Ledger*, April 30, 2003; Clint Riley (multiple stories), "Banking on Your Money," "'Genghis Khan' of N.J. Banking," "'Playing on the Edges' of Political Giving," "DiFrancesco's Parting Act Helped Commerce," all published in *Hackensack Record*, May 21, 2003; Shannon Harrington and Josh Gohlke, "Branching North in a Big Way," *Hackensack Record*, May 21, 2003; editorial, "Banking on Politics," *Hackensack Record*, May 21, 2003; David B. Caruso, Associated Press, "SEC Probing Commerce on Political Gifts," *Newark Star-Ledger*, October 30, 2003; Joe Donohue, "Investment Bankers Lavish Donations on State Politicians," *Newark Star-Ledger*, May 2, 2004; David Kinney and Josh Margolin, "Bank Caught Up in Fraud Case," *Newark Star-Ledger*, June 30, 2004; "They Have No Choice," *Philadelphia Magazine*, September 2005; Ed Beeson, "Court Battle between Bank, Founder Starts," *Newark Star-Ledger*, May 9, 2013.

**13.** Information about the corruption involving Commerce Bank and the city of Philadelphia is from the following: Alan Guenther, "Roberts and the Boss: Perfect Together," *Asbury Park Press*, September 30, 2007; Method, "South Jersey Power Broker Stepping Out from the Shadows"; Emilie Lounsberry and Nancy Phillips, "Probe Taps City, Piece by Piece; A Bug is Found in Mayor's Office," *Philadelphia Inquirer*, February 8, 2004; David B. Caruso, "Indictments in Phila. Allege Shakedowns," AP Online; Associated Press State Wire: Pennsylvania, June 30, 2004; Kinney and Margolin, "Bank Caught Up in Fraud Case"; Larry King and Emilie Lounsberry, "Pay-to-Play Indictment Is a Tale of Hubris, Greed," *Philadelphia Inquirer*, July 10, 2004.

**14.** Guenther, "Roberts and the Boss: Perfect Together"; Beeson, "Court Battle between Bank, Founder Starts."

**15.** Josh Margolin and Chris Mergerian, "In This County, They Play Power Politics," *Newark Star-Ledger*, October 4, 2009; editorial, "The Games They Play," *Newark Star-Ledger*, October 1, 2009; Chris Mergerian and Matt Friedman, "Sheila Oliver: Will She Go or Will She Stay?" *Newark Star-Ledger*, July 10, 2011; Max Pizarro, "Dem Leaders Done with Deal for Prieto," PolitckerNJ.com, October 11, 2013.

**16.** Tom Moran, "Newark Boss Faces a Moment of Truth," *Newark Star-Ledger*, April 22, 2012.

17. Margolin and Mergerian, "In This County, They Play Power Politics"; Mergerian and Friedman, "Sheila Oliver: Will She Go or Will She Stay?"; Pizarro, "Dem Leaders Done with Deal for Prieto."

18. Moran, "Newark Boss Faces a Moment of Truth."

19. Tom Moran, "Trenton's Feud Threatens Ed Reform," *Newark Star-Ledger*, July 10, 2011.

20. Report by the Office of State Comptroller, "On-Line Transparency of New Jersey's Local Authorities and Commissions," February 15, 2011. This report identified 587 local authorities and commissions, including many that do not play a significant role in patronage, such as 185 fire districts and 50 other miscellaneous entities that are not politically infected. Deducting these two quantities results in the estimated 350 net local authorities and commissions where patronage is commonly practiced. John Reitmeyer, "Bill Seeks to Shine Light on Agencies; Transparency Urged for Those Spending Public Funds in NJ," *Newark Star-Ledger*, March 8, 2011.

21. Neese, "'Shadow Government' Causing Trouble for Christie."

22. Information regarding the PVSC is from the following sources: Ted Sherman, "Jersey's Pipelines of Cash and Favors," *Newark Star-Ledger*, July 27, 2003; John Reitmeyer, "Christie to Sewer Agency: Lobbyists Won't Quiet Me," *Newark Star-Ledger*, February 4, 2010; John Reitmeyer and Elise Young, "Passaic Valley Sewerage Commission Faces More Scrutiny of Salaries, Hiring," *Newark Star-Ledger* (NJ.com), February 4, 2010, updated February 5, 2010; Jeff Pillets, "Embattled Sewer Agency Chief to Quit $313K Post," *Hackensack Record*, February 13, 2010; Clair Heininger, "Christie Wants Ex-prosecutor to Lead Sewer Panel; Governor Had Blasted Passaic Valley Commission," *Newark Star-Ledger*, May 27, 2010; Richard Cowen, "Passaic Valley Sewerage Agency Faces Criminal Probe," *Hackensack Record*, September 18, 2010; Ted Sherman, "Christie to Sewer Bosses: Get Out; Citing 'Pattern of Abuse,' He Fires Six of Seven Passaic Valley Commissioners," *Newark Star-Ledger*, January 26, 2011; Ted Sherman, "PVSC a Rich Source of Funding for Campaigns," *Newark Star-Ledger*, January 30, 2011; Ted Sherman, "Governor Fires Dozens at Sewer Agency," *Newark Star-Ledger*, February 8, 2011; Reitmeyer, "Bill Seeks to Shine Light on Agencies"; editorial, "More Power to Him; In Petty Moment, Senate Dems Refuse to Give Gov. Veto over Some Independent Boards," *Newark Star-Ledger*, April 3, 2011; Jeff Pillets, "Sewerage Agency Drops Health-Insurance Broker," *Hackensack Record*, December 2, 2011; Ted Sherman, "Former PVSC Administrator Admits Illegal Perks," *Newark Star-Ledger*, June 22, 2012.

23. Cowen, "Passaic Valley Sewerage Agency Faces Criminal Probe."

24. New Jersey legislative website (www.njleg.state.nj.us) shows no action in the 2012–2013 or 2014–2015 sessions on relevant bills.

25. "They Have No Choice," *Philadelphia Magazine.*

26. Information regarding the DRPA is from the following sources: Wendy Ruderman and Joel Bewley, "N.J. Fill-in Says He'll Run for Senate," *Philadelphia Inquirer*, February 28, 2003; Elisa Ung, "Senator Approved as Chief of DRPA," *Philadelphia Inquirer*, March 20, 2003; Elisa Ung, "Pension Issue Resolved for Sen. Matheussen," *Philadelphia Inquirer*, April 23, 2003; editorial, "Judge Them for Yourself," *Philadelphia Inquirer*, November 8, 2003. Information about the financial excesses of the DRPA is from the

Office of State Comptroller, Investigative Report, Delaware River Port Authority, March 29, 2012, as reported by Christopher Baxter, "Del. River PA Wasted Millions, Report Finds," *Newark Star-Ledger*, March 30, 2012.

27. Editorial, "A Promising Plan," *Newark Star-Ledger*, September 25, 2011.

28. UMDNJ awarded $718 million in no-bid contracts between 2001 and 2005. Josh Margolin, "Paid Adviser to UMDNJ, No Record of His Advice," *Newark Star-Ledger*, June 14, 2005.

29. Stapleton's patronage was not limited to the UMDNJ consultancy. As DiFrancesco was leaving the governor's office in 2001, he appointed Stapleton to the New York Harbor Pilots Commission, a $28,000 per year position with full family health benefits. Stapleton was reappointed to the Harbor Pilots Commission by Governor Christie. Senator Richard Codey's comment on the reappointment was: "Chip's been on the good ship Lollypop for a long time." The Auditor (column), "Of Christie, Stapleton, and UMDNJ," *Newark Star-Ledger*, October 10, 2010.

30. Josh Margolin and Dunstan McNichol, "McGreevey Backer's $75,000 Deal," *Newark Star-Ledger*, March 6, 2005; Kelly Heyboer and Josh Margolin, "UMDNJ Goes After Fees Paid to Pair of Consultants," *Newark Star-Ledger*, September 1, 2005.

31. Ted Sherman and Josh Margolin, "UMDNJ Ranked Job Applicants on Political Ties," *Newark Star-Ledger*, April 2, 2006.

32. Information regarding Senator Wayne Bryant's involvement with UMDNJ comes from the following sources: Dunstan McNichol, "It Pays to Have Him as a Friend," *Newark Star-Ledger*, August 3, 2003; Sherman and Margolin, "UMDNJ Ranked Job Applicants on Political Ties"; Ted Sherman and Josh Margolin, "UMDNJ Probe Finds Senator Had Phony Job," *Newark Star-Ledger*, September 17, 2006; Alan Guenther, "Two Sides of Bryant Long Evident," *Asbury Park Press*, October 2, 2007; George Anastasia, "Questions Swirl around Latest Charges against Former New Jersey Legislator Bryant," *Philadelphia Inquirer*, November 22, 2010.

33. David Kinney, "DiFrancesco Is Leaving but His Friends Won't Be," *Newark Star-Ledger*, December 13, 2001.

34. Barbara G. Salmore and Stephen A. Salmore, *New Jersey Politics and Government*, 3rd ed. (New Brunswick, NJ: Rutgers University Press, 2008), 203. Remarks transcribed by Lewis Thurston, former chief of staff to Governor Kean, at the Symposium on the Transition, November 20, 1989.

35. Associated Press, "Port Authority Hired 50 People Christie Recommended," *Newark Star-Ledger*, January 30, 2012; Steve Strunsky, "In the Name of Reforming PA, Christie Pushed 35 New Hires," *Newark Star-Ledger*, February 10, 2012.

36. Associated Press, "Port Authority Hired 50 People Christie Recommended." The patronage aspects of the referrals from the governor's office came to light through a wrongful termination suit filed by a Port Authority employee who had been appointed to a professional position by the previous Democratic administration. This person was terminated for what the suit claims were political reasons when Republican Christie came into office.

37. Kevin Manahan, "Gov. Chris Christie's Commandments Ring Hollow," *Newark Star-Ledger* (NJ.com), September 19, 2010.

**38.** Ibid.; Darryl R. Isherwood, "Speziale Still Sitting on $500K War Chest," PolitickerNJ.com, September 23, 2011.

**39.** Jeff Pillets and Clint Riley, "Paying for Power," *Hackensack Record*, June 16, 2002; Michael Jennings, "Says Gay Affair Left Him Open to Threats, False Allegations," *Times of Trenton*, August 13, 2004.

**40.** Jarrett Renshaw, "Christie's Actions Get Message to Codey," *Newark Star-Ledger*, December 14, 2011; Steve Strunsky, "More Changes at the Top for Port Authority," *Newark Star-Ledger*, May 2, 2012.

**41.** Salvador Rizzo, "Christie Accused of Interfering with Ethics Agency," *Newark Star-Ledger*, April 13, 2014.

**42.** Information about Corzine's payments to Katz and Riccio comes from the following sources: Tom Moran, "Come Clean, Gov. Corzine on Katz Cash," *Newark Star-Ledger*, March 8, 2007; David Kocieniewski and Serge F. Kovaleski, "Romance with Corzine Ended, Union Chief Keeps His Number," *New York Times*, May 23, 2007; Josh Margolin and John P. Martin, "Corzine Gave $15K to In-Law of Katz," *Newark Star-Ledger*, September 2, 2007; Josh Margolin and John P. Martin, "Corzine Fends Off Allegations of Cover-Up Involving Riccio," *Newark Star-Ledger*, September 6, 2007; Josh Margolin, "Corzine Pays Katz Relative $362,500," *Newark Star-Ledger*, November 30, 2008; Josh Margolin, "Key Democrat Seeks Probe of Katz In-Law," *Newark Star-Ledger*, December 11, 2007.

**43.** Margolin, "Corzine Pays Katz Relative $362,500." The $15,000 payment was claimed to be in violation of Corzine's agreement. The $362,500 was settlement of personal legal action.

**44.** Joe Donohue, "Investment Bankers Lavish Donations on State Politicians," *Newark Star-Ledger*, May 2, 2004; Dunstan McNichol, "Underwriter Terminates McGreevey Middleman," *Newark Star-Ledger*, February 16, 2005; ELEC contribution disclosure records. Much of this flow of tribute from consultants stopped when Governor Richard Codey issued an executive order in 2005 prohibiting consultants from negotiating with the state treasurer on bond underwriting.

**45.** McNichol, "Underwriter Terminates McGreevey Middleman."

**46.** By agreement with the State of New York, New Jersey's governor has the right to appoint the chair of the twelve-member Port Authority board as well as the Authority's deputy executive director. New York's governor appoints the executive director. Information about the Bridgegate episode is contained in: Steve Strunsky, "Motives behind Closed GWB Lanes Get a Closer Look," *Newark Star-Ledger*, November 13, 2013; Philip Rucker, "For Chris Christie, Lane Closures at N.J. Bridge Attract Scrutiny If Not Scandal," *Washington Post*, December 17, 2013; Max Pizarro, "Big Boy at the Brink: Chris Christie and the Discipline of Fear," http://observer.com, January 14, 2014; Kate Zernike, "Christie Linked to Knowledge of Shut Lanes," *New York Times*, January 31, 2014.

**47.** Steve Strunsky and Brent Johnson, "P.A. Cops: We Were Told to Shut Up on GWB Closings," *Newark Star-Ledger*, September 4, 2014.

**48.** "Assembly Aides' Pay Is Listed," *Times of Trenton*, March 10, 1972; ELEC, 1973.

**49.** Gene Racz, "Gary L. Guear Sr., 55, Former Assemblyman, D-Mercer," *Asbury Park Press*, October 1, 2007.

**50.** Dunstan McNichol, "Disgraced Legislator Put Family on Payroll," *Newark Star-Ledger*, November 21, 2004.

**51.** Paul D'Ambrosio, "Prosecutions, Ethics Laws Spell Progress, but Loopholes Remain," *Asbury Park Press*, September 30, 2007.

**52.** Racz, "Gary L. Guear Sr., 55, Former Assemblyman, D-Mercer."

**53.** Shannon D. Harrington, "Freeholders' Clerk Gets Raise, 3-Year Deal," *Hackensack Record*, December 10, 2004.

**54.** Colleen O'Dea, "Expanded Tax Boards Add Patronage Jobs," *Asbury Park Press*, October 6, 2007.

**55.** Ibid.

**56.** Dunstan McNichol and Ted Sherman, "Records Give Back-Room View of State Grant Process," *Newark Star-Ledger*, October 18, 2008; Ted Sherman and Robert Schwaneberg, "How Groups Got Funding at the Whim of Trenton," *Newark Star-Ledger*, October 19, 2008.

**57.** Kathy Barrett Carter, "Justices Back Judge Rejection but Split on Use of 'Courtesy,'" *Newark Star-Ledger*, December 24, 1993.

**58.** The two Supreme Court decisions were: Baker v. Carr, 369 U.S. 186 (1962), and Reynolds v. Sims, 377 U.S. 533 (1964).

**59.** Governor Brendan Byrne, interview by Michael Aron of New Jersey Network for the Rutgers Project on the Governor, August 14, 2007. Byrne served as counsel to Governor Meyner in the 1950s.

**60.** George Amick, "Senatorial Courtesy Rears Its Ugly Head Again," Capitol Talk, *Times of Trenton*, December 26, 2011; Jessica Calefati and Jeanette Rundquist, "Move Ends Stalemate over Cerf Approval," *Newark Star-Ledger*, January 19, 2012; Jenna Portnoy, "Christopher Cerf Is Confirmed as N.J. Education Commissioner," *Newark Star-Ledger*, July 30, 2012.

**61.** Jill Porter, "Farkas-Pellettieri Meeting Is Questioned," *Trentonian*, September 24, 1974; Editorial, "The Pellettieri Matter," *Trentonian*, October 5, 1974; John Reilly, "Pellettieri Replies: 'I Did Nothing Wrong,'" *Trenton Sunday Times Advertiser*, October 6, 1974; Joe Piscione, "Maybe It's Legal, but It Does Stink," *Times of Trenton*, October 8, 1974.

**62.** Steven Ford, "New Jersey Courts 'Tainted with Conflicts,'" *Times of Trenton*, December 17, 1975.

**63.** The Auditor, "Blackballed," *Newark Star-Ledger*, May 23, 2004.

**64.** Primary campaign finance report, Bill Baroni, 2008, 14th legislative district, New Jersey Election Law Enforcement Commission, Trenton.

**65.** Tom Baldwin, "Reform Advocates Want to Repeal Senatorial Courtesy," *Asbury Park Press*, October 11, 2007; report by Citizens for the Public Good, October 31, 2007, analyzing results of the survey.

**66.** Courier-Post Bureau, "Perskie Blocked by Farley as County Judge," *Camden Courier-Post*, June 7, 1966. Also, see Rules of the Senate 1966–67, number 15, Nominations, sec. 75.

**67.** Raymond Bateman, "Senatorial Courtesy the Only Way to Rein in a Governor," *Bridgewater Courier-News*, June 24, 2007.

**68.** The sick and vacation day payout scam is contained in the following newspaper stories by Jarrett Renshaw: "Politicians Due Healthy Payouts for Sick Time" and "Creating a Diverse Legislature Has Its Perks," *Newark Star-Ledger*, April 29, 2012; "Christie: No More Free Days Off for Lawmakers," *Newark Star-Ledger*, May 1, 2012; "Sacco Gives Up $188K in Sick Time," *Newark Star-Ledger*, May 3, 2012; "Officials Skirt Law on School Sick Time," *Newark Star-Ledger*, May 11, 2012; also, MaryAnn Spoto, "Top Court Upholds Cap on Sick Pay," *Newark Star-Ledger*, May 4, 2012; editorial, "The Sick Pay Scam," *Newark Star-Ledger*, April 30, 2012.

**69.** Renshaw, "Christie: No More Free Days Off for Lawmakers."

**70.** Mark Lagerkvist, "NJ Lawmakers Fiddle as Double-Dipping Burns State Pension Funds," New Jersey Watchdog.org, January 6, 2014; Dave Neese, "State Watch: Is Double-Dippergate Next?" *Trentonian*, January 27, 2014.

**71.** There are some minor exceptions in law enforcement pension systems.

**72.** Dunstan McNichol, "One-Year Stints Fatten Ex-legislators' Pensions," *Newark Star-Ledger*, February 5, 2003.

**73.** Tom Baldwin, "Great Perks for Part-Timers: It's No Joke," *Asbury Park Press*, October 1, 2007.

**74.** Renshaw, "Politicians Due Healthy Payouts for Sick Time."

**75.** Editorial, "Exploiting State Pensions," *Newark Star-Ledger*, July 27, 2009.

**76.** Editorial, "Cushy Deal," *Newark Star-Ledger*, September 29, 2010.

**77.** Christopher Baxter, "Part-Timers Illegally on Pension Rolls," *Newark Star-Ledger*, July 18, 2012; Renshaw, "Politicians Due Healthy Payouts for Sick Time"; Spoto, "Top Court Upholds Cap on Sick Pay."

**78.** Salvador Rizzo, "Christie Challenges Pension Lawsuits," *Newark Star-Ledger*, September 3, 2014.

**79.** Henry Bryan, "Naples Tells Story of Party Payoffs," *Times of Trenton*, January 22, 1977.

**80.** Ibid.

**81.** Ted Sherman, "PVSC a Rich Source of Funding for Campaigns," *Newark Star-Ledger*, January 30, 2011.

**82.** Ted Sherman, "Pay-to-Play Still Thriving at Local Government Level," *Newark Star-Ledger*, November 29, 2009.

**83.** Information regarding the political activities of the Elizabeth school board is from the following: Ted Sherman, "Education in Elizabeth: A Study in Politics," *Newark Star-Ledger*, May 22, 2011; editorial, "The Rot in Elizabeth," *Newark Star-Ledger*, May 24, 2011; Ted Sherman, "At Least $1.5M Paid Out Secretly by Elizabeth Schools, a Fraction of Workers' Settlements," *Newark Star-Ledger* (NJ.com), July 24, 2011; Kevin Manahan, "Check Yourself? Not in Elizabeth," *Newark Star-Ledger*, October 23, 2011; Ted Sherman, "Elizabeth Probe Takes New Twist with Court Filing," *Newark Star-Ledger*, November 4, 2011; Matt Friedman, "Bill Takes Aim at Political Fundraising Shakedowns," *Newark Star-Ledger*, January 6, 2012; Max Pizarro, "The LD20 Incumbent Democratic Ticket v. the Elizabeth Board of Education," Politickernj.com, June 19, 2012; Matt

Friedman, "Outside Groups, Money Taking Control of Race for Lesniak Seat," *Newark Star-Ledger*, May 20, 2013.

**84.** The Auditor, "Elizabeth Is No Hotbed of Ethical Culture," *Newark Star-Ledger*, March 2, 2014; Sherman, "At Least $1.5M Paid Out Secretly by Elizabeth Schools."

**85.** Sherman, "At Least $1.5M Paid Out Secretly by Elizabeth Schools."

**86.** Ibid.

**87.** MaryAnn Spoto, "Elizabeth Ed Board, Lesniak Clash over Election Campaigning," *Newark Star-Ledger*, March 27, 2014.

**88.** Max Pizarro, "Lesniak Celebrates Court Decision in Elizabeth BOE Case," politickernj.com, September 11, 2015.

## CHAPTER 7     THE ELECTORAL PROCESS

**1.** In this analysis, Republican counties are Hunterdon, Monmouth, Morris, Ocean, Somerset, Sussex, and Warren. Democratic counties are Camden, Cumberland, Essex, Gloucester, Hudson, Mercer, Middlesex, Passaic, and Union. Reasonably competitive counties are Atlantic, Bergen, Burlington, Cape May, and Salem. This analysis is based on Democrat versus Republican spread of 10 percent or more in votes for the assembly in the elections of 2001, 2005, and 2009. A spread of less than 10 percent is considered competitive. Also factored in is the party composition of the freeholder boards. For example, the spread of assembly vote in Passaic amounted to 9 percent, but the composition of the freeholder board averaged 75 percent Democratic. Passaic was thereby classified as a Democratic county. Data from *Fitzgerald's Legislative Manual* (Newark, NJ: Skinner-Strauss, 2002, 2006, 2010).

**2.** NJSA 19:49–2.

**3.** Matt Friedman, "New State Redistricting Could Make Elections More Competitive; Jersey Legislature, Lots of Races, Little Competition," *Newark Star-Ledger*, February 18, 2011.

**4.** Election Law Enforcement Commission White Paper 22, "Trends in Legislative Campaign Financing," September 2011, 12–13.

**5.** Eu v. San Francisco County Democratic Central Committee, 489 U.S. 214 (1989).

**6.** Miles Benson, Newhouse News Service, "First on Ballot Has an Edge," *Times of Trenton*, August 22, 2004.

**7.** Hunterdon election ballots for the years 1999 through 2009, provided to the author by the Hunterdon county clerk.

**8.** Information about Caputo's record of ballot draws is from Don Demaio, "The Man with the Golden Hand," *New Jersey Magazine*, November 1976.

**9.** Benson, "First on Ballot Has an Edge."

**10.** NJSA 19:1–1.

**11.** Data on number of votes to qualify as a political party are from: Richard Winger, editor, *Ballot Access News*, San Francisco, January 20, 1995; research compiled by New Jersey Office of Legislative Services, Trenton, NJ, as contained in letter from Leonard Lawson, First Assistant Legislative Counsel, to author, May 25, 1993.

**12.** Nicole Gordon, former executive director of New York City Campaign Finance Board, telephone discussion with author, June 13, 2012; http://www.elections.ny.gov/NYSBOE/elections/2010/general/2010GovernorRecertified09122012.pdf.

**13.** NJSA 19:5–1. In this legal citation, "party column" has the same context as "party line."

**14.** Information regarding the lawsuit by the NJ Conservative Party is from the following: John McLaughlin, "If Both Parties Played Fair, Even They'd Be Disqualified," *Newark Star-Ledger*, August 1, 1999; David Wald, "GOP and Democrats Could Lose Their Top Ballot Spots," *Newark Star-Ledger*, August 3, 1999; John McLaughlin, "A Major Victory for a Minor Party," *Newark Star-Ledger*, August 24, 1999; Sherry Sylvester, "State Political Sky Could Fall," *Trentonian*, August 27, 1999; Robert Schwaneberg, "Confusion Wins Top Spot on Ballots," *Newark Star-Ledger*, August 25, 1999; David Wald, "Two Major Parties Seek to Regain Top Billing on Ballots," *Newark Star-Ledger*, August 27, 1999; David Wald, "Major Parties Win Their Appeal to Regain Top Slots on Ballot," *Newark Star-Ledger*, August 28, 1999.

**15.** The 10 percent of votes for the assembly in the prior general election of the full assembly as applied to the 1999 primary turnout amounted to 428,304. There were 203,119 Republicans who voted and 257,606 Democrats. If all the candidates voted for by each voter were tallied, as per the math agreed to by the appellate judges, the aggregate totals amounted to 717,829 and 1,247,967 for Republicans and Democrats respectively, both in excess of the 428,304 threshold. Wald, "Major Parties Win Their Appeal."

**16.** Background material on IRV can be found in: http://www.instantrunoff.com; George Amick, "Doing Away with Election Spoilers," *Times of Trenton*, July 2, 2007; "Instant Runoff Voting—Majority Rule without a Separate Election," Center for Voting and Democracy, Takoma Park, Maryland, http://www.fairvote.org; Blair Bobier, "Instant Runoff: Easy as 1, 2, 3," *Times of Trenton*, December 14, 2008.

**17.** Matt Friedman, "Former Gov. Byrne Turns 90 Today; Here Are Some of His Best Jokes," N.J. Advance Media for NJ.com, April 1, 2014.

**18.** Ted Sherman, "Five More Ensnared in Alleged Vote Fraud," *Newark Star-Ledger*, December 2, 2009; Philip Read, "Essex Election Workers Admit Phony Absentee Ballots," *Newark Star-Ledger*, March 4, 2010.

**19.** Wayne Parry, Associated Press, "2 More Are Charged in A.C. Voter Fraud," *Newark Star-Ledger*, July 1, 2009; Local News Briefs, *Newark Star-Ledger*, October 14, 2009.

**20.** Information for this story is from the *Hunterdon Democrat* newspaper editions of October 21 and 28 and November 5, 12, and 19 of 1948.

**21.** Associated Press, "Secaucus Racetrack Runs out of the Money," *Times of Trenton*, November 8, 1967; "Gangsters Blamed for Secaucus Track Defeat," *Times of Trenton*, September 17, 1968.

**22.** "Gangsters Blamed for Secaucus Track Defeat."

**23.** Information about voter suppression in the 1981 gubernatorial campaign is from: Rick Nichols and Dale Mezzacappa, "Judge Bars Jersey GOP's Warning Signs at Polls," *Philadelphia Inquirer*, November 4, 1981; Robert Drogin, Dale Mezzacappa, and Susan Fitzgerald, "Florio, Kean Probe Voter Complaints," *Philadelphia Inquirer*, November 6,

1981; Karla Vallance, "N.J. Democrats Fight GOP Lead," *Christian Science Monitor*, November 9, 1981; David G. Savage, "Justices Deny RNC's Bid to End Voter-Fraud Decree," *Newport News (VA) Daily Press*, January 15, 2013.

24. Data on the trend for states imposing restrictions on voting eligibility are from "Voting Law Changes in 2012" by Brennan Center for Justice, New York University School of Law, 2011.

25. Jason Noble, "Final Report: 117 Fraudulent Voters Found in Investigation," *Des Moines Register*, May 8, 2014.

## CHAPTER 8    AGENDA FOR REFORM

1. Francis X. Clines, "Money 'Reigns Supreme in American Politics,'" *Charleston [WV] Gazette*, March 23, 1997.

2. Michael Kirkland, "Citizens United Rolls, SEC Rule Drifts," UPI.com, February 16, 2014.

3. These super PACs include 501(c)(3) and 501(c)(4) nonprofit entities. Those that are charitable organizations can channel up to 49 percent of the donations they receive to political causes.

4. McCutcheon v. Federal Election Commission, 134 S. Ct. 1434 (2014); Center for Public Integrity, "More Than a Dozen States Could Throw Out Donation Caps After McCutcheon Ruling," http://www.publicintegrity.org/2014/04/04/14517.

5. Center for Public Integrity, "More Than a Dozen States Could Throw Out Donation Caps After McCutcheon Ruling."

6. Laurel Rosenhall, "Gov. Brown Signs Law Requiring Political Nonprofits to Identify Donors," *Sacramento Bee*, May 14, 2014, http://www.sacbee.com/news/politics -government/election/article2598851.html.

7. Meredith McGehee, "What's Next for Campaign Finance Reform," *Huffington Post*, September 19, 2014, http://www.huffingtonpost.com/meredith-mcgehee/campaign -finance-reform_b_5847164.html.

8. Big New Jersey cities to be considered for public financing of mayoral elections would be Newark, Jersey City, Paterson, Elizabeth, Trenton, and Camden.

9. Trevor Potter, president and chief counsel of the Campaign Legal Center, speech to the California Fair Political Practices Commission, September 19, 2014.

10. New York City Campaign Finance Board, "2013 Limits, Requirements, and Public Funds," http://www.nyccfb.info.

11. Michael Barbaro, "Campaign Finance Law Changed Face of Elections, Report Shows," *New York Times*, September 1, 2010.

12. Quoted in Robert G. Kaiser, *So Damn Much Money: The Triumph of Lobbying and the Corrosion of American Government* (New York: Vintage Books, 2010), 348. Panetta served as secretary of defense under President Barack Obama.

13. Nixon v. Shrink Missouri Government PAC, 528 U.S. 377 (2000). This is the decision where Justice John Paul Stevens made his famous remark: "Money is property; it is not speech."

14. New Jersey pay-to-play laws cover contributions to state political parties, candidates for governor, legislative leadership PACs, county political party committees, and municipal political party committees, but not to PACs and nongubernatorial candidates.

15. Election Law Enforcement Commission, "Contribution Limits and Prohibited Contributions," October 1988, http://www.elec.state.nj.us; Herb Jackson, "Reforms Won't Close Campaign Cash Spigot," *Hackensack Record*, August 15, 2004.

16. Matt Friedman, "Easy Money," *Newark Star-Ledger*, January 29, 2012; Matt Friedman, "Getting Tough on Campaign Spending," *Newark Star-Ledger*, June 24, 2012; editorial, "Stronger Spending Rules," *Newark Star-Ledger*, August 20, 2012; editorial, "Bad, Worse, and Criminal," *Newark Star-Ledger*, September 16, 2012; editorial, "Feasting on Contractors' Dime," *Newark Star-Ledger*, April 14, 2013; Ted Sherman, "Pushing to Reform Campaign Fund Rules," *Newark Star-Ledger*, February 28, 2014.

17. "You Say Vendor, I Say . . . ," The Auditor, *Newark Star-Ledger*, February 5, 2012.

18. Diane C. Walsh, "Ex-Essex Exec Paid Himself $65,000," *Newark Star-Ledger*, August 18, 2002.

19. John Hassell, "DiFrancesco Drops Out; Awash in Scrutiny, Acting Governor Says, 'I've Just Had It,'" *Newark Star-Ledger*, April 26, 2001.

20. Dunstan McNichol, "Critics: Finance Law Ripe for Abuse," *Newark Star-Ledger*, June 8, 2003; Matt Friedman, "Ex-Gov. Donald DiFrancesco Pays Back $4,650 for Campaign Finance Violations, 9 Years Later," NJ Advance Media for NJ.com, October 6, 2011. This transaction was investigated by ELEC not because it circumvented pay-to-play but because CME officials had exceeded the maximum allowable contribution to each municipal candidate, which, at the time, was $2,200. It took nine years for ELEC to complete its investigation; DiFrancesco was fined $4,650 and was required to repay the two CME officials $4,800 each from his campaign account.

21. Information about this scandal is from: Matt Friedman, "How PACs Are Skirting the Law on Pay-to-Play," *Newark Star-Ledger*, April 8, 2012; Darryl R. Isherwood, "MCIA Vendors Contributed Heavily to Executive Director Pucci, Other Middlesex County Dems," PolitickerNJ.com, August 12, 2012.

22. "2012 Overview, Campaign Contribution Limits," *ELEC-tronic Newsletter*, May 2012.

23. Joe Donohue, "Casinos Donate $19,000 to PAC," *Newark Star-Ledger*, November 27, 1995.

24. Candidates Guide, Statewide Direct Primary Election, San Joachim County Register of Voters, June 2014.

25. This recommendation is contained in legislation S-1409 sponsored by Senator Loretta Weinberg in the 2016–17 legislative session.

26. Matt Friedman and Chris Megerian, "Municipalities Cut Funding after Drawing Governor's Ire," *Newark Star-Ledger*, March 10, 2011.

27. Sal Rizzo, "Christie Accused of Interfering with Ethics Agency," *Newark Star-Ledger*, April 14, 2014.

28. National Conference of State Legislatures, 50 State Chart, Personal Financial Disclosure for Legislators: Client Identification Requirements (accessed April 7, 2014), www.ncsl.org/research/ethics.

29. Max Pizarro, "Stockton Study: Vast Difference between Composition of State Legislature and NJ," PolitickerNJ.com, September 10, 2015.

30. Information about representation and salaries of legislators in California is from: ballotpedia.org/CaliforniaStateLegislature.

31. N.J.S.A. 10:4–6 et seq.

32. The legislation proposing this constitutional amendment was drawn up for the author in his early years in the assembly by Sam Alito, the director of Legislative Services. When handing over the draft, Alito removed his professional hat and offered some personal advice that saved the author considerable future pain. He said, "Assemblyman, if you introduce this legislation, you will never get another of your bills passed by the Senate." The advice was taken, and the measure was not introduced until two years later, when the author became a member of the senate.

33. Christopher Baxter and Tom Haydon, "Audit: Middlesex Officials Received 'Hidden' Bonuses," *Newark Star-Ledger*, August 2, 2012.

34. Editorial, "Naughty Norcross," *Newark Star-Ledger*, April 1, 2012.

35. Dave Neese, "State Watch: Is Double-Dippergate Next?" *Trentonian*, January 27, 2014; S-883 of 2014–2015 session.

36. Mark Magyar, "The Problem with Redistricting," *New Jersey League of Municipalities* magazine, February 2012; Benjamin Brickner, "Reading between the Lines," report published by Eagleton Institute of Politics, Rutgers University, May 2010. This report represents a policy analysis exercise and major writing credit submitted in partial fulfillment of the requirements for the concurrent degree of master in public policy from the Harvard University Kennedy School of Government and juris doctor from Columbia University School of Law.

37. Nicholas Stephanopoulos, "California Fixed Redistricting; Will the Supreme Court Break It Again?" *Los Angeles Times*, February 20, 2015.

38. Josh Goodman, "The Disappearance of Multi-Member Constituencies," Stateline, Governing.com, July 27, 2011, http://www.governing.com/blogs/politics/The-Disappearance-of-Multi-Member-Constituencies.html.

39. Ibid.

40. Final Report and Commentary to Proposed Title 19A of the New Jersey Statutes, vol. 2, by the State of New Jersey Election Law Revision Commission, March 25, 1975.

41. Joe Duggan, "Coming Soon to Nebraska: Online Voter Registration," Omaha.com, March 31, 2014, http://www.omaha.com/news/coming-soon-to-nebraska-online-voter-registration/article_ca8c62d9-77de-57d8-8e24-f64f2e7fd76d.html.

42. NJSA 19:13–20.

43. PL 2009 c135.

44. Eu v. San Francisco County Democratic Central Committee, 489 *U.S.* 214 (1989).

45. Editorial, "Missing Women—Why We Need Them in Elective Office," *Newark Star-Ledger*, September 10, 2012.

46. Miles Benson, "First on Ballot Has an Edge," *Times of Trenton*, August 22, 2004.

47. Jason Method, "Campaign Cash: No Clean Sweep," *Asbury Park Press*, October 6, 2007.

**48.** Paula Franzese and Daniel J. O'Hern, "Truth in Campaigning Law Would Restore Civility to Politics," *Asbury Park Press*, December 6, 2006.

## CHAPTER 9     HOW TO ACHIEVE REFORM

**1.** Background information about I & R is found in the following: David S. Broder, *Democracy Derailed* (New York: Harcourt, 2000); Larry J. Sabato, Howard R. Ernst, and Bruce A. Larson, *Dangerous Democracy?* (New York: Roman & Littlefield, 2001); Richard J. Ellis, *Democratic Delusions* (Lawrence: University Press of Kansas, 2002); Craig B. Holman, Brennan Center for Justice, "An Assessment of New Jersey's Proposed Limited Initiative Process," 2001; Jon Shure, New Jersey Policy Perspective, "When States Let People Speak . . . Campaign Reform Happens," report prepared for Citizens for the Public Good, Trenton, New Jersey, July 18, 2001; George Amick, "Following California Ill-advised," *Times of Trenton*, July 27, 2009.

**2.** Broder, *Democracy Derailed*, 1.

**3.** Ibid., 47.

**4.** Ellis, *Democratic Delusions*, 47, 63: Meyer v. Grant 486 U.S. 414 (1988).

**5.** Broder, *Democracy Derailed*, 171.

**6.** Shure, "When States Let People Speak . . . Campaign Reform Happens."

**7.** Broder, *Democracy Derailed*, 223.

**8.** Ibid., 225.

**9.** Ibid., 204.

**10.** Center for State Constitutional Studies, Rutgers University–Camden, "State Constitutions in the 2010 Elections," *Subnational Constitutional Chronicle* 13, no. 1 (Winter 2011).

**11.** Broder, *Democracy Derailed*, 45. Proposition 13 actually barred any tax rate increases on properties, except that it did allow local property assessments on which property taxes are based to be raised by as much as 2 percent per year. Further, properties when sold could be reassessed at their resale value, which, presumably, would be at a higher level than prior to the sale.

**12.** Editorial, "Bad Day's Work," *Times of Trenton*, May 13, 1996.

**13.** William Yardley, "Top Connecticut Legislators Agree on Strict Campaign Finance Reform," *New York Times*, November 29, 2005; Mark Pazniokas and Christopher Keating, "Legislature Passes Reform Package," *Hartford (CT) Courant*, December 1, 2005.

**14.** Broder, *Democracy Derailed*, 166–167; Shure, "When States Let People Speak . . . Campaign Reform Happens," 4.

**15.** "The Board and Its Mandates," New York City Campaign Finance Board, October 1998, 4; Nicole Gordon, past director of the New York City Campaign Finance Board, telephone conferences with author, September 27, 2010, October 11, 2010, and June 13, 2012.

**16.** Shure, "When States Let People Speak . . . Reform Happens," 10.

**17.** Ibid., 11. Among the ten states are some of the most prolific users of I & R, including Arizona, California, Colorado, Missouri, and Oregon.

**18.** California allows I & R at primary elections when voter turnout is lower than at general elections.

**19.** Holman, "An Assessment of New Jersey's Proposed Limited Initiative Process."

**20.** Before the motion to relieve can take effect, the bill would have to have been introduced at least sixty days prior, and senators would have to have twenty-four hours' notice of the vote.

**21.** Editorial, "Campaign Reform?" *Press of Atlantic City*, March 14, 1997; Christopher Hann, "Schluter Testifies in Campaign Finance Hearing," *Bridgewater Courier-News*, April 18, 1997.

**22.** John Kolesar, "Stop the Drift toward Plutocracy," *Times of Trenton*, December 18, 2000.

**23.** Arizona, Massachusetts, Michigan, Ohio, and Oklahoma approved I & R by means of a constitutional convention. Ellis, *Democratic Delusions*, 177.

**24.** James J. Florio, "The Color of Money," *Bridgewater Sunday Courier News Forum*, December 3, 2000.

**25.** Shure, "When States Let People Speak . . . Campaign Reform Happens," 4.

# INDEX

# ABOUT THE AUTHOR

WILLIAM E. SCHLUTER, longtime crusader for ethics and government reform, served as a Republican state senator and assemblyman during two stints in the New Jersey legislature, from 1968 to 1974 and from 1987 to 2002. He sponsored laws to regulate lobbying and disclosure of campaign contributions and expenditures. Schluter was a member of legislative committees on environmental quality and land use, and chair of the Joint Legislative Committee on Ethical Standards.

Schluter later served by gubernatorial appointment as chair of the New Jersey Citizens Clean Elections Commission and on the New Jersey State Ethics Commission. A Princeton University graduate, Schluter and his wife, Nancy, live in Pennington, where he served for six years as borough councilman.